BOULANGERIE AT HOME

BOULANGERIE AT HOME

RODOLPHE LANDEMAINE
BREAD BAKING AND INSTRUCTION

PHOTOGRAPHS BY JOERG LEHMANN
ILLUSTRATIONS BY YANNIS VAROUTSIKOS
TECHNICAL ADDITIONS BY ANNE CAZOR

HARPER
DESIGN

An Imprint of HarperCollinsPublishers

MAISON LANDEMAINE

———

Originally from Mayenne, in northwest France, Rodolphe Landemaine trained in both bread and pastry making at the school Les Compagnons du Devoir et du Tour de France. To perfect his craft, he joined the teams of renowned pastry houses Ladurée (alongside Pierre Hermé), Paul Bocuse in Lyon, then in Paris at the gastronomic restaurant Lucas Carton, and finally at Le Bristol hotel. In 2007, along with his wife, Yoshimi, he opened the first Maison Landemaine bakery in the 9th arrondissement of Paris before expanding to other parts of the city.

Maison Landemaine was founded on three important principles: work, excellence, and pleasure. Its products are made with the best raw ingredients: Red Label (*Label Rouge*) or organic flour, high-quality butter, and fresh and seasonal fruits and vegetables, together with artisanal know-how based on the use of natural starters, slow fermentations, and homemade products—all values that inspire the teams of this Parisian *maison*. Recently, Rodolphe's adventures have expanded to Japan, with a school dedicated to bread making and his first shop in the heart of Tokyo.

This book is the culmination of ten years of work and continuous improvement to provide high-quality products every day and for everyone. In this book, Maison Landemaine offers you the secrets of its recipes with explanations and tricks of its trade. We wish you happy baking—and happy tasting!

CONTENTS

THE BUILDING BLOCKS

Essential ingredients 12

Fermentation steps 30

Fundamental doughs.....................54

Fundamental custards

    and creams...............................76

THE RECIPES

Baguettes......................................84

Yeast-raised breads 96

Specialty breads 114

Filled breads..............................132

Breads made with oil

    (flat breads) 158

Soft breads and buns.................170

Leavened puff pastries 180

Traditional puff pastries............194

Puff pastry–based cakes

    and tarts 202

Yeast-raised sweet breads

    and doughnuts 208

Brioche 216

Brioche-style cakes 232

Tarts 248

Loaf and single-layer cakes

    (gâteaux de voyage)...............252

Small bites: sponge cakes, puffs,

    and crisp cookies 262

ILLUSTRATED GLOSSARY

Equipment 280

Dough skills defined..................282

Butter and egg techniques.........284

Basic skills 285

HOW TO USE THIS BOOK

THE BUILDING BLOCKS

In this section, you will discover all the essential ingredients and fundamental techniques and recipes necessary for baking breads—from wheat to flour, from kneading to baking, from bread dough to puff pastry. For each item there is an infographic and detailed explanations of the technique and preparation.

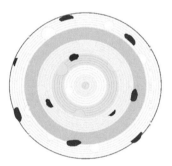

THE RECIPES

In this section, you will use the building blocks to make breads, pastries, brioches, tarts, and cakes. For each recipe there are references to the essential ingredients and fundamental techniques, an infographic to help you understand the concept of the recipe, and step-by-step photos for making each product.

ILLUSTRATED GLOSSARY

The details and illustrated techniques in the glossary will help deepen your knowledge of the ingredients and how to use them.

CHAPTER 1
THE BUILDING BLOCKS OF BREAD BAKING

ESSENTIAL INGREDIENTS

WHEAT FLOURS 12
ALTERNATIVE FLOURS 14
GLUTEN-FREE FLOURS 16
FRESH YEAST 18
SOURDOUGH STARTER (LEVAIN) 19
LIQUID STARTER 20
STIFF STARTER 22
POOLISH 24
WATER 26
SALT 27
FATS 28
MILK 28
SUGAR 29
EGGS 29

FERMENTATION STAGES

KNEADING BY HAND 30
KNEADING MECHANICALLY 32
FERMENTATION 34
FINAL SHAPING 40
GLAZING 48
SCORING 50
BAKING 52

FUNDAMENTAL DOUGHS

STRAIGHT DOUGH 54
"FRENCH TRADITION"
   STRAIGHT DOUGH 56
PIZZA DOUGH 58
VIENNA DOUGH 60
LEAVENED PUFF PASTRY 62
BRIOCHE DOUGH 66
INVERSE PUFF PASTRY 68
CHOUX DOUGH (PÂTE À CHOUX) 72
SWEET PASTRY DOUGH
   (PÂTE SUCRÉE/PÂTE SABLÉE) 74

FUNDAMENTAL CUSTARDS AND CREAMS

PASTRY CREAM (CRÈME PÂTISSIÈRE) 76
ALMOND CREAM
   (CRÈME D'AMANDES) 78
APPLE COMPOTE FILLING 80

WHEAT FLOURS

Understanding

WHAT THEY ARE

The powders obtained by milling the wheat berry.

COMPOSITION OF THE WHEAT BERRY

–Bran (the outer coating): 20 to 25 percent of the kernel. It is rich in minerals.
–Endosperm: 70 to 75 percent of the kernel. It contains 70 percent starch and about 12 percent gluten.
–Germ: 3 percent of the kernel. It contains vitamins.
–Note: The whiter a flour is, the less bran it has, and consequently the more gluten it has.

FROM WHEAT TO FLOUR

The wheat berry is ground, sifted, sorted, and ground again until a more (or less) refined powder is obtained according to the desired quality (white, whole wheat, etc.).

STONE-GROUND FLOUR

This is a flour that is ground between two stone wheels instead of metal cylinders. This traditional technique makes it possible to preserve the germ of the wheat berry and all, or part, of the bran. The flour retains most of its nutrients.

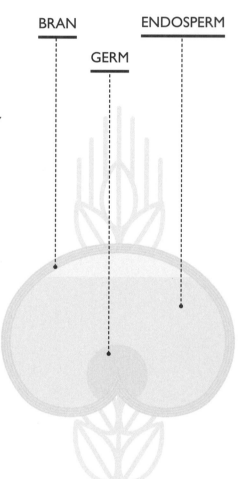

BRAN   ENDOSPERM

GERM

FLOURS RICH IN BRAN

The bran is the hard outer layer of the wheat berry. When milling, the bran is separated from the endosperm. Then, depending on the flour type desired, some of these layers are added back. The more bran there is in a flour, the less the bread dough is developed (in other words, the flour is coarser, making the formation of the gluten network more difficult) and the denser the bread's crumb will be. A flour rich in bran is rich in fiber, protein, vitamins, and minerals. It also lends a rustic flavor to the bread.

NOTE

These recipes were developed using European, specifically French, flour types. European and American flour types can vary in their manufacture and protein content, with European flours tending toward lower protein levels. Every attempt has been made in the recipes to indicate the closest equivalent of American flour types, but variations in the recipes can occur depending on the flour selected. Many American artisan flour mills have begun producing flours for bakers seeking to replicate classic European breads. Check online or with your local mills to find suppliers of these specialty flours.

WHAT IS THE "T" USED TO DESCRIBE SOME FLOUR TYPES?

This letter corresponds to the mineral content in 3½ ounces (100 g) of wheat flour. The more the flour is refined, the whiter it is and the less bran it contains, and consequently fewer minerals: from 0.45 percent for a T45 flour to 150 percent for T150 flour.

LOW-"T" FLOUR TYPES
–Appearance: white, fine
–Mineral content: low
–Gluten level: high to very high
–Uses: breakfast pastries (viennoiseries) and baked goods other than bread, white bread, brioche
–Result: a dough that rises fast and is elastic; an airy crumb with little chewiness; a thin crust; delicate flavors.

HIGH-"T" FLOUR TYPES
–Appearance: more or less gray, grainy
–Mineral content: high
–Gluten level: low
–Uses: rustic breads, specialty breads
–Result: a fragile dough, less elastic due to a lower gluten network; dense crumb. The breads made with these flours have more flavor because the flour is richer in bran.

WHAT IS GLUTEN?

Gluten is a protein contained in wheat flour. During kneading, bonds are formed between gluten proteins, creating a tight mesh (the gluten network). If the dough is kneaded too much (or not enough), this mesh is not tight enough and too porous. It will not retain enough gas from fermentation to allow the development of the dough. Gluten is the principal element that allows a dough to rise. The more gluten contained in a flour, the more easily the dough rises. Gluten-free flour is not suitable for traditional bread making.

1 T45 "FARINE DE GRUAU" FLOUR

Milled from a high-quality, protein-rich wheat, it contains more gluten than standard flour.
–Most similar to: pastry flour
–Appearance: white, fine
–Gluten level: very high (8 to 9 percent protein)
–Uses: brioche, breakfast pastries (*viennoiseries*), and baked goods other than breads

2 T55 FLOUR

–Most similar to: all-purpose flour
–Appearance: white, fine
–Gluten level: high (10.75 to 11.2 percent protein)
–Uses: white bread, tart dough, pizza dough, cakes, and pastries

3 T65 FLOUR

–Most similar to: high-protein all-purpose or bread flour
–Appearance: white, medium grain
–Gluten level: medium (12 to 13 percent protein)
–Uses: rustic loaves (*pain de campagne*), tart dough, pizza dough, cakes, and pastries

4 T65 "FRENCH TRADITION" WHEAT FLOUR

Guaranteed by the 1993 French decree on flour to be without additives.
–Appearance: white, medium grain
–Gluten level: medium
–Uses: "French tradition" breads

5 T80 FLOUR

–Most similar to: whole wheat pastry flour
–Appearance: light gray, medium grain
–Gluten level: medium (10 percent protein)
–Uses: specialty breads, cakes, and pastries

6 T110 FLOUR

–Most similar to: white whole wheat flour
–Appearance: gray, coarse grain
–Gluten level: low
–Uses: whole and light brown breads

7 T150 "INTEGRAL" FLOUR

–Most similar to: whole wheat flour
–Appearance: gray, coarse grain
–Gluten level: low
–Uses: bran bread

ALTERNATIVE
FLOURS

———

Understanding

RYE

SPELT

EINKORN

KHORASAN
(KAMUT)

WHY DO THESE FLOURS NEED TO BE MIXED WITH WHEAT FLOUR TO MAKE BREAD?

Because they do not contain enough gluten to allow the gluten network to form properly. The combination with wheat flour (rich in gluten) makes it possible to give more volume to the dough and to obtain an airy crumb.

1 RYE FLOUR

A product from the milling of rye, a grain from northern Europe.
– Composition: contains a low-quality gluten for bread making; fragile, less elastic than wheat, little gluten network.
– Use: can be used alone in bread making, but it is easier to work with when mixed with modern wheat flour in a ratio of 20 to 50 percent rye flour.
– Result: tight crumb, dense, dark brown, very chewy. Strong flavor.

2 SPELT FLOUR

A product of the milling of spelt grains, a subspecies of soft wheat and an ancestor of wheat.
– Composition: 12 percent gluten, rich in bran and nutrients.
– Use: an option between wheat and einkorn. It can be used alone in bread making.
– Result: a more dense crumb than from wheat, a darker color (light brown). Quite pronounced flavor.

3 EINKORN FLOUR

A product of the milling of einkorn wheat, this ancient grain variety is a popular grain for organic farming.
– Composition: 7 percent gluten, very well assimilated by the body. Suitable for people sensitive to gluten.
– Use: can be used alone in bread making, but is more often mixed with modern wheat flour in a ratio of 50 to 70 percent einkorn flour.
– Result: yellow crumb, dense. A slightly sweet, delicate taste.

4 KHORASAN (KAMUT FLOUR)

A product of the milling of Khorasan wheat (an ancestor of wheat originally from Egypt); considered a good candidate for an organic rotation. The trademark Kamut comes from an Egyptian word meaning "wheat."
– Composition: 10 to 12 percent gluten, well assimilated by the body. Suitable for people sensitive to gluten.
– Use: can be used alone in bread making, but is more often mixed with modern wheat flour in a ratio of 50 to 70 percent Khorasan flour.
– Result: tight crumb. A delicate taste, more pronounced than wheat. Light aromas of dried fruits.

GLUTEN-FREE
FLOURS

Understanding

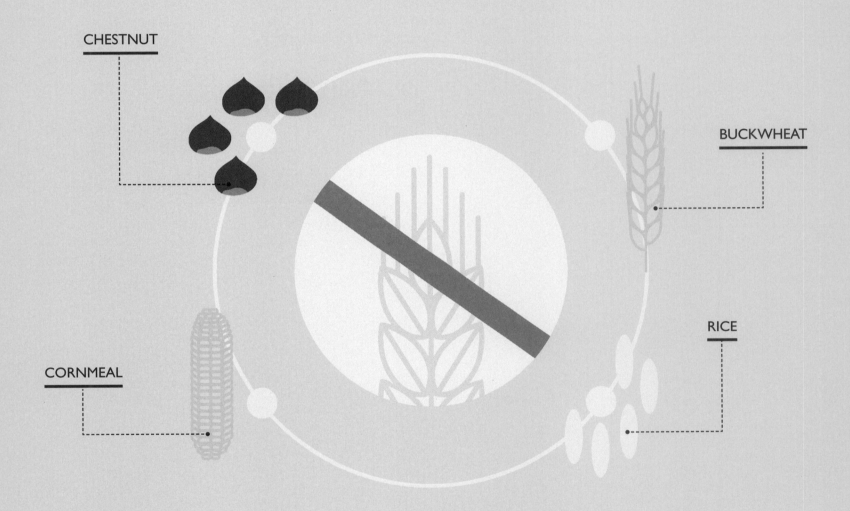

CHESTNUT

BUCKWHEAT

CORNMEAL

RICE

WHAT IS A GLUTEN-FREE FLOUR?

This is flour void of gluten. Without gluten, there is no gluten network formation, the tight mesh that traps the gases from fermentation and allows the dough to rise. You can make bread with them, but the crumb will be very dense.

1 CHESTNUT FLOUR

A product from the milling of chestnuts.
– Composition: 0 percent gluten.
– Use: not suitable alone for bread making; to be used mixed with wheat flour with no more than 5 to 20 percent being chestnut flour.
– Result: tight crumb, beige color. Sweet and intense taste.

2 CORNMEAL

A product from the milling of corn kernels.
– Composition: 0 percent gluten, granular texture.
– Use: not suitable alone for bread making; to be used mixed with wheat flour with no more than 5 to 20 percent being cornmeal.
– Result: very yellow crumb. Sweet taste.

3 BUCKWHEAT FLOUR

A product from the milling of buckwheat, a gray grain originating from northeast Asia.
– Composition: 0 percent gluten.
– Use: not suitable alone for bread making; to be used mixed with wheat flour with no more than 5 to 20 percent being buckwheat flour.
– Result: gray crumb, tight. Slightly acidic taste.

4 RICE FLOUR

A product from the milling of rice.
– Composition: 0 percent gluten, high in starch.
– Use: not suitable alone for bread making; to be used mixed with wheat flour with no more than 5 to 10 percent being rice flour.
– Result: gritty grain. Slightly sweet taste.

FRESH
YEAST

Understanding

WHAT IT IS

A ferment consisting of a group of microscopic fungi. This is one of the basic elements of bread making, along with flour and water.

ROLE

To start fermentation and make the dough rise.

RESULT

Breads with a very open crumb and a fairly neutral flavor and thin crust.

PRECAUTION

Yeasts die in contact with salt; start kneading immediately.

SHELF LIFE

Two weeks in the refrigerator.

PRINCIPLE

In the presence of oxygen (kneading), the yeasts multiply and are activated. In the absence of oxygen (rest), the yeasts eat the sugars in the flour and produce carbon dioxide (CO_2) and alcohol, causing fermentation. This is referred to as "alcohol fermentation."

PLACES TO PURCHASE

Bakeries, natural food stores, bread aisle of the supermarket.

WHAT IS THE ADVANTAGE OF FRESH YEAST OVER A SOURDOUGH STARTER?

Fresh yeast has a faster and more regular fermentation strength. Its use is immediate. Its small cube shape inhibits oxidation, and it crumbles easily.

CAN YOU USE DRIED YEAST?

Dried yeast has the same components as fresh yeast. It is dehydrated then ground to a powder and sold in packets. How much to use is more complicated, since it is more concentrated. For an equal weight of flour, less dried yeast is required than fresh. It also keeps longer than fresh yeast.

SOURDOUGH STARTER
(LEVAIN)

Understanding

WHAT IT IS

A living, natural ferment obtained by the cultivation of wild yeasts and bacteria from a mixture of warm water and flour. This is one of the basic elements of bread making, along with flour and water.

ROLE

To start fermentation and make a dough rise.

PRINCIPLE

Mix together an equal amount of water and flour. Wild yeasts and microorganisms naturally present in this mixture will eat the sugars in the flour, causing fermentation. The result is what's called the *chef*. Next, to prevent too much acidity, the yeast must be regularly refreshed by adding water and flour. After several days of refreshing and resting in a warm location, the starter is ready.

RESULT

Breads with a dense crumb (irregular), rustic flavor, and thick crust.

TWO TYPES OF SOURDOUGH STARTERS

– Liquid starter: refreshed with equal amounts of flour and water. This creates lactic fermentation.
– Stiff starter: refreshed with more flour than water. This creates acetic fermentation.

LIQUID STARTER OR STIFF STARTER, HOW DO YOU CHOOSE?

– Flavors: mild and lactic with a liquid starter; pronounced and acetic with a stiff starter.
– Crust: crispy with a liquid starter; crispy and thick with a stiff starter.
– Crumb: airy with a liquid starter; dense with stiff starter (because the acidity, which tends to tighten the crumb, is more pronounced).
– Storage: longer with a stiff starter than with a liquid starter.

WHAT IS THE ADVANTAGE OF A SOURDOUGH STARTER OVER FRESH YEAST?

The use of a sourdough starter produces breads with more traditional characteristics, including a more rustic appearance and a more acidic taste. The starter is also richer in nutrients and provides a longer shelf life for breads.

WHY IS A DOUGH MADE FROM A STARTER MORE ACIDIC?

The starter's particular composition of yeast (bacteria + wild yeasts) favors acidic fermentation, which gives the dough a particular acidity, too.

WHAT ABOUT USING A DRIED STARTER?

Sold in packets in natural foods stores, this powder is less effective than a natural starter. It offers less acidity and, thus, less flavor. But it is easier to use and keeps longer.

LIQUID STARTER

Understanding

WATER   FLOUR

WHAT IT IS

A mixture composed of an equal
amount of water and flour that
undergoes a lactic fermentation and
whose role is to raise the dough.

COMPARISON WITH
FRESH YEAST

–More sour flavor.
–Broader aromatic palate.
–Crunchier crust.
–Longer shelf life.

COMPLETION TIME

–Preparation time: 10 minutes
–Fermentation time: 8 to 9 days

TRADITIONAL USE

"French Tradition" Straight Dough (page 56)

OTHER USES

–Vienna Dough (page 60)
–Panettone (page 244)
–Ciabatta (page 158)

VARIATION

Stiff Starter (page 22)

SHELF LIFE

When refrigerated in an airtight
container it keeps indefinitely,
provided the starter is refreshed
every 2 to 3 days to keep it active.

IT'S READY

When, after 8 to 9 days, the
starter doubles its volume within
8 hours. At this point it is then
called the *chef* or "seed culture."
–Appearance: creamy beige yogurt.

WHY IS IT NECESSARY TO
"REFRESH" THE STARTER?

*During fermentation, yeasts and bacteria
eat the sugars found in the flour. Once all
the sugars have been eaten, the fermentation
stops. Consequently, if the starter has not
been sufficiently fed with sugar, it will be
too acidic and the bread will be sour.*

WHY DO YOU ADD HONEY?

*To accelerate the growth of microorganisms,
which allows the dough to rise more quickly.*

WHY MUST YOU REST IT IN A
WARM PLACE?

*So the microorganisms can grow in
sufficient quantity and "work" effectively.
Otherwise, the starter will be too acidic and
the bread too aggressive on the palate.*

CHALLENGE

Storing the starter. If the refreshings are
too frequent or if the temperature of
the storage area is not high enough, the
starter ferments less and the dough will
therefore rise less, resulting in a bread
that is less acidic and less aromatic. In
contrast, if the starter has fermented too
much between each refreshing, or if the
temperature of the storage area is too
high, the starter will be too acidic and the
bread will be too aggressive on the palate.

USEFUL TIP

The starter must have time to develop
to be active. It's better to wait longer
than to not wait long enough.

MAKES 10½ OUNCES (300 G) LIQUID STARTER

BEGIN THE STARTER (STAGE 1)

¾ cup (100 g) organic high-protein all-purpose flour (or use bread flour or T65 flour)

½ cup minus 1 tablespoon (100 g) warm water at 122°F (50°C)

1½ teaspoons (10 g) organic honey

FOR EACH REFRESHING (EVERY 36 TO 48 HOURS)

½ cup minus 1 tablespoon (100 g) water

¾ cup (100 g) organic high-protein all-purpose flour (or use bread flour or T65 flour)

DAY 1

Combine the flour, warm water, and honey in a mixing bowl. Place the mixture in an airtight container and let rest in a warm place (77°F/25°C minimum, such as on top of the refrigerator or a radiator) for 48 hours.

DAY 3

When small bubbles have formed, take 3½ ounces (100 g) of the starter, place it in a mixing bowl, and discard the rest. Refresh the dough by adding the ½ cup minus 1 tablespoon (100 g) water and the ¾ cup (100 g) flour. Stir to combine using a spatula. Store in an airtight container in a warm place for about 36 hours.

DAY 5

Repeat steps for Day 3. Let rest for an additional 36 hours in a warm place.

DAY 6 OR 7

Repeat the process one last time. Let rest for an additional 36 hours in a warm place. The starter is ready after 8 to 9 days.

STIFF STARTER

Understanding

WATER   FLOUR

WHAT IT IS
A liquid starter enriched with stone-ground flour and water.

COMPLETION TIME
–Preparation time: 10 minutes
–Fermentation time: 10 days

TRADITIONAL USE
Rustic Loaf with Rye (page 100)

CHALLENGE
Storing the starter.

IT'S READY
When the starter looks like a gray and dry bread dough.

SHELF LIFE
Refresh the starter every 2 to 3 days to keep it active: add 1½ cups (200 g) stone-ground flour and ½ cup minus 1 tablespoon (100 g) water at 122°F (50°C), and let rest for 24 hours.

COMPARISON OF A STIFF STARTER TO A LIQUID STARTER
–*Thick and crunchy crust.*
–*Strong, pronounced flavor.*
–*Longer shelf life.*

HOW ARE THESE DIFFERENCES EXPLAINED?
A stiff starter results in a thicker crust and a tighter crumb because the dough is denser. It has a more pronounced flavor because the dough is more acidic.

BEGIN THE STARTER (STAGE 1)
¾ cup (100 g) organic high-protein all-purpose flour (or use bread flour or T65 flour)
½ cup minus 1 tablespoon (100 g) warm water at 122°F (50°C)
1½ teaspoons (10 g) organic honey

FOR EACH REFRESHING (EVERY 24 TO 36 HOURS)
½ cup minus 1 tablespoon (100 g) water
1½ cups (200 g) organic high-protein all-purpose flour (or use bread flour or T65 flour)

TO TRANSFORM A LIQUID STARTER INTO A STIFF STARTER

1⅔ cups minus 1 tablespoon (200 g)
  whole wheat pastry flour (or stone-
  ground T80 or T110 flour)
3½ tablespoons (50 g) warm water at 122°F (50°C)

DAY 1

For days 1–7, follow the directions for a liquid starter on page 21, repeated here for your convenience. Combine ¾ cup whole wheat pastry flour, ½ cup warm water, and 1½ teaspoons honey in a mixing bowl. Place the mixture in an airtight container and let rest in a warm place (77°F/25°C minimum, such as on top of the refrigerator or a radiator) for 48 hours.

DAY 3

When small bubbles have formed, take 3½ ounces (100 g) of the starter, place it in a mixing bowl, and discard the rest. Refresh the dough by adding ½ cup minus 1 tablespoon (100 g) water and ¾ cup (100 g) flour. Stir to combine using a spatula. Press plastic wrap onto the surface (see page 285) and let rest in a warm place for 36 hours.

DAY 5

Repeat the previous steps. Let rest for an additional 36 hours in a warm place.

DAY 6 OR 7

Repeat the process one last time. Let rest for an additional 36 hours in a warm place.

DAY 8 OR 9

Take 3½ ounces (100 g) of liquid starter (the culture), place it in the bowl of a stand mixer fitted with the dough hook, add the 1⅔ cups minus 1 tablespoon (200 g) whole wheat pastry flour and the 3½ tablespoons (50 g) warm water, and knead for 5 minutes on the lowest speed (speed 1). Store the starter in the refrigerator in an airtight container for 24 hours before using.

POOLISH

Understanding

WHAT IT IS

A combination of equal amounts of flour and water mixed with fresh yeast. This is a kind of an "express" starter (taking only 10 hours instead of 8 days).

COMPLETION TIME

–Preparation time: 5 minutes
–Fermentation time: 10 hours

ROLE

Like sourdough starter and fresh yeast, poolish is a ferment. It ensures the fermentation and the rise of the dough.

RESULT

Lends a more interesting and pronounced flavor than when using fresh yeast, but a less acidic flavor than when using a sourdough starter. The holes of the crumb are irregular (as with a sourdough starter) and the crust is thin (as with fresh yeast).

TRADITIONAL USES

–White bread
–Breakfast pastries (helps with the development of the dough layer during baking)

COMPARISON TO A SOURDOUGH STARTER

–*Easy to use.*
–*No culture to produce.*
–*It takes only a few hours before the dough is ready for kneading.*

COMPARISON TO FRESH YEAST

–*The dough has more flavor.*
–*The rising time is more important in order to give the aromas more time to develop. Allows the gluten to soften and improves the extensibility of the dough.*
–*Better shelf life.*

CHALLENGE

Using the poolish when it's mature, which is the moment it deflates (an indentation will form in the center); if used too early, the dough lacks fermentation and flavor; if used too late, the dough will be acidic.

USEFUL TIP

Use tepid water to accelerate the fermentation.

MAKES 7 OUNCES (200 G)

Pinch of fresh yeast
½ cup minus 1 tablespoon (100 g) cold water
¾ cup (100 g) T65 "French tradition" wheat
    flour (or use organic high-protein
    all-purpose flour or bread flour)

1 Dilute the crumbled yeast in the water.

2 Add the flour and whisk to combine until smooth.

3 Cover the bowl with plastic wrap or a towel.

4 Let rest at room temperature for about 10 hours.

5 Mix the poolish with the other ingredients at the beginning of the kneading process.

WATER

Understanding

WHAT IT IS

An essential ingredient for use with flour and with ferments in bread making.

ROLES

– To hydrate the flour (to form a dough): use 1⅓ to 1½ pounds (600 to 700 g) water per 2¼ pounds (1 kg) flour.
– To dissolve salt and yeast.
– To aid the formation of the gluten network.
– To soften the gluten to give the dough its elasticity.
– To create a moist environment essential for yeasts to be active.

THE RIGHT TEMPERATURE

The temperature of the water is the main parameter used to create a dough of the right temperature (between 73 and 75°F/23 and 24°C).

A NOTE ABOUT LIQUID MEASUREMENTS

The recipes in this book provide both imperial and metric measurements for all ingredients. Liquid measurements are first provided as cups/tablespoons/teaspoons (volume), because this is the most convenient way to measure liquids, and then as grams (weight).

If you are a baker who likes to weigh your ingredients for precision like professional bakers do, you can weigh both the solid and liquid ingredients on a kitchen scale, taring the scale in between. Or, you can weigh the solids and measure the liquids in a measuring cup; this conversion is easy to do, as 100 grams water or other liquid equals 100 milliliters. (You will need a scale and a glass measuring cup that include metric measurements.)

WHY IS THE TEMPERATURE OF THE DOUGH SO IMPORTANT?

Because the yeasts present in the dough require a particular temperature (73 to 75°F/23 to 24°C) to be sufficiently active and to transform the sugars into carbon dioxide (CO_2). If the dough is too hot or too cold, the fermentation will not be optimal. The bread will not be "good."

HOW DO YOU CALCULATE THE RIGHT WATER TEMPERATURE?

The base temperature (T°) must be between 131 and 149°F (55 and 65°C):
  T° of the base = T° of the water + T° of the room + T° of the flour.
The room and flour temperatures are generally the same. Just add them up, then do the following subtraction:
  T° of the base - (T° of the flour + T° of the room) = T° of the water

WHAT HAPPENS IF THE WATER IS TOO COLD?

The base temperature will be too low, and the fermentation not optimal. The weaker dough causes the crumb to be less developed and the crust to be irregular.

WHAT HAPPENS IF THE WATER IS TOO HOT?

The base temperature will be too high. The dough will have too much strength and be sticky, the bread's texture will be more granular, and the crust paler.

WHAT IS THE HYDRATION RATE?

This is the amount of water incorporated into the flour during kneading to form the dough. For 2¼ pounds (1 kg) flour, use 2⅓ to 3¼ cups (550 to 750 g) water. This rate affects the moisture of the crumb and the crust: the less water contained in the dough, the more quickly its surface will dry when baked; the crust therefore has more time to form and will be thicker.

SALT

Understanding

WHAT IT IS
The last essential ingredient for use with flour, ferments, and water in bread making.

ROLES IN DOUGH
– Tightens the dough: it creates bonds between the proteins that ensure better stability of the gluten.
– Regulates fermentation: it limits the activity of the yeast; without salt, a dough ferments much faster.

WHICH SALT SHOULD YOU CHOOSE?
Fine or coarse sea salt.
– Proportion: 3 to 3⅓ teaspoons (18 to 20 g) of salt per 2¼ pounds (1 kg) of flour.

ROLES IN BAKED BREAD
– Acts as a flavor enhancer.
– Contributes to the browning of the crust.
– Holds moisture in the bread thanks to its hygroscopic properties: it assists with maintaining a soft crumb during and after baking.

PRECAUTION
Yeasts die in contact with salt; start kneading the dough immediately.

WHY DO YEASTS DIE IN CONTACT WITH SALT?
Because salt absorbs the water that the yeasts contain and, therefore, dehydrates them. This dehydration makes yeasts inactive, and can kill them.

FATS

Understanding

FATS

WHAT THEY ARE

Fatty acids of animal or vegetable origin.

ROLE

Fats reduce the formation of the gluten network, which impacts the crust and the crumb. When fats are introduced, the crumb will be silky and tender and the crust will be thin.

USES

–Breakfast pastries (*viennoiseries*)
–Brioches
–Italian breads

USEFUL TIP

Use butter or margarine at room temperature for easy incorporation.

ROLL-IN BUTTER (BEURRE DE TOURAGE)

This butter is richer in fat than standard butter and therefore contains less water. It is used for creating laminated doughs, such as puff pastry (*pâte feuilletée*). This butter has the advantage of being easier to handle since it has less water, allowing it to melt less quickly. It also does not combine with the dough layer during baking, helping to maintain the many layers that form the layering (or "lamination") of these doughs.

OIL

A vegetable fat that provides more moisture than butter, in equal parts, and which weighs the dough down less. Used most often in savory baked goods.

MILK

MILK

WHAT IT IS

Unless otherwise described, this refers to whole-fat cow's milk. It is composed of 87 percent water and 4 percent fat.

ROLES

– Contributes to the moisture of the dough due to its high water content.
– Contributes softness thanks to its fats.
– Influences the color and taste of the product.

USES

–Vienna dough
–Breakfast pastries (*viennoiseries*)
–Brioches

PLANT-BASED "MILKS"

They can be used as substitutes for cow's milk in equal quantities.
– For a neutral flavor use liquids derived from soy, rice, or oats.
– For a more distinctive flavor use liquids derived from hazelnuts, almonds, or spelt.

SUGAR

Understanding

SUGAR

WHAT IT IS
A substance extracted from sugarcane or sugar beets.

ROLES
- Provides a higher tolerance of the dough to mechanical and physical manipulation: the sugar reduces the formation of the gluten network. Doughs containing sugar, therefore, are easier to handle.
- Improves fermentation. Sugar is fermentable, that is to say it is directly assimilated by the yeasts. As a result, it refines aromas and improves flavor.
- Promotes browning during baking due to the Maillard reaction (page 285).

WHAT TYPE OF SUGAR SHOULD YOU CHOOSE?
- White granulated sugar: the most often used in bread baking.
- Cane sugar: lends a more distinctive flavor.
- Confectioners' sugar: this is a granulated sugar that has been ground into a very fine powder. It is used often for making pastries as it combines into a mixture more easily.

EGGS

EGGS

WHAT ARE THEY
In bread baking, only chicken eggs are used.
1 large egg = 1¾ ounces (50 g) out of shell, of which:
- 1⅛ ounces (32 g) = the egg white (high in water)
- ⅔ ounce (18 g) = the egg yolk (high in protein)

ROLES
- Add color to the dough.
- Used as a glaze before baking.
- Act as an excellent binder.
- Allow for better leavening of the dough.

TRADITIONAL USES
- Brioche dough (page 66)
- Glazing (page 48)
- Pastries

WHY DO EGGS PROMOTE AN AIRY CRUMB?
The proteins contained in eggs have surfactant properties that promote the incorporation of air into the dough. They have the ability to bind water and air at the same time.

KNEADING
BY HAND

Understanding

WHAT IT IS

The action that combines all the ingredients of the dough by hand.

ROLES

– Activates and develops yeasts by incorporating air into the dough. This is called the "aerobic" phase.
– Develops the gluten network in the dough. It is the movement of the dough during kneading, among other actions, that allows the formation of bonds between the gluten proteins. These bonds form the gluten network. The dough therefore develops its "strength" and is thus ready for the fermentation phase.

COMPLETION TIME

15 minutes

EQUIPMENT

Instant-read thermometer

CHALLENGES

– Storing the dough at the correct temperature (between 73 and 75°F/23 and 24°C).
– Kneading the dough sufficiently. The gluten must be stretched well and the dough elastic, otherwise the gases may escape and the dough will not rise.

USEFUL TIP

Tear off a small piece of dough at the end of the kneading time and stretch it; the dough is ready if it does not tear (because the gluten resists).

IT'S READY

When the dough is homogeneous, smooth, elastic, and not sticky.

WHAT HAPPENS IF YOU KNEAD TOO LONG?

The bonds between the gluten proteins are reduced, therefore the dough weakens and becomes sticky.

WHAT HAPPENS IF YOU DO NOT KNEAD LONG ENOUGH?

The gluten network will not be strong enough to retain the gases in the dough at the time of fermentation and baking. The bread will therefore rise less in the oven.

WHY MUST THE DOUGH BE BETWEEN 73 AND 75°F (23 AND 24°C)?

The microorganisms present in yeasts and starters are living organisms. They use the sugars present in the flour to form carbon dioxide (CO_2) during fermentation. It is between 73 and 75°F (23 and 24°C) that they are most active and effective.

INGREDIENTS

Salt
Fresh yeast
Water
Flour

1   Dilute the salt and the yeast in the water in a mixing bowl.

2   Pour the flour onto a work surface and form a well in the center. Pour the water mixture into the well, and incorporate the flour as you go.

3   The resulting rough ball of dough is referred to as the "mixing" (*frasage*).

4   Form a rough rectangle with the resulting dough. Cut away a quarter of the dough from the left edge.

5   Reapply this piece of dough onto the right side of the dough rectangle. Repeat Steps 4 and 5 several times for about 3 minutes. The purpose of these steps is to stretch the gluten and make the dough elastic.

6   Take a portion of dough and throw it very forcefully onto the work surface. Fold the dough over onto itself to trap the maximum amount of air inside. This is the stretching and expanding.

7   Continue to fold the dough over onto itself until it becomes less sticky. Shape the dough into a round.

8   Check that the temperature of the dough is between 73 and 75°F (23 and 24°C) using an instant-read thermometer.

KNEADING
MECHANICALLY

___

Understanding

WHAT IT IS

The action that combines all the ingredients of the dough using an electric mixer.

ADVANTAGES OF AN ELECTRIC MIXER

Faster, less tiring, and often more effective.

ROLES

– Activates and develops yeasts through the incorporation of air into the dough. This is called the "aerobic" phase.
– Develops the gluten network in the dough. It is the movement of the dough during kneading, among other actions, that allows the formation of bonds between the gluten proteins. These bonds form the gluten network. The dough therefore develops its "strength" and is thus ready for the fermentation phase.

COMPLETION TIME

10 minutes

EQUIPMENT

– Stand mixer fitted with the dough hook
– Instant-read thermometer

STEPS

– Mixing: occurs on the lowest speed.
– Kneading: occurs on medium speed to incorporate air.
– Spritzing (optional): adds additional water at the end of the kneading time.

CHALLENGE

Storing the dough at the correct temperature (between 73 and 75°F/23 and 24°C).

IT'S READY

When the dough detaches from the sides of the mixing bowl. It must be smooth, homogeneous, elastic, extensible, and not sticky.

DO YOU GET THE SAME RESULT KNEADING BY HAND AS WITH A MIXER?

The stretching and compression forces are greater during mechanical kneading, resulting in a more elastic dough with better resistance to rising during fermentation because the gluten network is better developed.

WHY IS THE KNEADING DURATION IMPORTANT?

The kneading time changes according to the desired result. A short kneading time preserves the flavors of the flour, but does not create optimal gluten development (this is counteracted by a long proofing time, and with "turning," which restores strength to the dough). This is for large loaves in which a typical bread flavor is desired. A long kneading time increases dough strength, but results in a loss of flavor. The proofing is short because the dough does not need to regain strength. This is the case with baguettes, in which a neutral flavor and presence of large holes in the crumb are desired.

WHAT IS SPRITZING?

This is the additional water incorporated at the end of the kneading time to soften a dough that is too firm. It makes it possible to obtain a thinner crust (the more water in the dough, the less quickly it dries out and the less the crust has time to form) and a more developed bread.

WHY MIX FIRST ON SLOW SPEED THEN ON MEDIUM SPEED?

The first kneading mixes the ingredients, which must be done slowly to form a homogeneous dough. The second kneading develops the gluten network and incorporates air. This is achieved on medium speed.

INGREDIENTS

Flour
Water
Yeast
Salt

1 Place all the ingredients in the mixing bowl and mix them on the lowest speed (speed 1) for 4 minutes. This is referred to as the "mixing" (*frasage*).

2 Increase the speed of the mixer to medium and continue kneading until the dough is smooth and homogeneous and detaches from the sides of the bowl; this will take about 6 minutes. This is referred to as the "kneading."

3 Check that the temperature of the dough is between 73 and 75°F (23 and 24°C) using an instant-read thermometer.

FERMENTATION

Understanding

WHAT IT IS

The transformation of the sugars contained in the flour into carbon dioxide (CO_2) and alcohol, under the action of the microorganisms present in the ferments (starters and fresh yeast). The gas released causes the swelling of the dough.

ROLE

To allow the optimal development of the dough and to lend flavor and aroma to the bread.

TEMPERATURE OF FERMENTATION

The dough needs to be at a temperature between 73 and 75°F (23 and 24°C) so that the microorganisms contained in the ferments can develop. This is also the temperature at which the flavors develop optimally.

WHAT TYPE OF FERMENTATION DOES EACH FERMENT CREATE?

–*Fermentation with fresh yeast: the rising is pronounced and fast because the yeast produces a great deal of carbon dioxide (CO_2). It also produces alcohol (which evaporates). This is referred to as "alcohol fermentation." The crumb is airy and the flavor neutral.*
–*Fermentation with a liquid starter: the rising is slow and complex (often aided by the addition of fresh yeast) and requires heat and moisture. This is referred to as "lactic fermentation" (it produces an acid), which develops more aromas.*
–*Fermentation with a stiff starter: the rising is even longer and must be achieved under refrigeration. This is referred to as "acetic fermentation." The flavor is rustic and acidic.*

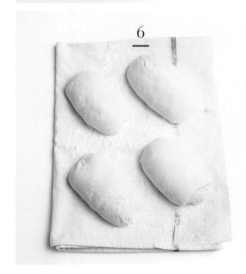

1 KNEADING

The activation of yeasts in the presence of oxygen.

2 FIRST RISE (START)

Anaerobic phase: in the absence of oxygen, the yeasts attack the sugars in the flour and produce carbon dioxide (CO_2). Gas is released, resulting in the first rise of the dough.

3 TURNING

Reactivation of the yeasts from fermentation by incorporating air (oxygen) into the dough.

4 FIRST RISE (END)

Anaerobic phase: deprived of oxygen, the yeasts attack the sugars again. Rising continues.

5 PRESHAPING

Cutting the dough to the desired shape before resting, in preparation for final shaping and proofing.

6 RESTING

This step is necessary before final shaping so that the dough relaxes and does not tear.

7 FINAL SHAPING

8 PROOFING

The second rise; the same process as the first rise, but the bread maintains its final shape.

FERMENTATION:
FIRST RISE

Understanding

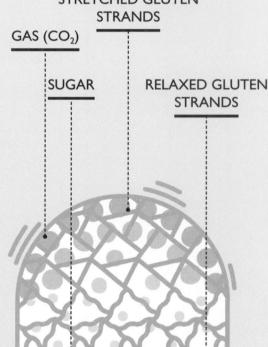

GAS (CO₂)

STRETCHED GLUTEN
STRANDS

SUGAR

RELAXED GLUTEN
STRANDS

WHAT IT IS

The second fermentation phase and the first rise of the dough. It begins after kneading and ends before final shaping. This is the "anaerobic" phase: there is no more oxygen in the dough, and the enzymes in the yeast begin to eat the sugars and transform them into carbon dioxide (CO_2).

ROLES

– Raises the dough: the gases produced by the fermentation are retained in the dough thanks to the gluten network (which forms a tight mesh). The dough swells.
– Develops the aromas and acidity of the dough.
– Makes the dough ready for final shaping: because of the correct balance between strength and elasticity, the dough can be stretched and lengthened without being damaged.

FERMENTATION TIMES

– At room temperature, this can take from 30 minutes to 3 hours.
– In the refrigerator, from 12 to 48 hours.

IT'S READY

When the dough:
– has a slight increase in volume;
– retracts a little: it becomes firmer, and holds better;
– is smoother;
– is more elastic and extensible.

A SPECIAL CASE: WHAT IS THE ADVANTAGE OF RISING IN THE REFRIGERATOR?

– Develops aromas: the fermentation is slower, of higher quality, and the ferments have the time to develop fully.
– Develops the gluten network: the cold tightens the "mesh" of the network.
– Increases the moisture content of the bread to achieve a better crumb and a thinner crust. The cold will allow the dough to tighten and to have more resistance to baking.
– By being less dependent on the rising of the dough, the moment when the dough should be baked is more flexible.

WHY DOES THE DURATION OF RISING VARY FROM ONE DOUGH TO ANOTHER?

It depends on the rate of hydration and the quantity of ferments present in the dough. The fewer the ferments, the longer the rising time (because the yeasts, in smaller quantities, take longer to eat the sugars, thus the dough takes longer to rise). Similarly, if the dough contains a great deal of water, it has less strength. A long rise helps to restore strength.

FERMENTATION CONDITIONS FOR DOUGH

– Directly in the bowl of the mixer or in a mixing bowl.
– Covered with plastic wrap or a towel, protected from the ambient air (to prevent the development of a crust and disturbing the fermentation).
– At room temperature.

FERMENTATION:
TURNING

Understanding

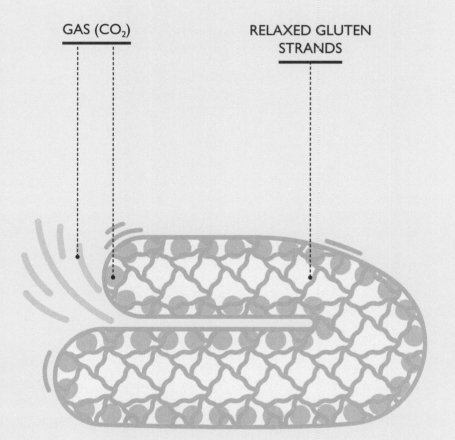

GAS (CO$_2$)

RELAXED GLUTEN
STRANDS

ROLE
Restart fermentation by
restoring strength to the dough.

PRINCIPLE
On a floured work surface, fold
2 sides in to meet in the center
of the dough. Flip the dough
over seam side down. Make 1 to
2 turns during the rising time.

WHAT IT IS
The action of folding the
dough onto itself in order
to restart fermentation.

HOW DOES TURNING RESTART FERMENTATION?

*Over the course of rising, the activity of the yeasts gradually slows down. Turning
the dough results in:*
*–expelling the excess carbon dioxide (CO$_2$), which has the effect of developing yeast
cells and of multiplying them (by division); it boosts fermentative activity;*
–tightening the gluten network: the dough becomes very extensible.
Turning makes it more elastic and thus gives it more resistance (firmness).
The dough regains strength and the rising can resume.

FERMENTATION:
PRESHAPING AND RESTING

Understanding

WHAT IT IS

Preshaping of the dough
(preceded by weighing)
and the resting phase after
the first stages of rising
and before final shaping.

ROLE

Allows the gluten network
to relax and loosen to
facilitate shaping and
avoid tearing the dough.

GAS (CO_2)

RELAXED GLUTEN
STRANDS

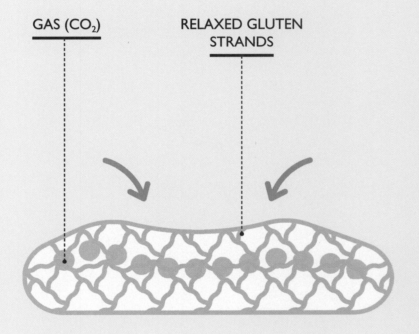

FERMENTATION TIME

Very short, 15 to 40 minutes.

IT'S READY

When, at the time of final
shaping, the dough does
not tear and is sufficiently
extensible (it does not
offer resistance).

PRESHAPING A ROUND

For round or oblong loaves, the dough should
be preshaped into a round after rising, in
preparation for resting. Bring the ends of
the dough to the center. Flip the round over.
Pinch the dough with your hands underneath
the round in order to stretch the top.

PRESHAPING AN OBLONG

– For baguettes, breadsticks, or épis, it
  is necessary to preshape a dough after
  rising until it is slightly elongated,
  in preparation for resting.
– Form a round with the dough
  then roll it under the palms of the
  hands to lengthen it slightly.

WHY SHOULD YOU NOT TEAR THE DOUGH?

*If the dough is torn, the gases
escape and the dough will not rise,
causing the bread to be dense.*

CONDITIONS FOR RESTING

Under a towel on a floured work surface or
in a mixing bowl covered with plastic wrap,
seam side down, at room temperature.

FERMENTATION:
PROOFING

Understanding

GAS (CO$_2$)   STRETCHED GLUTEN
                              STRANDS

SUGAR

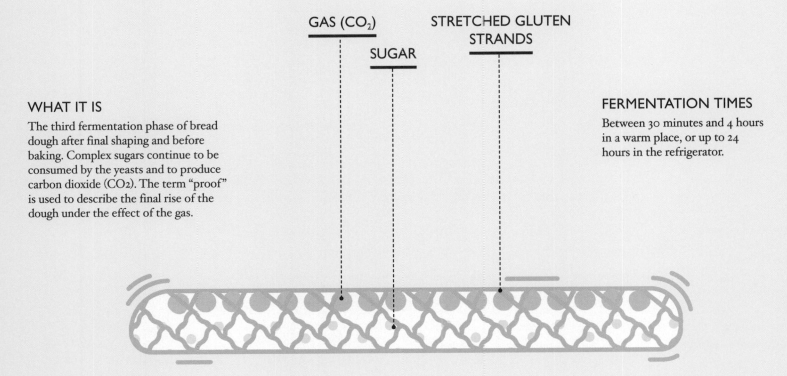

WHAT IT IS

The third fermentation phase of bread dough after final shaping and before baking. Complex sugars continue to be consumed by the yeasts and to produce carbon dioxide (CO2). The term "proof" is used to describe the final rise of the dough under the effect of the gas.

FERMENTATION TIMES

Between 30 minutes and 4 hours in a warm place, or up to 24 hours in the refrigerator.

ROLE

To restart the expansion from gases until the ideal moment of development prior to baking. This determines the final volume of the bread once baked.

IT'S READY

When a light press into the dough with the fingertip leaves no mark.

WHY DOES PROOFING NEED TO BE IN A WARM PLACE?

During this phase, some of the starch is transformed into simple sugars. These are then broken down into alcohol and carbon dioxide (CO$_2$) by the enzymes in the yeast. To be successful, and to allow the enzymes to do their job properly, this step must take place in a warm place, between 77 and 82°F (25 and 28°C).

FERMENTATION CONDITIONS

In a warm place (between 77 and 82°F/25 and 28°C), such as on top of the refrigerator or a radiator, and covered with a towel to prevent a crust from forming.

FINAL SHAPING

Understanding

WHAT IT IS

Manipulating the dough before baking to give it its final shape. This step follows rising and precedes proofing.

COMPLETION TIME

Between 5 and 15 minutes depending on the complexity of the desired shape.

CHALLENGES

– Handling the dough without crushing or tearing it.
– Forming a uniform shape.
– Tightening the dough: this is adapting the level of tightening (which can be more or less accentuated) according to the consistency of the dough. With a soft dough, securing a tight shape is important; with a firm dough, the tightening should be less pronounced.

WHAT IS SEAMING?

This is where the edges of the dough are joined during shaping. During fermentation, the seams are usually placed underneath, except in special cases. For baking, the seam is also placed underneath, except where it is desired for the dough to split during baking; in this case, this approach would replace scoring.

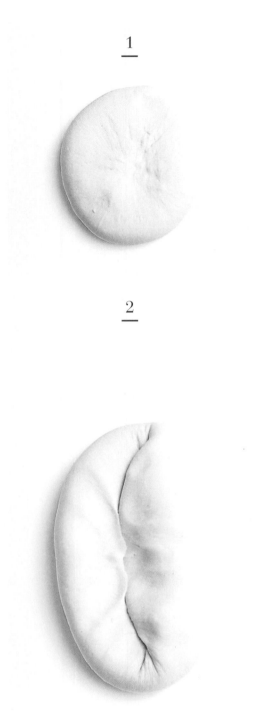

Final shaping consists of three basic steps (two only for boules). For each type of shaping, it is necessary to flatten and fold. For elongated breads (baguettes, bâtards, épis), the shaping includes a step to lengthen them. For specialized shapes, see pages 42 to 47.

1 FLATTENING

Once the preshaping and resting are complete, turn the dough over, make a seam on top, and smooth it gently to level the surface and release the excess gas.

2 FOLDING

Bring the ends of the dough to the center in successive folds while maintaining the shape and strength of the dough (it is necessary to stretch the outer membrane of the dough so that it can expand during baking). This creates the seam.

3 ELONGATING (EXCEPT FOR BOULES)

Shape the desired length of the dough by rolling it under your palms, starting from the center and moving out toward the ends.

Shaping a boule (ball)

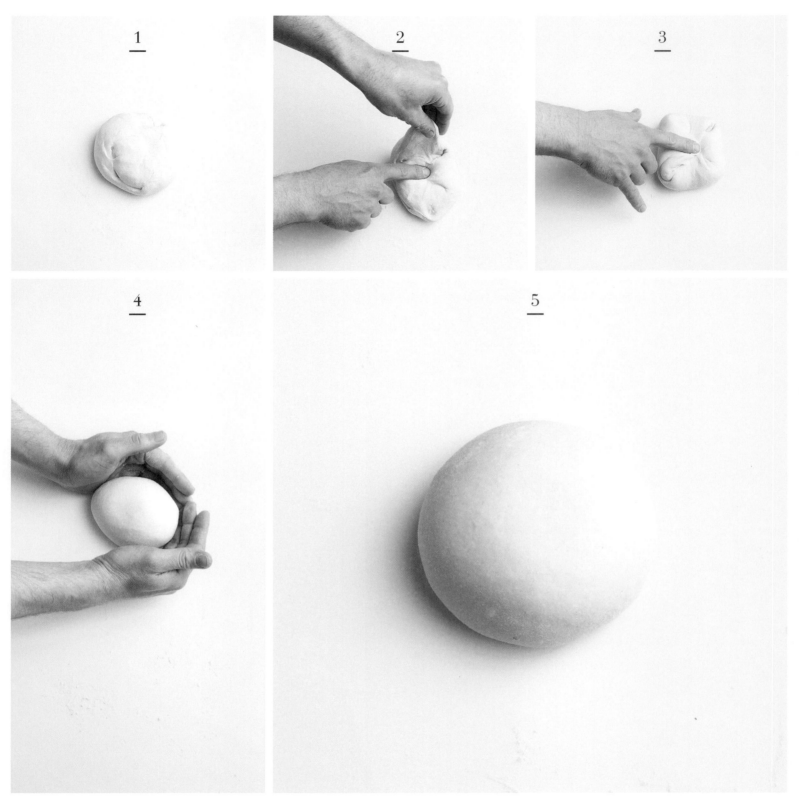

1 Place a piece of dough seam side up onto a lightly floured work surface.

2 Place your index finger with your right hand in the center of the dough without pressing. With the left hand, fold each corner into the middle of the dough.

3 Secure the edges with the index finger of your right hand.

4 Turn the boule over. Pinch the dough with your hands moving under it, to stretch the top, and turn the dough one quarter.

5 Repeat Step 4 three times.

Shaping a baguette

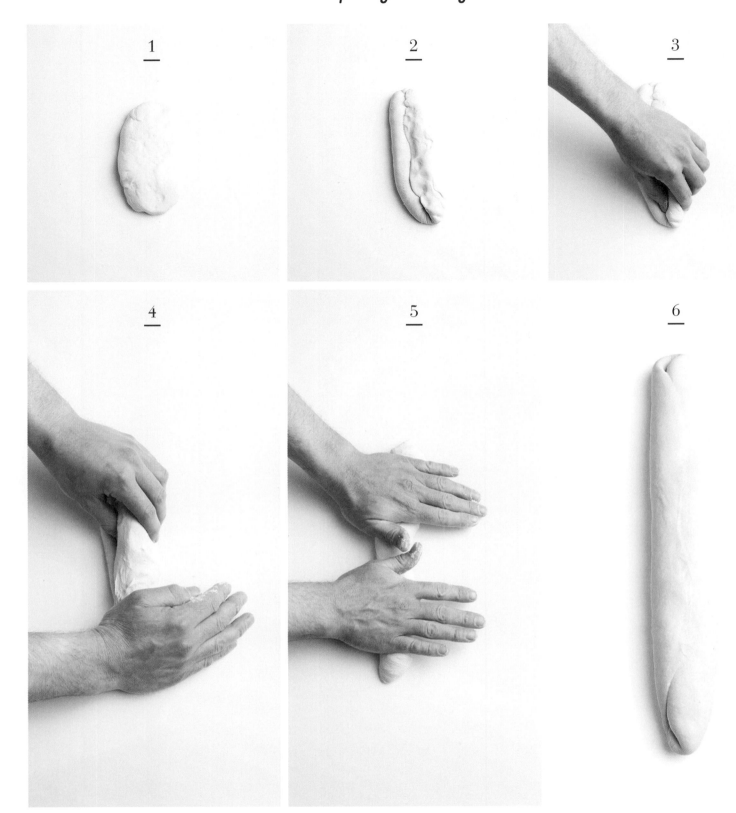

1 Place a piece of dough smooth side down (seam on top) onto a lightly floured work surface. Shape it into a rectangular form.

2 Fold the dough lengthwise three times.

3 Place the left thumb on the right end of the dough pressing lightly on the seam. Enclose the thumb using three other fingers of the same hand.

4 Slide the thumb down the length of the dough and seal the entire length of it, creating a seam using the palm of the opposite hand.

5 Place your palms in the middle of the top of the baguette. Lengthen it by rolling the baguette with both hands, starting from the center and moving out toward the ends.

6 Continue rolling to adjust the length.

Shaping a ficelle (long, thin loaf)

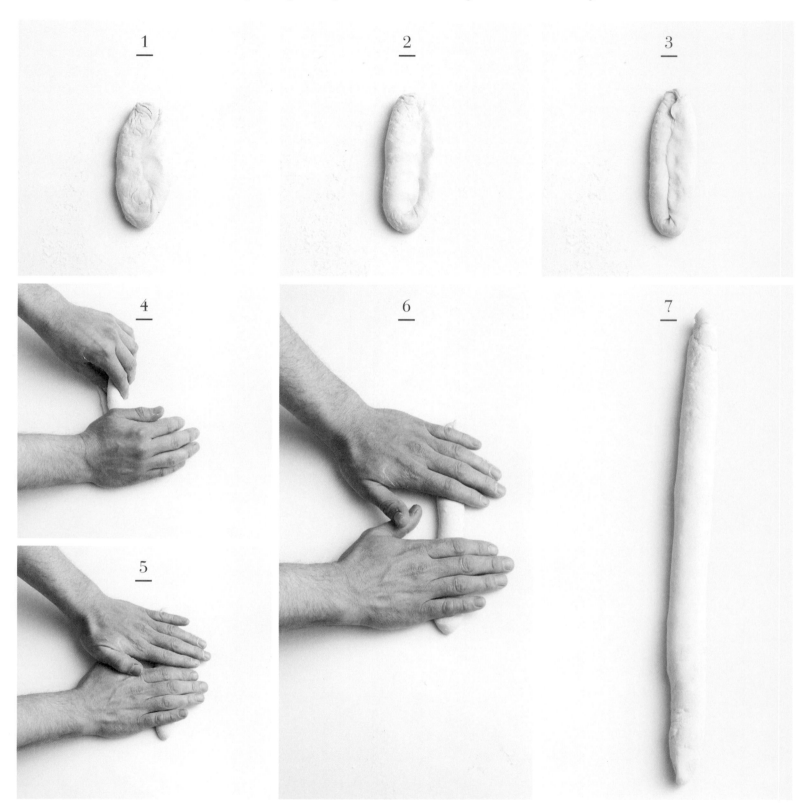

1 Place a piece of dough smooth side down (seam on top) onto a lightly floured work surface.

2 Shape the dough into a rectangle. Take one side of the dough and fold it toward the center of the dough.

3 Take the other side of the dough and fold it over into the middle so that each side overlaps.

4 Place your left thumb at one end of the seam, thumb on the seam. Gather the top of the dough with your left hand and fold it down and toward your left thumb. Continue this gather and fold motion down the length of the dough, while using the heel of your right hand to press and seal the seam.

5 Repeat this gather and fold motion down the length of the dough again.

6 Place your palms in the middle of the top of the ficelle. Press down while rolling it with both hands, starting from the center and moving out toward the ends.

7 Continue to roll and elongate the dough until it is the length of your baking sheet or to your desired length.

Shaping a bâtard (torpedo)

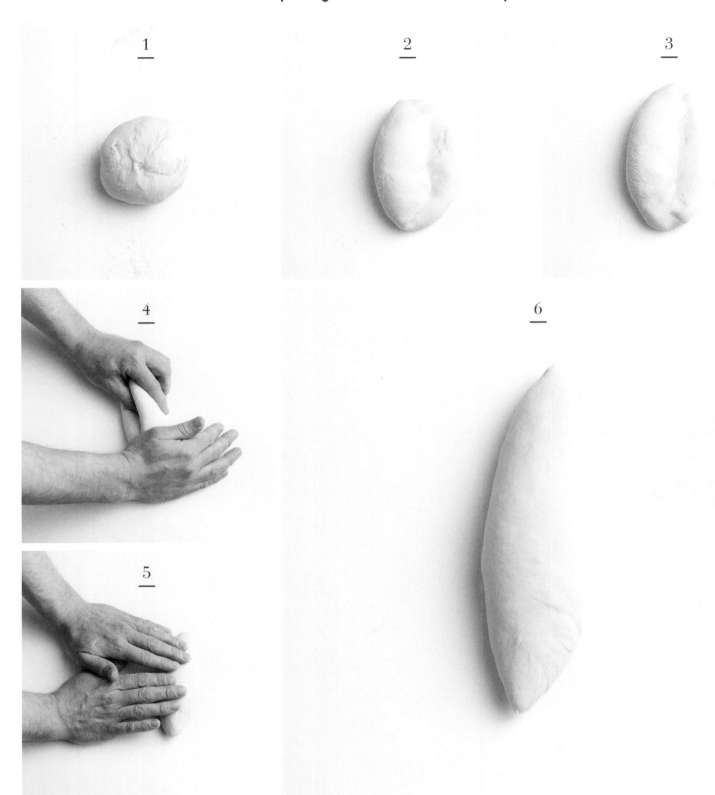

1 Take a piece of dough previously shaped into a boule. Place it on a lightly floured work surface.

2 Take one side of the dough and fold it over into the middle.

3 Rotate the dough and repeat the operation with the other side.

4 Place your left thumb at one end of the seam, thumb on the seam. Gather the top of the dough with your left hand and fold it down and toward your left thumb. Continue this gather and fold motion down the length of the dough, while using the heel of your right hand to press and seal the seam.

5 Place your hands in the middle of the bâtard and lengthen it slightly by rolling the dough with both hands, starting from the center and moving out toward the ends.

6 Continue to roll and elongate the dough until it is the length of the baking sheet or to your desired length. To create the tapered ends, roll the dough more at the ends.

Shaping a couronne (ring)

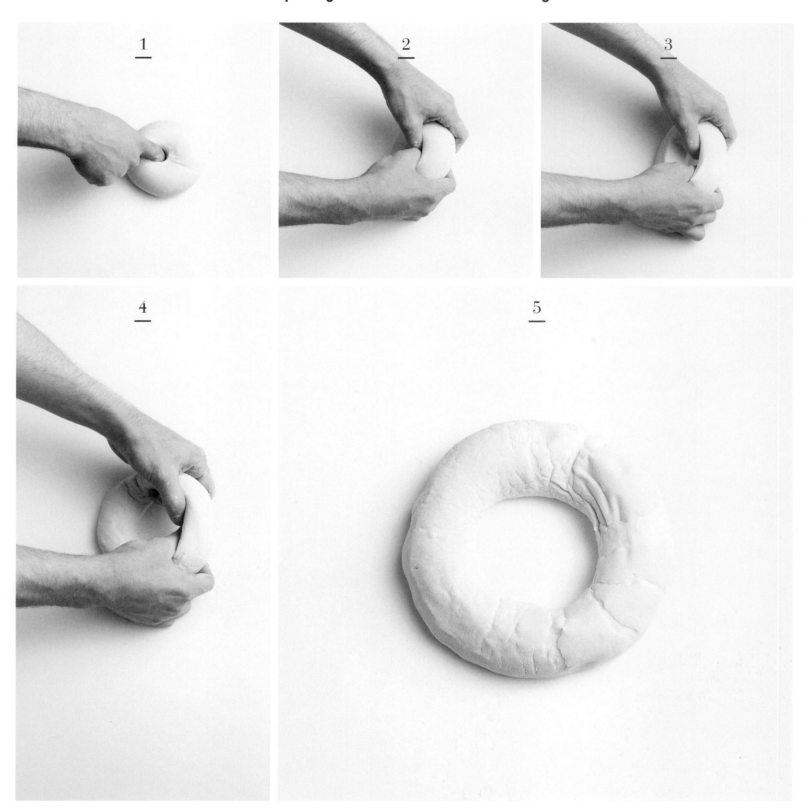

1 Take a piece of dough previously shaped into a boule and place it on a work surface seam side down. Lightly flour the center of the dough and press into the center with your index finger until you reach the work surface.

2 Flour your fingers, then grasp the dough between the thumb and index finger of one hand.

3 With the other hand, gently slide the dough through your hands to enlarge the center hole while at the same time reducing the thickness of the ring. When the dough no longer stretches, let it rest for 5 minutes.

4 Repeat this procedure until you have a diameter of 4 inches (10 cm) inside the ring.

5 The center hole should be large enough to not close during proofing or baking.

Shaping a braid

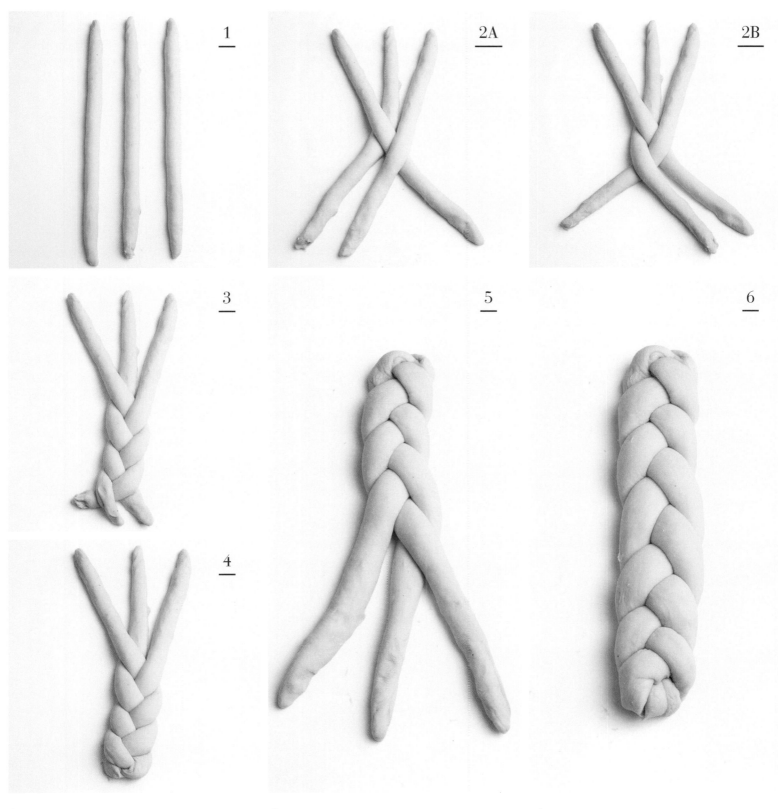

1   Shape three long strands of dough of the same length and place them parallel to one another. The one on the left is number 1, the one in the middle is number 2, and the one on the right is number 3.

2   Begin braiding at the center point of the three strands: take strand 2 and cross it under in place of strand 1; take strand 1 and cross it under in place of strand 3. Take strand 3 and cross it over in place of strand 2.

3   Repeat this operation all the way down to the ends of the strands.

4   Seal the ends of the three strands together.

5   Turn the dough around and finish the braiding toward the other end, crossing the strands one over the other as previously described. Do not tighten the braid too much to prevent it from tearing during proofing.

6   Seal the ends of the three strands together.

GLANCING

Understanding

WHAT IT IS

A mixture of egg, milk, and salt brushed onto doughs before baking them to obtain a golden and shiny crust once baked.

COMPLETION TIME

Preparation time: 5 minutes

EQUIPMENT

–Strainer
–Pastry brush

SKILL TO MASTER

Straining (page 285)

SHELF LIFE

Use immediately.

TRADITIONAL USES

–Breakfast pastries (*viennoiseries*)
–Brioche (page 216)
–King Cake (page 204)

USEFUL TIP

Avoid silicone brushes, as they do not allow you to brush the glaze on evenly. Brush the dough several times to brown it well.

WHAT IS THE PURPOSE OF GLAZING?

It plays an aesthetic role by giving shine to the dough and an attractive golden color. It also lightly crisps the crust.

WHY ADD MILK TO THE EGG?

During baking, egg proteins and milk sugars react (Maillard reaction; page 285). This makes it possible to obtain the typical golden color.

WHY MUST GLAZING OCCUR BEFORE AND AFTER PROOFING?

To glaze the areas of the dough that appear once the dough has risen and to obtain a more even color when baking.

ENOUGH TO GLAZE 1 BRIOCHE OR 6 CROISSANTS

1 large (50 g) egg
½ teaspoon (3 g) whole milk
Pinch of salt

1 Lightly beat the egg, milk, and salt together with a whisk in a bowl until the mixture is well blended.

2 Strain through a sieve to create a smooth mixture.

3 Apply the glaze using a pastry brush, brushing lightly and without pressing too firmly to prevent changing the shape of the surface of the dough.

SCORING

Understanding

WHAT IT IS

A blade is used to slash through the dough before baking to form cuts or notches.

COMPLETION TIME

Between 5 and 10 minutes

EQUIPMENT

Lame, razor blade, or serrated knife

ROLES

– Allows gas to escape and the bread to rise sufficiently without splitting the crust.
– Provides a visual identification to finished breads.

CHALLENGE

Adjusting the blade stroke: cut deeply into a dough that has risen very little, but make shallow cuts in a dough that has risen too much.

USEFUL TIPS

– For breads, lightly flouring the surface of the dough before scoring it lends a more aesthetic result.
– For a traditional slash (a straight slash down the length of the dough), start from the end farthest from you.

WHAT HAPPENS IF THE SLASHES ARE TOO DEEP?

Sagging and loss of volume of the dough could occur when baked. If the slashes are too wide, the bread could stale more rapidly.

WHAT HAPPENS IF THE SLASHES ARE TOO SHALLOW?

Resulting from the build up of gases and from steam, the crust could burst and cause deformities. The slashes could also close up, causing the bread to lack volume, making the bread's appearance less attractive.

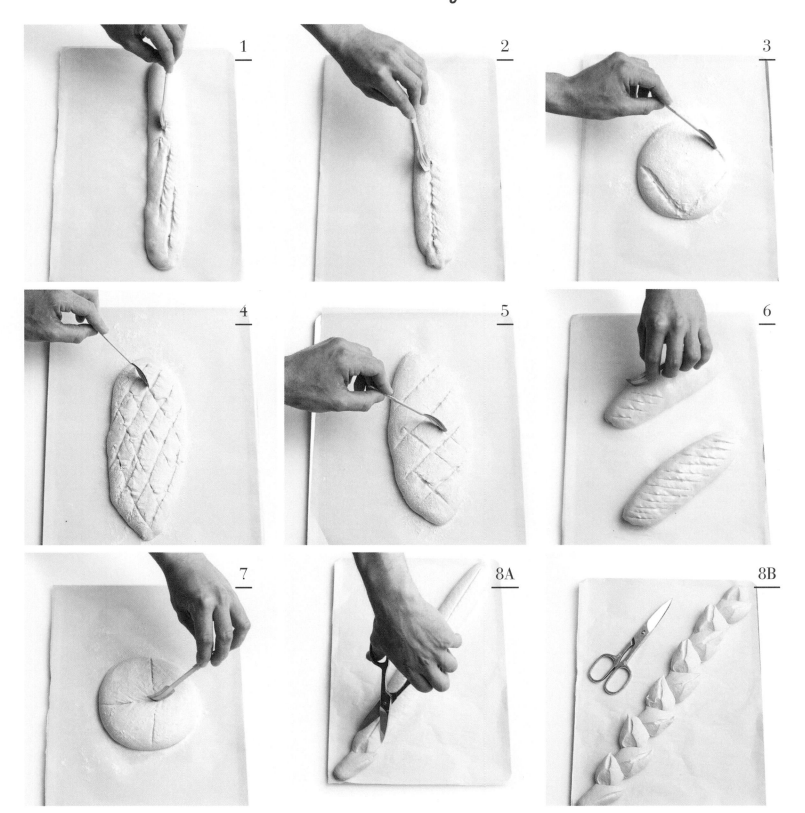

1 BAGUETTE

Tilt the blade thirty degrees to one side. Make 2-inch-long (5 cm) diagonal slashes, moving down toward the end of the dough, repeating the slashing at even intervals; make five to seven slashes down the baguette.

2 TRADITIONAL

Tilt the blade thirty degrees to one side. With a precise and continuous motion, slash a long line down the center of the dough.

3 DIAMOND

Hold the blade at an angle and make four straight slashes close to the edges of the dough, extending the ends to the edges, to form a large diamond shape.

4 CRISSCROSS

Tilt the blade at an angle and make shallow slashes spaced ⅓ to ¾ inch (1 to 2 cm) apart. Repeat along the opposite diagonal to form a diamond pattern.

5 LARGE CRISSCROSS

Make four parallel blade strokes diagonally across the dough. Repeat along the opposite diagonal, making one slash ending at the beginning point of the second slash. Make two more slashes to form three diamond shapes down the center of the dough.

6 DIAGONAL

Hold the lame close to the blade. Make quick, parallel and deep slashes, very close together, and at an angle across the top of the dough.

7 SINGLE CROSS

Flour the dough. Make slashes from top to bottom through the center, then from left to right.

8 ÉPI (WHEAT STALK)

Tilt the blade thirty degrees to one side. Make a long slash down the center of the baguette. Using scissors angled at forty-five degrees, make cuts through the top two-thirds portion of the dough every 4 inches (10 cm). Move each cut piece of dough to one side of the baguette, alternating the sides. Be careful when moving the dough to the oven as the baguette is very fragile.

BAKING

Understanding

WHAT IT IS

The last fermentation phase (the yeasts die at 122°F/50°C). Transformation of the fermented dough into bread occurs under the heat of the oven.

OVEN TEMPERATURE

– Small doughs: bake quickly at a high and constant temperature to ensure a soft crumb.
– Large doughs (more than 14 ounces/400 g of raw dough): bake at a preheated high temperature, then reduce the temperature as soon as the dough is placed in the oven. Slightly prop open the oven door 5 to 10 minutes before the end of the baking time so that the crumb can dry without burning the crust.

STEAMING

Creating steam in the oven as soon as the dough is placed in the oven. Place a bowl filled with water in the oven while it is preheating. When baking, spritz the bottom of the oven with a spray bottle to release a maximum amount of steam.

IT'S BAKED

When the crust is crisp and slightly shiny, and the interior crumb is soft.

NOTE

Some breads, such as rye bread, are better when staling has begun (see page 53).

WHY DOES THE BREAD STOP DEVELOPING AT 212°F (100°C)?

Because at this temperature the flour's starch gelatinizes and thickens the dough, causing the gluten network to congeal. This stops the development of the bread.

WHAT PURPOSE DOES STEAMING SERVE?

–It delays the formation of the crust to allow time for the dough to finish swelling.
–It assists with the development of a thinner and shinier crust.
–It assists with the formation of the slashes.

WHAT HAPPENS IF THERE IS NOT ENOUGH STEAM?

–The slashes may tear open because the crust will form too quickly.
–The crust will be dull and thick.

WHAT HAPPENS IF THERE IS TOO MUCH STEAM?

–The slashes may stick together.
–The bread may be too shiny and smooth: the crust will not be crispy and will have a rubbery texture.

CAN YOU EAT A BREAD THAT IS STILL HOT?

Hot bread has a strong smell, but less flavor. It is not digested as easily because all the gases have not yet escaped.

1

2

STAGES DURING BAKING

The volume of the dough increases as the high heat from the oven expands the gases contained in the dough, giving the bread its final volume. The crust and crumb form. Evaporation of water and gases occurs (this is an advantage of scoring, which aids evaporation). Once the bread reaches 212°F (100°C), it stops swelling and the crust hardens. The final caramelization of the sugars occurs, which gives the crust color and provides flavor and aromas to the bread (Maillard reaction, page 285).

STAGES AFTER BAKING

COOLING

–What it is: cooling of the bread after it is removed from the oven.
–Roles: steam, carbon dioxide (CO_2), and alcohol in the crumb escape. The crumb absorbs moisture from the ambient and dry air. The aromas are established.
–Conditions and duration: on a rack, until completely cooled, from 30 minutes for small loaves to a few hours for large loaves.

STALING

–What it is: the bread dries gradually; it begins to age at the end of the cooling process.
–Duration: fast for baguettes and small loaves. It accelerates over time for large loaves.

BAKING RESULTS

1 POOR BAKING

–The crumb is sticky and gummy.
–The crust is dull and barely crisp

2 SUCCESSFUL BAKING

–The crust is well browned (Maillard reaction, page 285).
–The bottom of the bread is firm.
–The crumb is not wet.

STRAIGHT DOUGH

Understanding

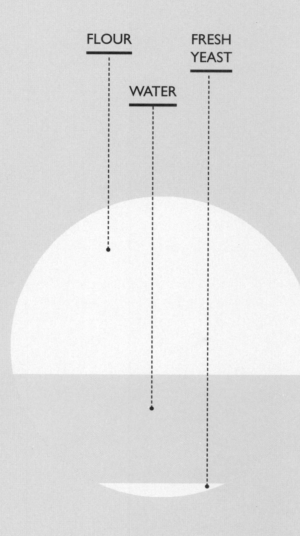

FLOUR

WATER

FRESH YEAST

WHAT IT IS

A classic bread dough made from wheat flour, water, fresh yeast, and salt, and which needs a rather short fermentation time.

COMPLETION TIME

–Preparation time: 20 minutes
–Fermentation time: 30 minutes

EQUIPMENT

–Stand mixer fitted with the dough hook (optional)
–Instant-read thermometer

TRADITIONAL USE

Baguette (page 84)

CHALLENGE

Storing the dough at the correct temperature (see "It's Ready," below).

SKILL TO MASTER

Kneading (pages 30 and 32)

IT'S READY

When the ball of dough is homogeneous and smooth, and its temperature is between 73 and 75°F (23 and 24°C).

SHELF LIFE

Twenty-four hours in the refrigerator, wrapped in plastic wrap.

WHAT IS THE ADVANTAGE OF THE FRESH YEAST IN THIS DOUGH?

To obtain a dough with a neutral flavor that can be enriched with cheese, bacon, dried fruits, etc. Fresh yeast also allows for a rapid rise. The crumb will be very airy as a result.

VARIATION: FERMENTED DOUGH (*PÂTE FERMENTÉE*)

A straight dough that has rested for 24 hours (also referred to as "old dough"). It allows additional flavors to develop in the dough without having to use a starter. It is used in the Cheese Bread (page 146) and Cheese Ficelles with Seeds (page 150) recipes specifically.

MAKES 1¾ POUNDS (800 G) DOUGH

3¾ cups (500 g) high-protein all-purpose
    flour (or use bread flour or T65 flour)
1¼ cups plus 1 teaspoon (300 g) water
1¼ packed teaspoons (10 g) fresh yeast
1½ teaspoons (9 g) salt

1 Place the flour, water, crumbled yeast,
and salt in the bowl of a stand mixer.

2 Knead (see page 32) for 4 minutes
on the lowest (speed 1).

3 Knead for 6 minutes on medium speed.
The dough should detach from the sides of the
bowl. (For kneading by hand, see page 30.)

4 Check that the temperature of the
dough is between 73 and 75°F (23 and 24°C)
using an instant-read thermometer.

5 Let rise (see page 36) for 30 minutes on a
floured work surface covered with a towel.

"FRENCH TRADITION"
STRAIGHT DOUGH

Understanding

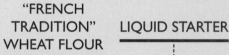

"FRENCH
TRADITION"
WHEAT FLOUR
LIQUID STARTER

WATER

WHAT IT IS

Dough made using a liquid starter and wheat flour processed without additives (aka "French tradition" wheat flour).

COMPLETION TIME

– Preparation time: 30 minutes
– Fermentation time: 1 hour

EQUIPMENT

– Stand mixer fitted with the dough hook (optional)
– Instant-read thermometer

TRADITIONAL USE

"French Tradition" Baguette (page 88)

CHALLENGES

– Storing the dough at the correct temperature (see "It's Ready," below).
– Not overworking the dough.

SKILLS TO MASTER

– Kneading (pages 30 and 32)
– Turning (page 37)

IT'S READY

When the ball of dough is homogeneous and smooth, nonelastic, and its temperature is between 73 and 75°F (23 and 24°C).

SHELF LIFE

Twenty-four hours in the refrigerator, wrapped in plastic wrap.

WHAT IS "FRENCH TRADITION" WHEAT FLOUR?

This flour does not contain any of the additives used to make dough more homogeneous. The absence of additives creates a crumb that is more irregular and flavorful.

WHAT DOES THE STARTER OFFER?

Like yeast, sourdough starter is a ferment. It allows the dough to rise. The starter also creates aromatic notes and acidity, which create the characteristic flavor of traditional breads and facilitates the formation of a more rustic crust.

WHAT ARE THE DIFFERENCES BETWEEN THIS DOUGH AND STANDARD STRAIGHT DOUGH?

"French tradition" dough uses "French tradition" wheat flour, and often more water. Its kneading is slower and its rising time is longer.

WHY MUST THE DOUGH BE TURNED?

During rising, the yeasts consume the sugars of the flour and release gases. These gases remain trapped in the gluten network formed during kneading, which

causes the dough to rise. After a while, the yeasts are exhausted and the gluten network relaxes. The result is less gas and a dough that holds gas less well, so the dough collapses. The turning can reactivate the yeast and tighten the gluten network, restoring strength to the dough. This is especially needed with "French tradition" dough because "French tradition" wheat flour contains more complex sugars than standard wheat flour. The yeasts first consume the simple sugars. The fermentation must be reactivated to allow time for the complex sugars to be consumed by the yeasts.

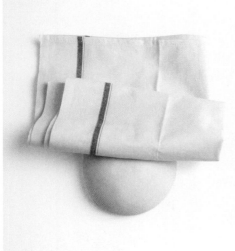

MAKES 2 POUNDS (910 G) "FRENCH TRADITION" STRAIGHT DOUGH

3¾ cups (500 g) T65 "French tradition"
    wheat flour (or use organic high-protein
    all-purpose flour or bread flour)
1½ cups minus 2 teaspoons (345 g) water
1¾ ounces (50 g) Liquid Starter (page 20)
⅝ packed teaspoon (5 g) fresh yeast
1⅔ teaspoons (10 g) salt

1   Knead (see page 32) the flour, water, starter, crumbled yeast, and salt in a stand mixer for 4 minutes on the lowest speed (speed 1).

2   Knead for 6 minutes on medium speed. The dough should detach from the sides of the bowl. (For kneading by hand, see page 30.)

3   Check that the temperature of the dough is between 73 and 75°F (23 and 24°C) using an instant-read thermometer.

4   Let the dough rise (see page 36) for 30 minutes on a floured work surface at room temperature, covered with a towel.

5   Turn the dough (see page 37), and let rise again for 30 minutes on a floured work surface, covered with a towel.

PIZZA DOUGH

Understanding

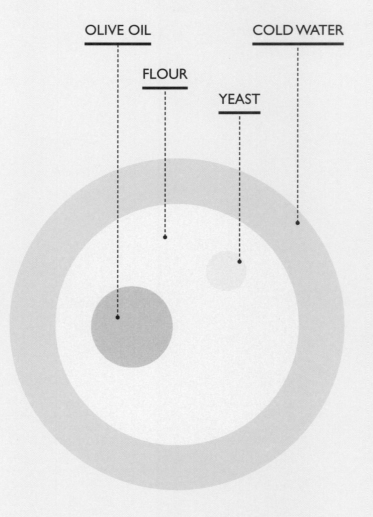

OLIVE OIL

FLOUR

YEAST

COLD WATER

WHAT IT IS
A straight dough enriched
with olive oil.

COMPLETION TIME
–Preparation time: 20 minutes
–Fermentation time: 2½ to 3 hours
 (30 minutes rising, 30 minutes
 resting, 1½ to 2 hours proofing)

EQUIPMENT
–Stand mixer fitted with the
 dough hook (optional)
–Bench scraper
–Rolling pin

TRADITIONAL USE
Pizza

OTHER USE
Fougasse (page 164)

VARIATION
Focaccia (page 160)

IT'S READY
When the dough ball is
homogeneous and smooth and
its temperature is between
73 and 75°F (23 and 24°C).

SHELF LIFE
Twenty-four hours, wrapped
in plastic wrap.

WHAT DOES THE ADDITION OF THE OIL DO FOR THIS DOUGH?
With this dough, oil is incorporated at the end of the kneading time. The
addition of the fat changes the formation of the gluten network, limiting
the development of holes during baking and providing suppleness.

CHALLENGE
The dough must be sufficiently
elastic to be thinly rolled out.

SKILLS TO MASTER
–Kneading (pages 30 and 32)
–Preshaping a Round (page 38)

USEFUL TIP
Roll out the dough several times
so that it relaxes and can be thinly
rolled out without tearing.

**MAKES 2 RECTANGULAR CRUSTS
MEASURING 15¾ × 12 INCHES
(40 × 30 CM)**

DOUGH

3¾ cups (500 g) high-protein all-purpose
   flour (or use bread flour or T65 flour)
1¼ cups plus 1 teaspoon (300 g) cold water
1⅞ packed teaspoons (15 g) fresh yeast
1⅔ teaspoons (10 g) salt
½ cup (100 g) olive oil

1 Knead (see page 32) the flour, water, crumbled
yeast, and salt in a stand mixer for 5 minutes on the
lowest speed (speed 1), then for 6 minutes on medium
speed; the dough should detach from the sides of
the bowl. (For kneading by hand, see page 30.)

2 Incorporate the oil little by little on speed 1.

3 Let the dough rise in the bowl for
30 minutes at room temperature.

4 Divide the dough into two pieces, shape
them into rounds, and let rest for 30 minutes,
covered with a towel, at room temperature.

5 Flour the bottoms and tops of the rounds,
then roll them out using a rolling pin, moving
from top to bottom and right to left so that
the dough is a uniform rectangular shape.

6 Let rest for 1½ to 2 hours, covered with a
towel, in a warm place, for the proofing.

VIENNA DOUGH

Understanding

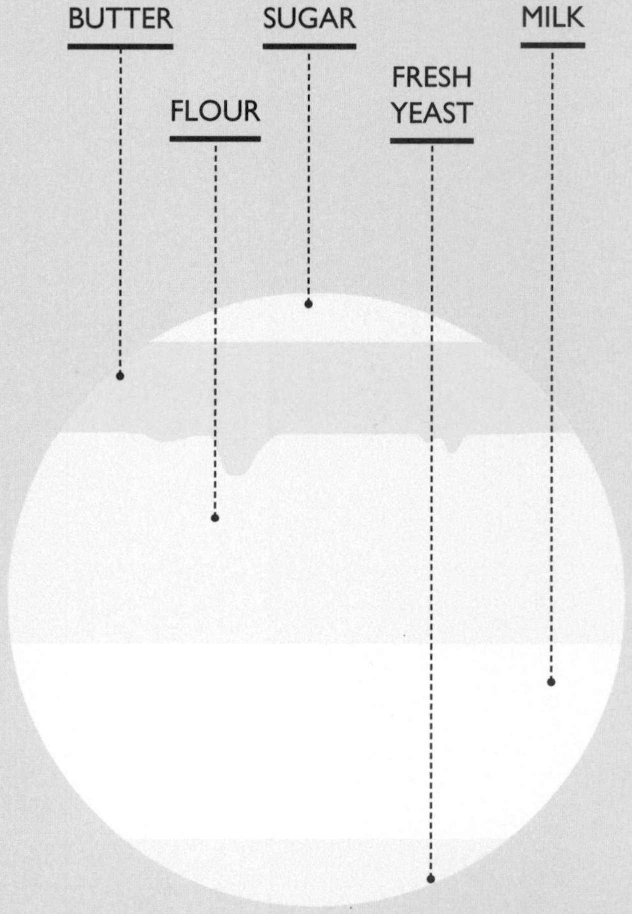

BUTTER   SUGAR   MILK

FLOUR   FRESH YEAST

WHAT IT IS

A slightly sweet yeast-raised dough made with milk.

OTHER USES

–Chocolate Vienna bread
–Small Muesli Loaves (page 144)

COMPLETION TIME

–Preparation time: 25 minutes
–Resting time: 5 hours

IT'S READY

When the dough ball is homogenous and smooth.

EQUIPMENT

–Stand mixer fitted with the dough hook (optional)
–Instant-read thermometer

SHELF LIFE

Twenty-four hours in the refrigerator, wrapped in plastic wrap.

CHALLENGE

Incorporating the butter without melting it to maintain the proper consistency of the dough.

TRADITIONAL USE

Plain Vienna bread

SKILL TO MASTER

Kneading (pages 30 and 32)

WHAT CHARACTERIZES VIENNA DOUGH?

Compared to a brioche or other soft loaves (such as pain au lait), Vienna dough contains less butter, less sugar, and no egg. These differences explain its drier and less aerated texture

MAKES I POUND (450 G) DOUGH

2 cups minus 2½ tablespoons (250 g)
    high-protein all-purpose flour (or
    use bread flour or T65 flour)
⅔ cup minus 2 teaspoons (150 g) whole milk
⅝ packed teaspoon (5 g) fresh yeast
1½ tablespoons (20 g) sugar
¾ teaspoon (5 g) salt
2 tablespoons plus 2 teaspoons (40 g)
    unsalted butter, cut into cubes

1 Place the flour, milk, crumbled yeast,
sugar, and salt in the bowl of a stand
mixer fitted with the dough hook.

2 Knead (see page 32) for 4 minutes on the lowest
speed (speed 1), then for 6 minutes on medium
speed. The dough should detach from the sides of
the bowl. (For kneading by hand, see page 30.)

3 Add all the butter pieces at once, and
knead on speed 1 until fully incorporated.

4 Wrap the dough in plastic wrap, and
let rest for 5 hours in the refrigerator.

LEAVENED PUFF PASTRY

Understanding

WHAT IT IS

A yeast-raised dough in which a layer of butter is inserted into a dough (the *détrempe*) then folded several times like a wallet in order to obtain layered flakiness during baking.

COMPLETION TIME

–Preparation time: 45 minutes
–Fermentation time: 3 hours

EQUIPMENT

–Stand mixer fitted with the dough hook (optional)
–Rolling pin

TRADITIONAL USE

Croissant (page 180)

OTHER USES

–Chocolate-Filled Croissant Rolls (page 184)
–Raisin and Cream Croissant Spirals (page 186)
–Pain Suisse (page 190)
–Almond Croissant (page 192)

USEFUL TIP

The combination of flours provides a structure that allows the dough to layer more easily. Use a butter of excellent quality to obtain a more generous layering.

IT'S READY

When the layers of the dough are distinguishable from the layers of butter.

SHELF LIFE

Twenty-four hours in the refrigerator, wrapped in plastic wrap.

CHALLENGE

Folding the dough into a "wallet" and rolling it out properly to keep distinctive layers of butter and dough. If the layers combine by being pressed too firmly, the flaky leaves will not develop.

SKILLS TO MASTER

–Kneading (pages 30 and 32)
–Shaping a Boule (page 42)
–Making a Single Turn (page 283)

HOW DO YOU OBTAIN THE PUFFED LAYERS?

This is a bread dough that is folded together with butter to form the layers. The layers of butter waterproof the dough layers and thus create the flaky leaves. During baking the butter melts, causing steam and air to lift and separate the layers.

HOW DOES THIS DOUGH COMPARE TO TRADITIONAL PUFF PASTRY?

Leavened puff pastry dough contains fresh yeast, which provides lift during the proofing of the pastries. The number of turns, therefore, is less important for leavened puff pastry, which will consequently have fewer layers than traditional puff pastry. Because the base is made from bread dough, leavened puff pastry is also wetter and therefore softer than traditional puff pastry.

Learning

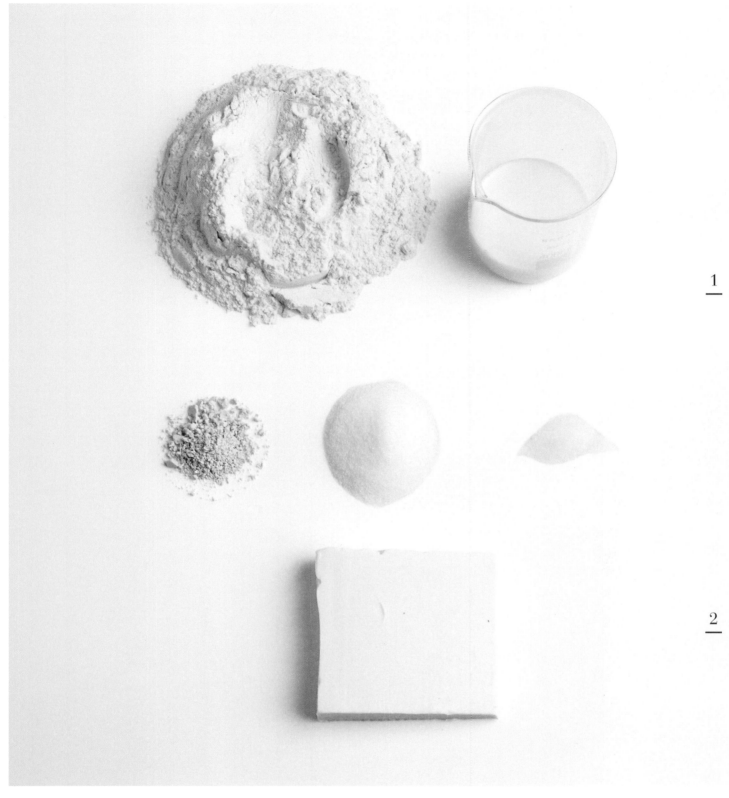

MAKES 13 OUNCES (370 G) DOUGH	**2** ROLL-IN BUTTER

2 ROLL-IN BUTTER

8½ tablespoons (120 g) unsalted butter, chilled

1 DOUGH LAYER (DÉTREMPE)

¾ cup plus 1 tablespoon (110 g) high-
protein all-purpose flour (or use
bread flour or T65 flour)
1 cup minus 1 tablespoon (110 g) pastry
flour (or use T45 flour)
⅓ cup plus 1½ tablespoons (105 g) whole milk
⅞ packed teaspoon (7 g) fresh yeast
2½ tablespoons (30 g) sugar
⅔ teaspoon (4 g) salt

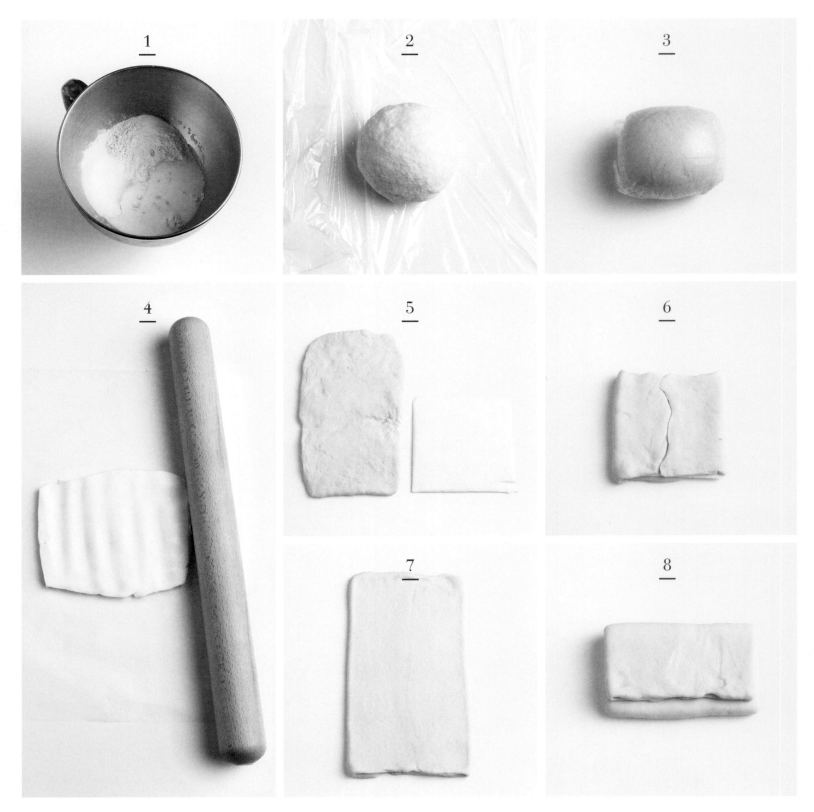

1   Make the dough layer: Place the flours, milk, crumbled yeast, sugar, and salt in the bowl of a stand mixer fitted with the dough hook. Knead (see page 32) for 5 minutes on the lowest speed (speed 1), then for 5 minutes on medium speed. (For kneading by hand, see page 30.)

2   Shape into a very tight boule (see page 42).

3   Wrap the dough in plastic wrap, and let rest for 1 hour in the refrigerator.

4   Using the rolling pin, tamp down the butter to soften it. Roll it out to obtain a uniform square ⅓ inch (1 cm) thick with 3-inch (8 cm) sides.

5   Roll out (see page 283) the dough to the same width as the butter square but twice as long (6 inches/16 cm). Place the butter square in the center of the dough.

6   Fold both sides of the dough together to form a seam in the middle. Turn the dough a quarter of a turn.

7   Make a single turn: roll out the dough in front of you with the seam vertical to you using the rolling pin to make a strip of dough measuring 9½ inches (24 cm) long.

8   Fold the dough over in thirds onto itself (like a wallet) to form a rectangle. Wrap the dough in plastic wrap and place it in the freezer for 10 minutes, then for 30 minutes in the refrigerator. Repeat Steps 7 and 8 twice more; the dough should have three single turns.

BRIOCHE DOUGH

Understanding

BUTTER   SUGAR   EGGS

FLOUR

FRESH
YEAST

WHAT IT IS

A yeast-raised dough enriched
with eggs and butter to create
a rich and airy crumb.

COMPLETION TIME

– Preparation time: 40 minutes
– Fermentation time:
  30 minutes proofing
– Resting time: 1 night

EQUIPMENT

– Stand mixer fitted
  with the dough
  hook (optional)
– Instant-read
  thermometer

TRADITIONAL USE

– Brioches
– Kugelhopf (page 240)
– Panettone (page 244)

SHELF LIFE

Twenty-four hours in the refrigerator,
wrapped in plastic wrap.

CHALLENGE

Do not overwork the dough
after incorporating the butter
as this may cause the butter
to melt and change the
consistency of the dough.

SKILLS TO MASTER

– Kneading (pages 30 and 32)
– Turning (page 37)

IT'S READY

When the ball of dough
is homogeneous, smooth,
and well chilled.

WHY ADD BUTTER AT THE END OF THE KNEADING TIME?

The butter coats the gluten proteins and thus limits the development of the gluten network. However, in order to obtain an airy and soft texture, the gluten network must be well developed. The first two kneadings without butter ensure the gluten's formation. The addition of the butter then provides softness to the dough.

WHY INCORPORATE THE BUTTER AT COOL ROOM TEMPERATURE?

So that it is easily incorporated into the dough. The temperature of the butter, and therefore its consistency, influences the texture of the crumb of the brioche. A butter at an ambient temperature provides a soft crumb (if the butter is too cold or too hot, the crumb will be dry).

WHAT DOES THE FLOUR DO?

It's rich in gluten and helps the development of the gluten network. The gluten will trap the gases formed during fermentation. As a result, the crumb will be very airy.

WHY DOES THE FIRST RISE OCCUR IN THE REFRIGERATOR?

The cold temperature retards the rise of the dough and thus avoids too quick of a rise, which would not allow the gluten network to develop sufficiently.

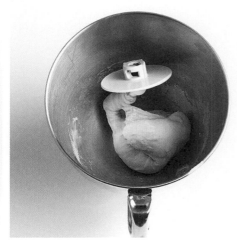

MAKES 1¼ POUNDS (580 G) DOUGH

2 cups plus 1 tablespoon (250 g) pastry
  flour (or use T45 flour)

3 large (150 g) eggs

1 packed teaspoon (8 g) fresh yeast

2 tablespoons plus 2½ teaspoons (35 g) sugar

¾ teaspoon (5 g) salt

9 tablespoons (125 g) unsalted butter,
  cut into cubes

1 Place all the ingredients in the refrigerator the day before making the dough. The next day, bring the cubes of butter to cool room temperature (see page 66). Place the flour, eggs, crumbled yeast, sugar, and salt into the bowl of a stand mixer. Knead (see page 32) for 4 minutes on the lowest speed (speed 1).

2 Knead for 6 minutes on medium speed. The dough should detach from the sides of the bowl. (For kneading by hand, see page 30.)

3 Add all the butter at once on speed 1, then continue kneading until the butter is completely incorporated into the dough.

4 Transfer the dough to a large mixing bowl.

5 Cover the bowl with a towel and let rest for 30 minutes.

6 Turn the dough (see page 37).

7 Place the dough back in the mixing bowl, press plastic wrap onto its surface (see page 285), and let rest in the refrigerator overnight.

INVERSE PUFF PASTRY

Understanding

WHAT IT IS

A delicate and crisp pastry, rich in fat, made by wrapping a dough (the *détrempe*) in a mixture of butter and flour (*beurre manié*) in successive folds to create layers when baking.

COMPLETION TIME

–Preparation time: 45 minutes
–Refrigeration time: 12 hours

EQUIPMENT

–Stand mixer with the paddle and dough hook
–Rolling pin

TRADITIONAL USES

–Millefeuille
–King Cake (page 204)
–Flaky Apple Tart (page 202)

OTHER USES

–Apple Turnover (page 194)
–Palmiers (page 264)

IT'S READY

When the layers of dough are distinguishable from the layers of butter.

SHELF LIFE

Use immediately.

HOW DOES THIS DOUGH DIFFER FROM
TRADITIONAL PUFF PASTRY DOUGH?

–*The flavor: the butter is filled with flour, which provides flavor during baking, such as with a roux.*
–*The process: the roll-in butter surrounds the dough during the first folding, while in a traditional puff pastry the butter is placed inside the dough before folding.*
–*The amount of butter: one and a half times more butter than in traditional puff pastry.*

CHALLENGE

Rolling out the dough. Do not press down too firmly. There must be distinctive layers of butter and dough, otherwise the flaky layers will not develop.

SKILLS TO MASTER

–Kneading (page 32)
–Making a Single Turn (page 283)
–Making a Double Turn (page 283)
–Making a Beurre en Pommade (page 284)

USEFUL TIP

Always roll out the dough moving away from you to make it easier and to achieve more regular layers.

MAKES 1⅓ POUNDS (600 G) DOUGH

1 BEURRE MANIÉ

14 tablespoons (200 g) unsalted butter, cut into cubes, softened

½ cup plus 2 tablespoons (80 g) high-protein all-purpose flour (or use bread flour or T65 flour)

2 DOUGH LAYER (DÉTREMPE)

1⅓ cups (180 g) high-protein all-purpose flour (or use bread flour or T65 flour)

1¼ teaspoons (8 g) salt

⅓ cup (80 g) cold water

4 tablespoons (60 g) Beurre en Pommade (page 284)

⅓ teaspoon (2 g) white wine vinegar

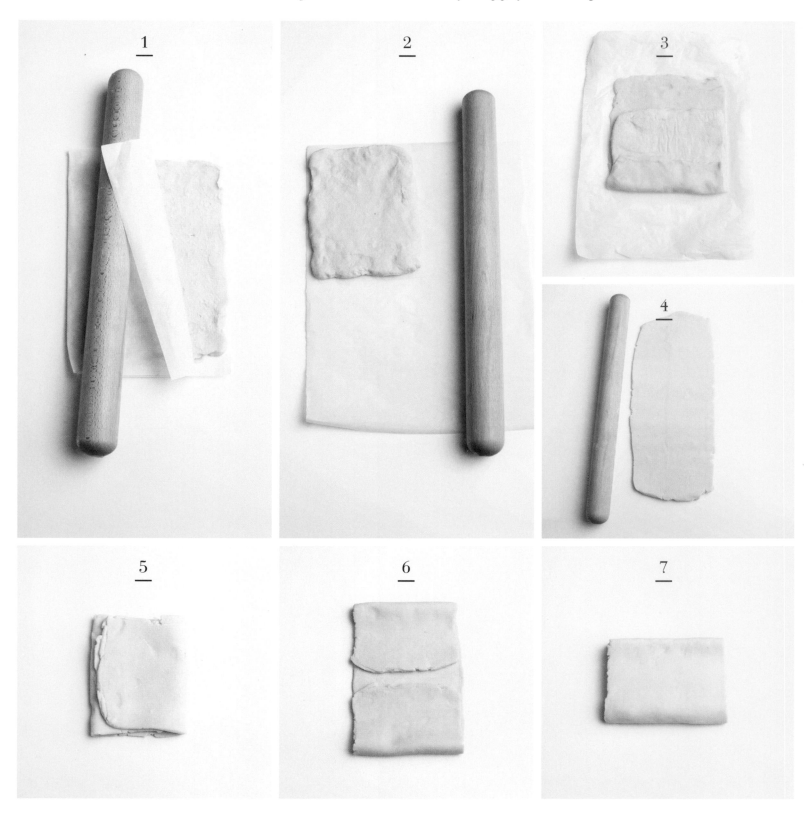

1 Make the beurre manié: Combine the butter and flour for 5 minutes in the bowl of a stand mixer fitted with the paddle. Turn the mixture out onto a floured work surface and roll it into a rectangle measuring 8 × 12 inches (20 × 30 cm). Wrap it in plastic wrap and refrigerate it for 2 hours.

2 Make the dough layer: Combine the flour, salt, water, beurre en pommade, and vinegar in the bowl of a stand mixer fitted with the paddle for 7 minutes on the lowest speed (speed 1). Turn the dough out onto a floured work surface and roll it into a rectangle measuring 6 × 8 inches (15 × 20 cm). Wrap it in plastic wrap and refrigerate it for 2 hours.

3 Place the dough in the center of the beurre manié and fold over both ends to enclose it.

4 Make a single turn: roll out (see page 283) the dough so that it is three times longer than it is wide (24 × 8 inches/60 × 20 cm).

5 Fold the dough over in thirds onto itself (like a wallet) to form a rectangle. Wrap it in plastic wrap and refrigerate it for 2 hours.

6 Place the chilled dough in front of you with the folded edge running vertically and make a double turn: roll out (see page 283) the dough so that it is three times longer than it is wide (24 × 8 inches/60 × 20 cm). Fold one-fourth of the dough from each end in toward the center.

7 Fold the dough in half again in the middle (like a book). Wrap it in plastic wrap and refrigerate it for 2 hours.

8 Place the chilled dough in front of you with the folded edge running vertically and make another double turn: roll out (see page 283) the dough so that it is three times longer than it is wide. Fold one-fourth of the dough from each end in toward the center. Fold the dough in half again in the middle. Wrap it in plastic wrap and refrigerate it for 2 hours.

9 Place the chilled dough in front of you with the folded edge running vertically and make a single turn: roll out (see page 283) the dough so that it is three times longer than it is wide, fold the dough in thirds (like a wallet), wrap it in plastic wrap and refrigerate it for 2 hours.

CHOUX DOUGH
(PÂTE À CHOUX)

Understanding

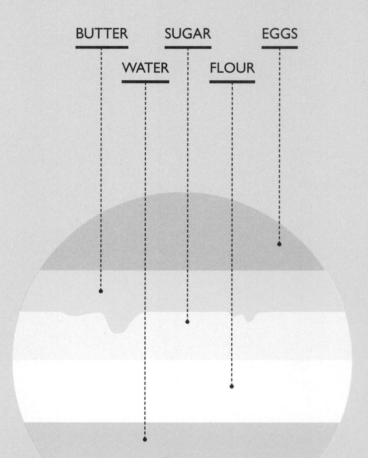

BUTTER   SUGAR   EGGS

WATER   FLOUR

WHAT IT IS

Dough made from eggs, butter, flour, and milk, cooked until dried out, then piped. It puffs when baked.

COMPLETION TIME

Preparation time: 10 minutes

EQUIPMENT

–Stand mixer fitted with the paddle (optional)
–Wooden spoon
–Plastic dough scraper

TRADITIONAL USE

Cream puffs

VARIATIONS

–Gougères
–Pommes Dauphines
–Parisian gnocchi

OTHER USES

–Sugar Puffs (page 276)
–Éclairs
–Religieuses
–Paris-Brest
–Saint-Honoré

IT'S READY

When the dough is homogeneous and forms a peak when the beater is lifted.

SHELF LIFE

Use immediately.

HOW DOES CHOUX DOUGH (PÂTE À CHOUX) PUFF?

When baked at 350°F (180°C), the water contained in the dough evaporates as steam. Because the dough is thick from being cooked in the pan prior to baking, it will contain the steam and puff.

WHY DOES IT DEFLATE IF THE OVEN IS OPENED TOO SOON?

Because the oven temperature will fall, causing the steam to condense into water. The water creates less volume than steam, and this causes the puffs to fall.

CHALLENGE

Thoroughly drying the dough when cooking it, but without burning it.

SKILL TO MASTER

Scraping (page 282)

USEFUL TIP

Drying out the dough allows for better development of the puffs when baked.

Learning

MAKES 1½ POUNDS (700 G) DOUGH

⅔ cup (165 g) whole milk
⅓ cup plus 2½ teaspoons (90 g) water
8 tablespoons minus ¾ teaspoon
    (110 g) unsalted butter
½ teaspoon (2 g) sugar
⅓ teaspoon (2 g) salt
1 cup plus 2 tablespoons (150 g) high-
    protein all-purpose flour (or use
    bread flour or T65 flour)
4 large (200 g) eggs

1   Add the milk, water, butter, sugar, and salt to a saucepan and bring it to a boil.

2   Add the flour all at once. Stir the dough continuously with the wooden spoon for 1 minute to dry it; keep stirring until it detaches from the sides of the pan. This mixture is called the *panade*.

3   Transfer the mixture to the bowl of a stand mixer fitted with the paddle and beat for 1 to 2 minutes on the lowest speed (speed 1), or mix it using the wooden spoon.

4   Incorporate the eggs one by one, while continuously beating, until fully incorporated.

5   Scrape (see page 282) the bowl and the beater clean, and beat for an additional 1 minute, or until the mixture is homogeneous and free of lumps.

73

SWEET PASTRY DOUGH
(PÂTE SUCRÉE/PÂTE SABLÉE)

Understanding

WHAT IT IS
A sweet and crumbly dough.

COMPLETION TIME
Preparation time: 15 minutes

EQUIPMENT
Stand mixer fitted with the paddle and dough hook (optional)

TRADITIONAL USES
–Tart crust
–As a base for cakes

OTHER USE
Small sablé cookies

IT'S READY
When the ball of dough is homogeneous and smooth.

SHELF LIFE
Twenty-four hours in the refrigerator, wrapped in plastic wrap.

WHY DO YOU GET A FRIABLE AND SANDY-TEXTURED DOUGH?
Because the action of mixing the dough in this way avoids incorporating the ingredients together too much. Using this mixing approach, the gluten network is not developed, resulting in a dough with no elasticity. In addition, the sugar does not dissolve in the fat, allowing a certain amount of sugar to remain in a crystallized form. The solid sugar crystals play a part in creating the sandy texture.

CHALLENGE
Not overworking the dough to prevent melting the butter and making the dough too elastic.

SKILL TO MASTER
Kneading (page 32)

USEFUL TIP
In the absence of a stand mixer, combine the flour, confectioners' sugar, salt, and almond flour in a bowl. Form a well in the center, and add the cubes of butter and the egg. Stir quickly to combine, then smear the dough (page 282) one or two times across the work surface.

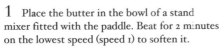

MAKES ONE 9½- TO 10¼-INCH (24 TO 26 CM) DIAMETER CRUST

11 tablespoons (155 g) unsalted
  butter, cut into cubes
1 cup (100 g) confectioners' sugar
¼ cup (30 g) almond flour
2 cups minus 1 tablespoon (260 g) high-
  protein all-purpose flour (or use
  bread flour or T65 flour), sifted
⅛ teaspoon (1 g) salt
1 large (50 g) egg

1 Place the butter in the bowl of a stand mixer fitted with the paddle. Beat for 2 minutes on the lowest speed (speed 1) to soften it.

2 Sift the confectioners' sugar and almond flour together and add them to the bowl. Beat for 2 minutes on speed 1.

3 Add the flour and salt; replace the paddle with the dough hook and mix on speed 1 until the dough is homogeneous.

4 Add the egg and beat for 5 minutes on speed 1.

5 Turn the dough out onto a work surface and shape it into a rectangle, wrap it in plastic wrap, and place it in the refrigerator until ready to use.

PASTRY CREAM
(CRÈME PÂTISSIÈRE)

Understanding

WHAT IT IS
A heated, thickened cream made from milk and egg yolks.

COMPLETION TIME
– Preparation time: 20 minutes
– Refrigeration time: 1 hour

TRADITIONAL USES
– Pain Suisse (page 190)
– Raisin and Cream Croissant
  Spirals (page 186)
– Eclairs
– Millefeuille

VARIATIONS
– Chiboust cream = pastry
  cream + Italian meringue
– Diplomat cream = pastry cream
  + whipped cream + gelatin
– Frangipane = pastry cream + almond cream
– Mousseline = pastry cream + butter

CHALLENGE
Avoiding burning the cream while cooking it.

SKILL TO MASTER
Whisking until Lightened (page 284)

IT'S READY
When the cream is thick, traces of the whisk appear in the cream, and large bubbles rise to the surface.

SHELF LIFE
Use the same day.

HOW DO YOU GO FROM A LIQUID STATE TO A CREAM?

Using cornstarch. When mixed with other ingredients, the starch releases water (contained in the eggs and milk). When cooked, the eggs coagulate and the starch gelatinizes, releasing amylose and amylopectin, which thicken the mixture. The texture will still develop during the cooling time in the refrigerator because the bonds will continue to form between the starch molecules.

WHY DOES A SKIN FORM ON THE SURFACE WHILE THE CREAM IS COOLING?

This is due to the coagulation of proteins that occur during heating (in the same way that a skin forms on milk when heated) and dehydration of the surface.

WHAT IS THE DIFFERENCE BETWEEN A PASTRY CREAM MADE USING FLOUR AND ONE MADE USING CORNSTARCH?

By changing the thickening ingredient, you change the source of the starch and therefore the texture of the cream. All starches have different properties. In equal quantities, a pastry cream made using cornstarch will be lighter than one made using flour.

MAKES 1⅓ POUNDS (600 G) PASTRY CREAM (CRÈME PATISSIÈRE)

2 cups plus 1 tablespoon (500 g) whole milk
½ cup (100 g) sugar
½ vanilla bean
⅓ cup (45 g) cornstarch
2 large (100 g) eggs

1   Pour the milk and half the sugar into a saucepan.

2   Flatten the vanilla bean with the back of a small knife. Cut the bean lengthwise in half and scrape out the seeds with the tip of the knife. Add the seeds to the saucepan and gently bring it to a boil; remove from the heat.

3   Stir together the cornstarch and the remaining sugar. Add the eggs and whisk until lightened (see page 284).

4   Pour some of the hot milk mixture into the lightened egg mixture. Whisk while pouring to create a smooth mixture. Pour the mixture back into the saucepan with the remaining milk and sugar-cornstarch mixture. While whisking, place the pan back over the heat. When the mixture begins to boil, cook for an additional 1 minute while whisking continuously.

5   Pour the cream onto a sheet pan and press plastic wrap onto its surface (see page 285) to prevent a skin from forming. Refrigerate for at least 1 hour.

6   Before using, whisk the cream to bring it back to a smooth consistency.

ALMOND CREAM
(CRÈME D'AMANDES)

Understanding

WHAT IT IS

An equal mixture of almond flour, butter, sugar, and egg.

COMPLETION TIME

Preparation time: 15 minutes

EQUIPMENT

Whisk

TRADITIONAL USES

–Chocolate-filled almond croissant rolls
–Almond Croissant (page 192)
–King Cake (page 204)
–Tarts

VARIATIONS

–Pistachio almond cream
–Hazelnut cream

IT'S READY

When the mixture is homogeneous and smooth.

SHELF LIFE

Five days maximum in the refrigerator.

VARIATION

Frangipane: almond cream + ⅓ pastry cream

SKILL TO MASTER

Whisking until Lightened (page 284)

WHY BEAT THE BUTTER AND SUGAR UNTIL LIGHTENED?

This action dissolves the sugar in the water contained in the butter to prevent the formation of sugar crystals in the cream.

WHY DOES IT PUFF WHEN COOKED?

When cooked, the air bubbles incorporated during the various mixing stages will expand and inflate the cream, giving it a mousse-like appearance.

MAKES 14 OUNCES (400 G) CREAM

7 tablespoons (100 g) Beurre en
   Pommade (page 284)
½ cup (100 g) sugar
1 cup minus 2 tablespoons (100 g) almond flour
1 tablespoon (10 g) cornstarch or flour
2 large (100 g) eggs

1   Whisk the beurre en pommade and sugar together
in a mixing bowl until lightened (see page 284).

2   Add the almond flour and cornstarch; whisk
to combine.

3   Add the eggs and whisk until the mixture is
smooth and creamy. Press plastic wrap onto the
surface (see page 285) of the cream, and place in
the refrigerator to cool.

APPLE COMPOTE
FILLING

Understanding

BUTTER

VANILLA   APPLES

SUGAR

WHAT IT IS

A mixture of apples cooked with
sugar, then crushed or pureed.

COMPLETION TIME

–Preparation time: 20 minutes
–Baking time: 1 hour

EQUIPMENT

Saucepan

TRADITIONAL USES

–Apple Turnover (page 194)
–Apple Tart with
  Lattice (page 198)
–Flaky Apple Tart
  (page 202)

IT'S READY

When the apples have
cooked down to a sauce.

SHELF LIFE

Three days in the refrigerator.

WHAT DOES THE BUTTER DO?
----

*It adds aromatic notes and softens the texture. The butter will melt and coat the palate,
creating a better mouthfeel and a longer finish as compared to a compote with no fat.*

USEFUL TIP

For a smooth result, process the compote
through a food mill after cooking and do not
add the diced apple.

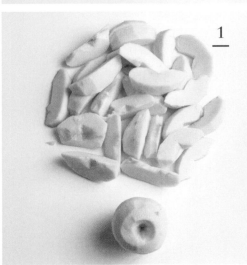

**MAKES 2¼ POUNDS (1 KG)
COMPOTE**

2 pounds (880 g) apples
5 tablespoons (70 g) unsalted butter
¼ cup (50 g) sugar
½ vanilla bean

1 Peel and core all the apples. Set 1 apple
aside and quarter the rest of the apples.

2 Cook the apple quarters, butter, sugar, and
vanilla bean that has been cut lengthwise in half
with the seeds scraped out and added to the
pan along with the empty pod. Cover and cook
for 1 hour over medium heat. Stir regularly.

3 Let cool. Dice the remaining apple,
then add it to the pan. Stir to combine.

CHAPTER 2
THE RECIPES

BAGUETTES

BAGUETTE 84
"FRENCH TRADITION" BAGUETTE 88
"FRENCH TRADITION" BAGUETTE
    WITH MIXED SEEDS.......................... 92

YEAST-RAISED BREADS

BASIC POOLISH LOAF (PAIN MAISON) 96
RUSTIC LOAF WITH RYE
    (PAIN DE CAMPAGNE) 100
OLD-WORLD LOAF (PAIN D'ANTAN).......104
STONE-GROUND WHEAT LOAF................106
MULTIGRAIN LOAF 108
WHOLE WHEAT SOURDOUGH 112

SPECIALTY BREADS

SOURDOUGH RYE.................................114
LEMON SOURDOUGH RYE 118
MULTIGRAIN BROWN LOAF
    (PAIN NOIR) 120
CHESTNUT SOURDOUGH.........................122
CORNMEAL LOAF.................................124
GLUTEN-FREE LOAF.............................126
BEER BREAD 128

FILLED BREADS

MIXED SEEDS RING 132
WALNUT LOAF....................................136
CHOCOLATE LOAF.................................138
SMALL HAZELNUT-FIG LOAVES 142
SMALL MUESLI LOAVES 144
CHEESE BREAD...................................146
SMALL ITALIAN LOAVES 148
CHEESE FICELLES WITH SEEDS 150
"SURPRISE" LOAF...............................154

BREADS MADE WITH OIL (FLAT BREADS)

CIABATTA.......................................158
FOCACCIA.......................................160
FOUGASSE.......................................164
CRUNCHY BREADSTICKS (GRISSINI)......168

SOFT BREADS AND BUNS

PULLMAN LOAF SANDWICH BREAD
    (PAIN DE MIE)..............................170
BAGEL..172
SESAME SEED BUN 176

LEAVENED PUFF PASTRIES

CROISSANT......................................180
CHOCOLATE-FILLED CROISSANT ROLLS
    (PAIN AU CHOCOLAT) 184
RAISIN AND CREAM CROISSANT SPIRALS
    (PAIN AUX RAISINS)........................186
PAIN SUISSE....................................190
ALMOND CROISSANT..............................192

TRADITIONAL PUFF PASTRIES

APPLE TURNOVER
    (CHAUSSON AUX POMMES) 194
APPLE TART WITH LATTICE.....................198

PUFF PASTRY–BASED CAKES AND TARTS

FLAKY APPLE TART..............................202
KING CAKE (GALETTE DES ROIS)............204

YEAST-RAISED SWEET BREADS AND DOUGHNUTS

SWEET LOAVES...................................208
VIENNA BAGUETTE...............................210
FILLED DOUGHNUTS..............................212

BRIOCHE

PARISIAN BRIOCHE..............................216
PINK PRALINE BRIOCHE.........................220
BRAIDED BRIOCHE (CHALLAH)............ 224
FLAKY BRIOCHE.................................. 228

BRIOCHE-STYLE CAKES

SUGAR TART (TARTE AU SUCRE)...............232
BRIOCHE BORDELAISE GARNISHED
    WITH CANDIED CITRUS 234
CREAM-FILLED BRIOCHE CAKE
    (TARTE TROPÉZIENNE) 236
KUGELHOPF......................................240
PANETTONE......................................244

TARTS

PISTACHIO-APRICOT TART......................248
FLAN TART (FLAN PÂTISSIER).................. 250

LOAF AND SINGLE-LAYER CAKES (GÂTEAUX DE VOYAGE)

SPICED LOAF CAKE (PAIN D'ÉPICE)..........252
FRUIT CAKE 254
GENOA CAKE (PAIN DE GÊNES) 258

SMALL BITES: SPONGE CAKES, PUFFS, AND CRISP COOKIES

SABLÉS 262
PALMIERS (PALM LEAVES)......................264
RASPBERRY STRIPS..............................266
FINANCIERS 270
MADELEINES.....................................272
ALMOND TUILE 274
SUGAR PUFFS (CHOUQUETTES)...............276

BAGUETTE

Understanding

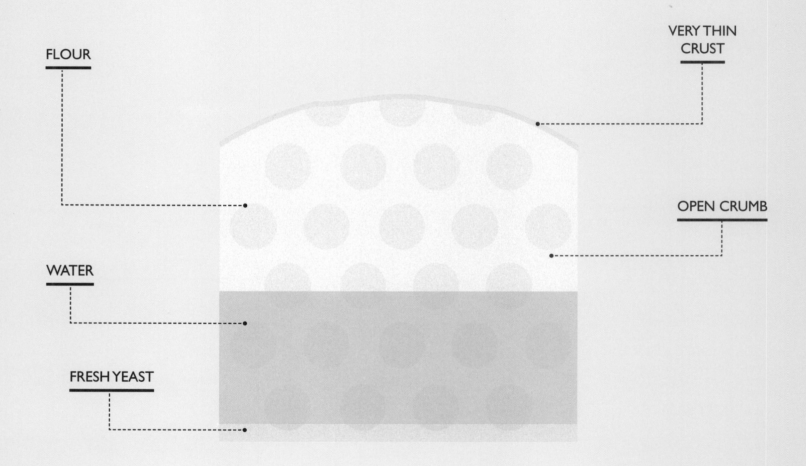

FLOUR

VERY THIN CRUST

WATER

OPEN CRUMB

FRESH YEAST

WHAT IT IS
A straight dough shaped into a baguette.

CHARACTERISTICS
–Weight: 9 ounces (250 g)
–Size: 24 inches (60 cm)
–Crumb: open, regular
–Crust: very thin
–Taste: neutral

EQUIPMENT
–Stand mixer fitted with the
  dough hook (optional)
–Bench scraper
–Lame

COMPLETION TIME
–Preparation time: 35 minutes
–Fermentation time: 2½ hours
  (30 minutes resting, 2 hours proofing)
–Baking time: 20 to 25 minutes

SKILLS TO MASTER
–Kneading (pages 30 and 32)
–Shaping a Baguette (page 43)
–Scoring (page 50)

IT'S READY
When the crust is slightly golden.

HOW DO YOU EXPLAIN THE MOIST CRUMB?
The large amount of yeast allows the dough to swell very quickly. In a short period of time (2 hours of proofing only) a very moist crumb is achieved.

HOW DO YOU EXPLAIN THE THIN CRUST?
The dough contains a great deal of water, so it begins to dry late in the baking time. Consequently, the crust has very little time to form.

MAKES 2 LOAVES

3 cups minus 2½ tablespoons (390 g)
high-protein all-purpose flour (or
use bread flour or T65 flour)
1 cup plus ¾ teaspoon (240 g) water
at 68 to 77°F (20 to 25°C)
¾ packed teaspoon (6 g) fresh yeast
1⅛ teaspoons (7 g) salt

Making a baguette

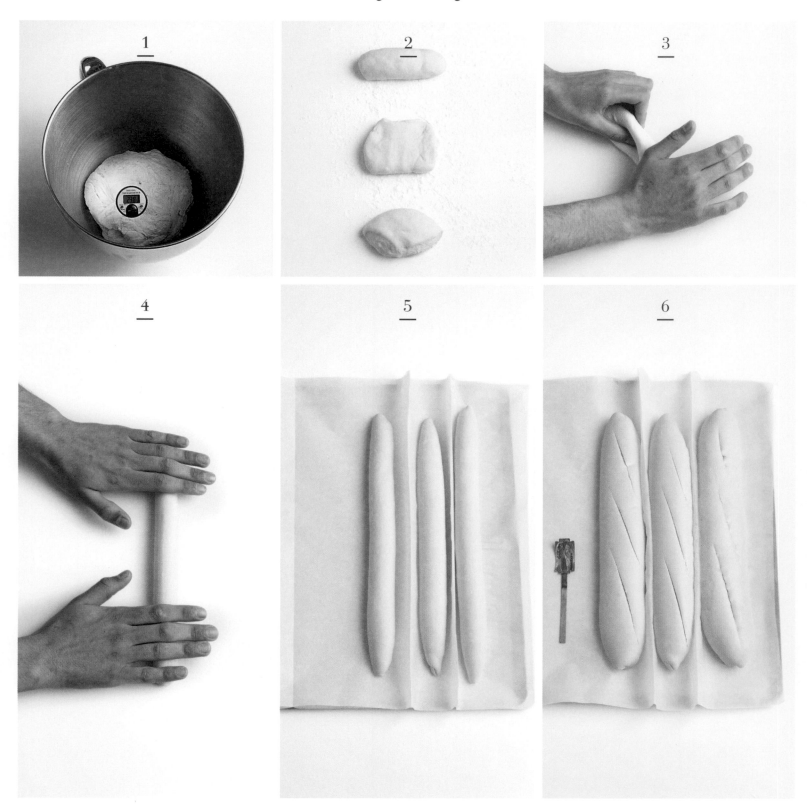

1 Knead the flour, water, crumbled yeast, and salt in the bowl of a stand mixer fitted with the dough hook for 4 minutes on the lowest speed (speed 1), then for 6 minutes on medium speed. The dough should detach from the sides of the bowl. (For kneading by hand, see page 30.)

2 Divide the dough into two pieces, 11¼ ounces (320 g) each, using the bench scraper. Lightly flour the work surface. Take each piece of dough and turn it over with the smooth side down. Flatten it to give it a rectangular form. Allow it to rest for 30 minutes at room temperature, covered with a towel.

3 Shape the dough pieces into baguettes: Fold the bottom and top edges of one of the dough pieces in toward the center, overlapping them to create a seam. Place the left thumb on the right end of the dough by pressing lightly on the seam. Enclose the

thumb using three other fingers of the same hand. Slide the thumb down the length of the dough and seal the entire length of it creating a seam using the palm of the opposite hand. Flatten the dough again and seam it closed in the same way a second time. Repeat these steps with the second piece of dough.

4 Place your palms in the middle of the top of the baguette. Lengthen it by rolling the baguette with both hands, starting from the center and moving out toward the ends. Repeat with the second piece of dough.

5 Place the baguettes on a towel, seam side down, and cover them with a second towel to prevent a crust from forming. Let the dough rise for 2 hours in a warm place, 77 to 82°F (25 to 28°C), for the proofing; the dough has sufficiently risen when gently pressing into it with your fingertip leaves no mark.

6 Preheat the oven to 500°F (260°C) with a baking sheet and a bowl of water placed in the oven. Place the baguettes seam side down onto parchment paper. Score the baguettes with three slashes each (see page 51). When the oven comes to temperature, place the parchment paper with the baguettes onto the hot baking sheet. Spritz the bottom of the oven with water and bake for 20 to 25 minutes (keeping the bowl of water in the oven).

"FRENCH TRADITION"
BAGUETTE

Understanding

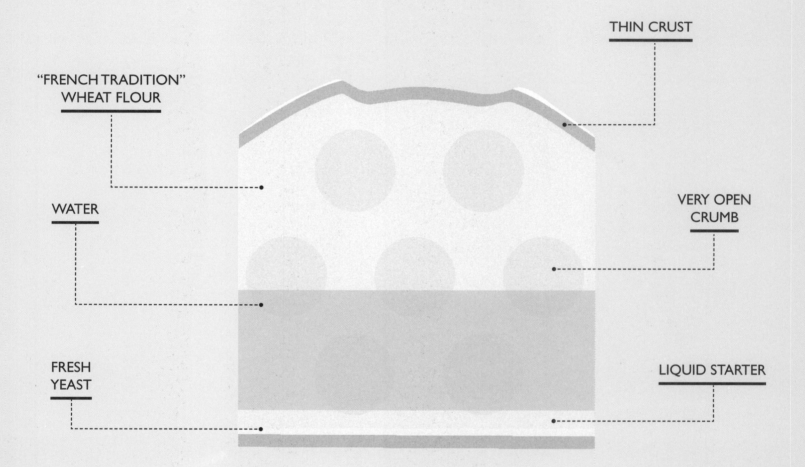

THIN CRUST

"FRENCH TRADITION" WHEAT FLOUR

WATER

VERY OPEN CRUMB

FRESH YEAST

LIQUID STARTER

WHAT IT IS

A dough made from "French tradition" wheat flour and a sourdough starter, with a long rising time, and shaped into a baguette. A baguette "made in the French tradition" is an appellation defined in France by the decree of September 13, 1993.

CHARACTERISTICS

–Weight: 9½ ounces (270 g)
–Size: 18 inches (45 cm)
–Crumb: very open, irregular
–Crust: thin
–Taste: slightly sour

COMPLETION TIME

–Preparation time: 15 minutes
–Fermentation time: 3½ hours (1 hour rising, 30 minutes resting, 2 hours proofing)
–Baking time: 20 to 25 minutes

EQUIPMENT

–Stand mixer fitted with the dough hook (optional)
–Lame
–Bench scraper

SKILLS TO MASTER

–Kneading (pages 30 and 32)
–Preshaping an Oblong (page 38)
–Shaping a Baguette (page 43)
–Scoring (page 50)
–Turning (page 37)

IT'S READY

When the crust is golden and crisp, and the bread sounds hollow when tapped.

HOW DO YOU EXPLAIN THE VERY OPEN CRUMB?

Fermentation occurs in two stages (the first rise and the proofing), allowing for a very good rise. What's more, the sourdough starter creates a more open crumb than would occur if using only fresh yeast.

MAKES 4 LOAVES

DOUGH

5¼ cups minus 1 tablespoon (700 g) T65 "French tradition" wheat flour (or use organic high-protein all-purpose flour or bread flour)

2 cups plus 1 tablespoon plus ¾ teaspoon (490 g) water, at room temperature

2½ ounces (70 g) Liquid Starter (page 20)

⅝ packed teaspoon (5 g) fresh yeast

2⅓ teaspoons (14 g) salt

SIFTING

2½ tablespoons (20 g) T65 "French tradition" wheat flour (or use organic high-protein all-purpose flour or bread flour)

Making a "French tradition" baguette

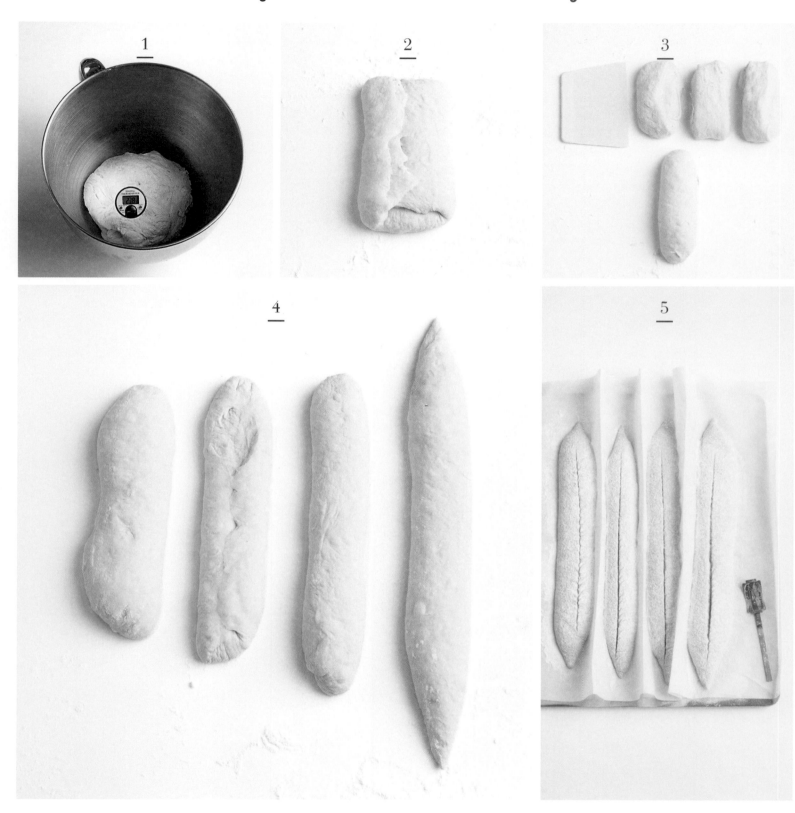

1 Knead (see page 32) together the flour, water, starter, crumbled yeast, and salt in the bowl of a stand mixer fitted with the dough hook for 4 minutes on the lowest speed (speed 1), then for 6 minutes on medium speed. The dough should detach from the sides of the bowl. (For kneading by hand, see page 30.)

2 Let the dough rise for 30 minutes on a floured work surface, covered with a towel. Turn the dough (see page 37). Let the dough rise again for 30 minutes on a floured work surface, covered with a towel.

3 Divide the dough into four pieces, 11½ ounces (330 g) each, using the bench scraper. Press them into oblongs (see page 38). Let stand for an additional 30 minutes on a floured work surface, covered with a towel.

4 Shape the dough pieces into baguettes (see page 43), place them on a towel seam side down, and cover them with a second towel to prevent a crust from forming. Let rise for 2 hours in a warm place, 77 to 82°F (25 to 28°C). The dough has sufficiently risen when gently pressing into it with your fingertip leaves no mark.

5 Preheat the oven to 500°F (260°C) with a baking sheet and a bowl of water placed in the oven. Place the baguettes seam side down onto parchment paper. Sift the 2½ tablespoons (20 g) flour over the baguettes. Score the baguettes with a lame or razor blade angled at thirty degrees, making a single stroke of the blade down the entire length of the baguette (see page 51). When the oven comes to temperature, place the parchment paper with the baguettes onto the hot baking sheet.

6 Spritz the bottom of the oven with water and bake for 20 to 25 minutes (keeping the bowl of water in the oven).

"FRENCH TRADITION"
BAGUETTE WITH MIXED SEEDS

Understanding

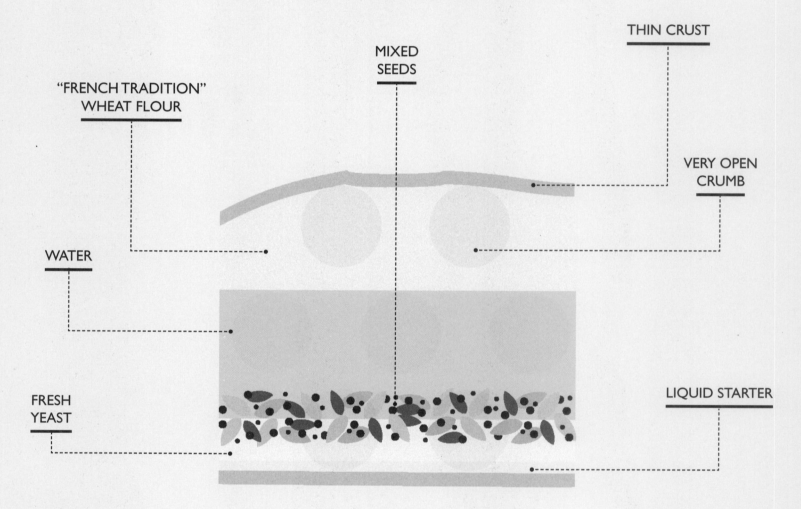

THIN CRUST

MIXED
SEEDS

"FRENCH TRADITION"
WHEAT FLOUR

VERY OPEN
CRUMB

WATER

FRESH
YEAST

LIQUID STARTER

WHAT IT IS
A dough made from "French tradition" wheat flour, mixed with toasted seeds, and shaped into an épi ("wheat stalk").

CHARACTERISTICS
–Weight: 9½ ounces (270 g)
–Size: 18 inches (45 cm)
–Crumb: very open, irregular
–Crust: thin
–Taste: slightly sour

COMPLETION TIME
–Preparation time: 25 minutes
–Fermentation time: 3½ hours (1 hour rising, 30 minutes resting, 2 hours proofing)
–Baking time: 20 to 25 minutes

EQUIPMENT
–Stand mixer fitted with the dough hook (optional)
–Lame

SKILLS TO MASTER
–Kneading (pages 30 and 32)
–Preshaping an Oblong (page 38)
–Shaping a Baguette (page 43)
–Cutting an Épi (page 51)
–Turning (page 37)

USEFUL TIP
The dough has sufficiently risen when gently pressing into it with your fingertip leaves no mark.

IT'S READY
When the baguette is golden brown.

MAKES 2 LOAVES

1 THE DOUGH

2⅔ cups minus 1 tablespoon (350 g) T65 "French
   tradition" wheat flour (or use organic high-
   protein all-purpose flour or bread flour)
1 cup plus 2 teaspoons (245 g) water
   at 68 to 77°F (20 to 25°C)
1¼ ounces (35 g) Liquid Starter (page 20)
¼ packed teaspoon (2 g) fresh yeast
¾ teaspoon (5 g) salt

2 SEEDS

½ cup (60 g) mixed seeds (flax, poppy,
   sesame, etc.)
¼ cup (60 g) water

Making "French tradition" baguette with mixed seeds

THE DAY BEFORE

1 Toast the seeds for 10 to 15 minutes in an oven preheated to 350°F (180°C). Place them in a mixing bowl with the water and let soak at room temperature overnight; the seeds will absorb all the water. If any water remains, drain it.

THE SAME DAY

2 Knead (see page 32) together the flour, water, starter, crumbled yeast, salt, and seeds for 4 minutes on the lowest speed (speed 1), then for 6 minutes on medium speed. The dough should detach from the sides of the bowl. (For kneading by hand, see page 30.)

3 Let the dough rise for 30 minutes on a floured work surface, covered with a towel.

4 Turn the dough (see page 37) and let rise again for 30 minutes on a floured work surface, covered with a towel.

5 Divide the dough into two pieces, preshape them into oblongs (see page 38), and let rest for 30 minutes at room temperature. Shape them into baguettes (see page 43).

6 Place the baguettes on a sheet of parchment paper, seam side down, and cover them with a towel to prevent a crust from forming. Let rise for 1½ to 2 hours in a warm place, 77 to 82°F (25 to 28°C), for the proofing. Cut them into an épi (see page 51).

7 Preheat the oven to 500°F (260°C) with a baking sheet and a bowl of water placed in the oven. When the oven comes to temperature, slide the parchment paper with the loaves onto the hot baking sheet. Spritz the bottom of the oven with water and bake for 20 to 25 minutes (keeping the bowl of water in the oven).

BASIC POOLISH LOAF
(PAIN MAISON)

Understanding

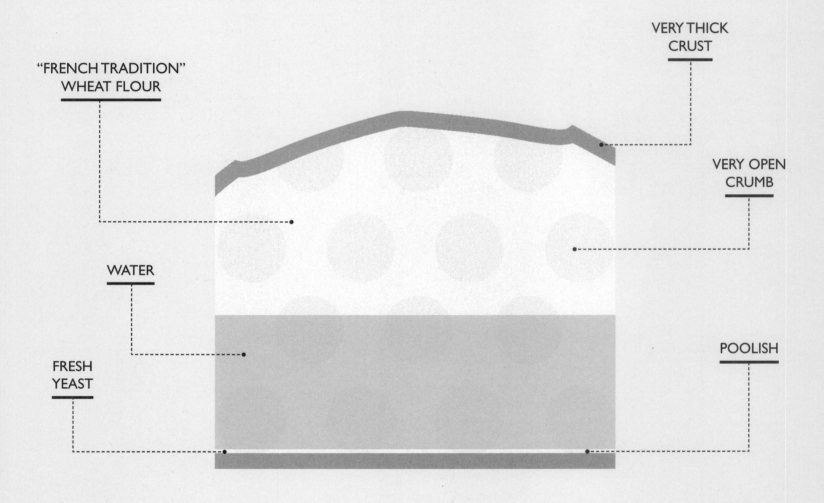

"FRENCH TRADITION" WHEAT FLOUR

VERY THICK CRUST

VERY OPEN CRUMB

WATER

FRESH YEAST

POOLISH

WHAT IT IS

A dough made from "French tradition" wheat flour, prepared with a poolish starter, and shaped into small bâtards.

CHARACTERISTICS

−Weight: 9 ounces (250 g)
−Size: 8 inches (20 cm)
−Crumb: very open, irregular
−Crust: thick
−Taste: sweet, slightly sour

COMPLETION TIME

−Preparation time: 40 minutes
−Fermentation time: 16 hours for the poolish, 1 hour rising, 45 minutes proofing
−Baking time: 20 to 25 minutes

EQUIPMENT

−Stand mixer fitted with the dough hook (optional)
−Bench scraper

CHALLENGE

Making the poolish.

SKILLS TO MASTER

−Kneading (pages 30 and 32)
−Turning (page 37)

USEFUL TIP

When making the poolish, use a container that's large enough, as the poolish will double in volume.

IT'S READY

When the bread is golden brown.

SHELF LIFE

Four to five days.

2

1

WHAT IS THE PURPOSE OF THE POOLISH?

A poolish is a pre-ferment that is easy to use and can replace a sourdough starter while providing a more standard bread flavor than when using fresh yeast.

MAKES 4 LOAVES

1 POOLISH

⅓ packed teaspoon (1 g) fresh yeast

¾ cup minus ¼ teaspoon (175 g) water at 68°F (20°C)

1¼ cups plus 1½ teaspoons (175 g) T65 "French tradition" wheat flour (or use organic high-protein all-purpose flour or bread flour)

2 DOUGH

3¾ cups (500 g) T65 "French tradition" wheat flour (or use organic high-protein all-purpose flour or bread flour)

1⅓ cups plus 2 teaspoons (325 g) water at 68 to 77°F (20 to 25°C)

⅛ packed teaspoon (1 g) fresh yeast

1¾ teaspoons (11 g) salt

Making basic poolish loaf

THE DAY BEFORE

1 Make the poolish: dilute the crumbled yeast in the water. Add the flour and whisk to obtain a smooth mixture.

2 Cover the bowl with plastic wrap and let stand at room temperature for about 16 hours.

THE SAME DAY

3 Knead (see page 32) together the flour, water, crumbled yeast, salt, and poolish in the bowl of a stand mixer fitted with the dough hook for 10 to 15 minutes on the lowest speed (speed 1). The dough should detach from the sides of the bowl. (For kneading by hand, see page 30.)

4 Place the dough in a mixing bowl, cover the bowl with plastic wrap, and let rise for 1 hour.

5 Turn the dough (see page 37) after 20 minutes, then again after 40 minutes.

6 Divide the dough into four pieces, 9 ounces (250 g) each, using the bench scraper. Shape each piece into a fairly rough rectangle by tucking a small portion of the two ends underneath.

7 Place the dough rectangles seam side down on a well-floured towel.

8 Let the dough rise for 45 minutes in a warm place, 77 to 82°F (25 to 28°C), for the proofing.

9 Preheat the oven to 500°F (260°C) with a baking sheet and a bowl of water placed in the oven. Turn the loaves over, seam side up, and place them on parchment paper. When the oven comes to temperature, slide the parchment with the loaves onto the hot baking sheet. Spritz the bottom of the oven with water, and bake for 20 to 25 minutes (keeping the bowl of water in the oven).

RUSTIC LOAF WITH RYE
(PAIN DE CAMPAGNE)

Understanding

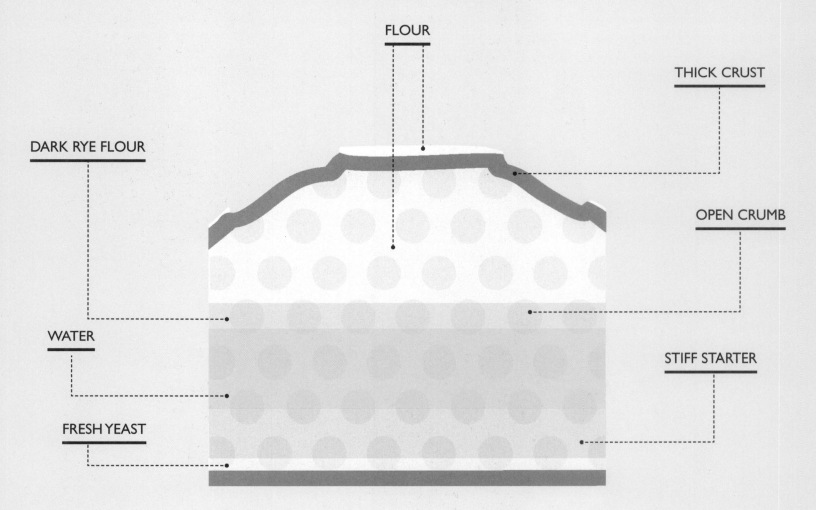

FLOUR

THICK CRUST

DARK RYE FLOUR

OPEN CRUMB

WATER

STIFF STARTER

FRESH YEAST

WHAT IT IS

A bread dough made of wheat flour, rye flour, and stiff starter, in the shape of a bâtard.

CHARACTERISTICS

–Weight: 7 ounces (200 g)
–Size: 8 inches (20 cm)
–Crumb: open
–Crust: thick
–Taste: complex and sour

COMPLETION TIME

–Preparation time: 30 minutes
–Fermentation time: 3 to 3½ hours
   (1 hour rising, 30 minutes resting,
   1½ to 2 hours proofing)
–Baking time: 25 to 30 minutes

EQUIPMENT

–Stand mixer fitted with the
   dough hook (optional)
–Bench scraper
–Lame

SHELF LIFE

Five days well wrapped, if not sliced;
two to three days if unwrapped.

SKILLS TO MASTER

–Kneading (pages 30 and 32)
–Turning (page 37)
–Shaping a Bâtard (page 45)
–Scoring a Large Crisscross (page 51)

CHALLENGE

Spritzing the dough: ensuring it
is wet enough to make it soft, but
not so wet that it is sticky.

IT'S READY

When the scored diamond shapes have
spread open and the bread is golden
and sounds hollow when tapped.

<u>1</u>

<u>2</u>

HOW DO YOU EXPLAIN THE LIGHT TEXTURE OF THE CRUMB?

There is enough wheat flour contained in the dough to provide the amount of gluten needed for the formation of the gluten network. The gases from fermentation are trapped, the bread rises, and the crumb is lightened—in addition to having the flavor of rye.

MAKES 2 LOAVES

1 DOUGH

1 cup plus 2 tablespoons (155 g) high-protein all-purpose flour (or use bread flour or T65 flour)
½ cup minus 2 teaspoons (60 g) dark rye flour (or use T170 flour)
⅔ cup minus 1 teaspoon (150 g) water
3½ ounces (100 g) Stiff Starter (page 22)
¼ packed teaspoon (2 g) fresh yeast
1 teaspoon (6 g) salt

2 SPRITZING

2 tablespoons (30 g) water

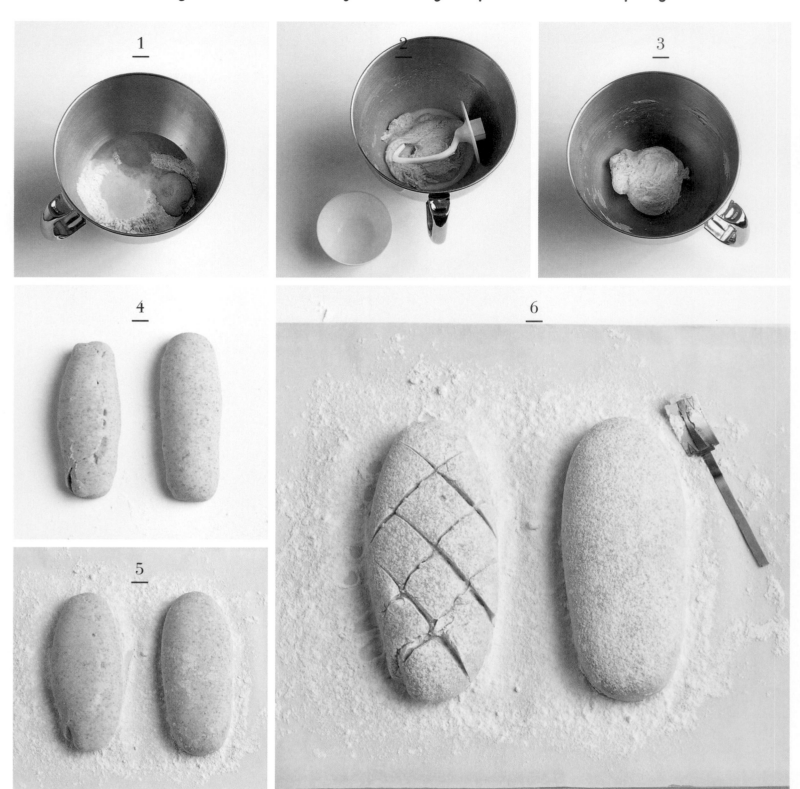

1 Knead (see page 32) together the wheat and rye flours, water, starter, crumbled yeast, and salt in the bowl of a stand mixer fitted with the dough hook for 4 minutes on the lowest speed (speed 1), then for 6 minutes on medium speed. The dough should detach from the sides of the bowl. (For kneading by hand, see page 30.)

2 Spritz the dough (see page 282) with water at the end of the kneading time to adjust the consistency of it.

3 Knead until the additional water is fully incorporated into the dough. Let the dough rise for 1 hour on a floured work surface, covered with a towel. After 30 minutes, turn the dough (see page 37). Cut the dough into two pieces, 9 ounces (250 g) each, using the bench scraper. Preshape the pieces

into rounds (see page 38) and let rest for 30 minutes, covered with a towel, at room temperature.

4 Shape them into bâtards (see page 45).

5 Turn the loaves seam side up and place them on a baking sheet lined with parchment paper. Cover them with a towel to prevent a crust from forming. Let rise for 1½ to 2 hours in a warm place, 77 to 82°F (25 to 28°C), for the proofing. The dough has sufficiently risen when gently pressing into it with your fingertip leaves no mark.

6 Preheat the oven to 500°F (260°C) with a baking sheet and a bowl of water placed in the oven. Turn the loaves over and, with your hands, brush off the tops to remove any excess flour. Slide the loaves seam side down onto the parchment paper. Score the loaves in a large crisscross (see page 51) with the lame or razor blade angled at thirty degrees. When the oven comes to temperature, slide the parchment with the loaves onto the hot baking sheet. Spritz the bottom of the oven with water and bake for 25 to 30 minutes (keeping the bowl of water in the oven).

OLD-WORLD LOAF
(PAIN D'ANTAN)

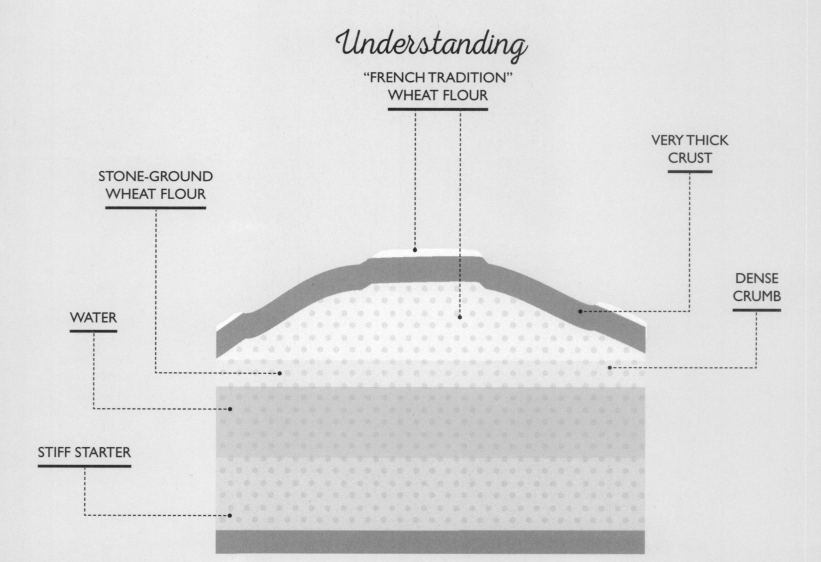

Understanding

"FRENCH TRADITION"
WHEAT FLOUR

VERY THICK
CRUST

STONE-GROUND
WHEAT FLOUR

DENSE
CRUMB

WATER

STIFF STARTER

WHAT IT IS

A bread dough made with a stiff starter and a mixture of "French tradition" and stone-ground flours (which retain their bran), shaped into a long loaf.

CHARACTERISTICS

– Weight: 1⅛ pounds (500 g)
– Size: bâtard measuring 19½ to 22 inches (50 to 55 cm)
– Crumb: dense
– Crust: very thick
– Taste: standard, sour

COMPLETION TIME

– Preparation time: 40 minutes
– Fermentation time: 4½ hours (2 hours rising, 30 minutes resting, 2 hours proofing)
– Baking time: 40 minutes

EQUIPMENT

– Stand mixer fitted with the dough hook (optional)
– Lame

SKILLS TO MASTER

– Kneading (pages 30 and 32)
– Turning (page 37)
– Preshaping an Oblong (page 38)
– Shaping a Bâtard (page 45)
– Scoring a Large Crisscross (page 51)

IT'S READY

When the bread is golden and sounds hollow when tapped.

SHELF LIFE

Four to five days, when not exposed to air.

MAKES I LOAF

DOUGH

½ cup minus I tablespoon (60 g) T65 "French
    tradition" wheat flour (or use organic high-
    protein all-purpose flour or bread flour)
I cup (130 g) whole wheat pastry flour (or
    stone-ground T80 or T110 flour)
⅔ cup plus I teaspoon (160 g) water
5¼ ounces (150 g) Stiff Starter (page 22)
I teaspoon (6 g) salt

SIFTING

2½ tablespoons (20 g) T65 "French tradition"
    wheat flour (or use organic high-protein
    all-purpose flour or bread flour)

1   Knead (see page 32) together the wheat and
stone-ground flours, water, crumbled starter, and
salt in the bowl of a stand mixer fitted with the
dough hook for 4 minutes on the lowest speed
(speed 1), then for 6 minutes on medium speed.
The dough should detach from the sides of the
bowl. (For kneading by hand, see page 30.)

2   Place the dough in a mixing bowl, cover the
bowl with plastic wrap, and let rise for I hour
at room temperature.

3   Turn the dough (see page 37), then place
the dough back in the mixing bowl, cover
the bowl with plastic wrap, and let rise for an
additional I hour at room temperature.

4   Preshape the dough into an oblong (see page 38)
and let rise for 30 minutes at room temperature.

5   Shape the dough into a bâtard (see page 45).

6   Place the dough seam side down onto a sheet of
parchment paper, cover, and let rest for 2 hours in a
warm place, 77 to 82°F (25 to 28°C), for the proofing.

7   Preheat the oven to 500°F (260°C) with a baking
sheet and bowl of water placed in the oven. Place the
dough seam side down onto parchment paper. Sift the
2½ tablespoons (20 g) flour over the dough and score it
in a large crisscross (see page 51) using a lame or razor
blade. When the oven comes to temperature, slide the
parchment with the loaf onto the hot baking sheet.

8   Spritz the bottom of the oven with water, and
bake for 40 minutes (leaving the bowl of water in
the oven). Slightly prop open the oven door 5 to
10 minutes before the end of the baking time.

STONE-GROUND
WHEAT LOAF

Understanding

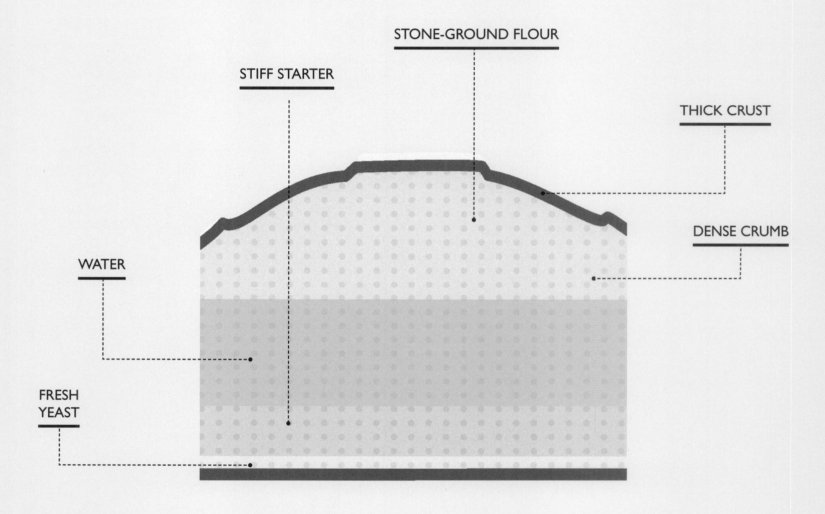

STONE-GROUND FLOUR

STIFF STARTER

THICK CRUST

WATER

DENSE CRUMB

FRESH
YEAST

WHAT IT IS

A bread dough made from stone-ground flour (a process that retains the bran) and a stiff starter, shaped into a large round.

CHARACTERISTICS

–Weight: 1¼ pounds (550 g)
–Size: 8 inches (20 cm) in diameter
–Crumb: dense
–Crust: thick
–Taste: slightly sour

COMPLETION TIME

–Preparation time: 30 minutes
–Fermentation time: 5 to 5½ hours
 (3 hours rising, 2 to 2½ hours proofing)
–Baking time: 35 to 40 minutes

EQUIPMENT

–Stand mixer fitted with the
 dough hook (optional)
–Lame

SKILLS TO MASTER

–Kneading (pages 30 and 32)
–Turning (page 37)
–Shaping a Boule (page 42)
–Scoring (page 50)

USEFUL TIP

Slightly open the oven door for about ten minutes before the end of the baking time to dry the crumb.

IT'S READY

When the crust is a very deep brown.

SHELF LIFE

Four to five days, when not exposed to air.

MAKES 1 LOAF

DOUGH

1¾ cups (220 g) whole wheat pastry flour
    (or stone-ground T80 flour)
4 ounces (110 g) Stiff Starter (page 22)
½ packed teaspoon (4 g) fresh yeast
¾ cup plus 1½ tablespoons (200 g)
    water at 77°F (25°C)
1 teaspoon (6 g) salt

SIFTING

1½ tablespoons (15 g) high-protein all-purpose
    flour (or use bread flour or T65 flour)

1 Knead (see page 32) together the flour, crumbled starter, crumbled yeast, water, and salt in the bowl of a stand mixer fitted with the dough hook for 4 minutes on the lowest speed (speed 1), then for 6 minutes on medium speed. The dough should detach from the sides of the bowl. (For kneading by hand, see page 30.)

2 Transfer the dough to a mixing bowl, cover the bowl with plastic wrap, and let rise for 1 hour in a warm place, 77 to 82°F (25 to 28°C).

3 Turn the dough (see page 37), then let rise for an additional 1 hour.

4 Turn the dough again (see page 37) and let rise for an additional 1 hour.

5 Shape the dough into a boule (see page 42). Place it seam side up on top of a well-floured towel set inside a mixing bowl. Cover the bowl with another towel.

6 Let rest for 2 to 2½ hours in a warm place, 77 to 82°F (25 to 28°C), for the proofing.

7 Preheat the oven to 500°F (260°C) with a baking sheet and a bowl of water placed in the oven. Turn the loaf over and place it seam side down on parchment paper. Sift the 1½ tablespoons flour over the dough and score the dough to form a large diamond shape in the center (see page 51). When the oven comes to temperature, slide the parchment with the loaf onto the hot baking sheet.

8 Spritz the bottom of the oven with water and bake for 35 to 40 minutes (keeping the bowl of water in the oven). Slightly prop open the oven door 5 to 10 minutes before the end of the baking time.

MULTIGRAIN LOAF

Understanding

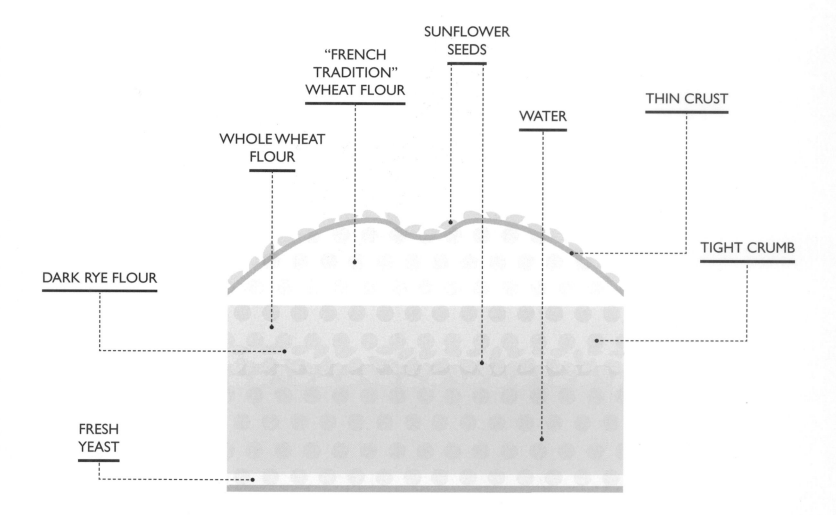

DARK RYE FLOUR

WHOLE WHEAT FLOUR

"FRENCH TRADITION" WHEAT FLOUR

SUNFLOWER SEEDS

WATER

THIN CRUST

TIGHT CRUMB

FRESH YEAST

WHAT IT IS

A bread dough made from a mixture of "French tradition" and rye flours, filled and covered with sunflower seeds.

CHARACTERISTICS

–Weight: 14 ounces (400 g)
–Size: 6 inches (15 cm) in diameter
–Crumb: tight
–Crust: thin
–Taste: of seeds

COMPLETION TIME

–Preparation time: 30 minutes
–Fermentation time: 3 hours (1 hour rising, 30 minutes resting, 1½ hours proofing)
–Baking time: 25 to 30 minutes

EQUIPMENT

–Stand mixer fitted with the dough hook (optional)
–Lame
–Pastry brush

SKILLS TO MASTER

–Kneading (pages 30 and 32)
–Preshaping a Round (page 38)
–Turning (page 37)
–Shaping a Boule (page 42)
–Scoring a Single Cross (page 51)

IT'S READY

When the crust is brown and the bread sounds hollow when tapped.

SHELF LIFE

Three to four days when covered with a towel and not exposed to air.

<u>1</u>

<u>2</u>

WHY IS THE CRUST THIN?

Compared to other large loaves such as a whole wheat loaf, multigrain bread does not contain a sourdough starter (which creates thick crusts) but instead fresh yeast (which does not create thick crusts).

MAKES 1 LOAF

1 BREAD DOUGH

¾ cup (100 g) T65 "French tradition" wheat flour (or use organic high-protein all-purpose flour or bread flour)

¼ cup plus 2 tablespoons (50 g) whole wheat flour (or use T150 flour)

1¼ cups plus 1 tablespoon (170 g) dark rye flour (or use T170 flour)

⅔ cup minus 1 teaspoon (150 g) water

½ packed teaspoon (4 g) fresh yeast

⅔ teaspoon (4 g) salt

3 tablespoons (25 g) sunflower seeds

2 FINISHING

1½ tablespoons (10 g) sunflower seeds

Making a multigrain loaf

1 Knead (see page 32) together the wheat, whole wheat, and rye flours, water, crumbled yeast, and salt in the bowl of a stand mixer fitted with the dough hook for 4 minutes on the lowest speed (speed 1), then for 6 minutes on medium speed. The dough should detach from the sides of the bowl. (For kneading by hand, see page 30.)

2 Add the sunflower seeds and knead on speed 1 to incorporate them.

3 Transfer the dough to a mixing bowl.

4 Cover the bowl with plastic wrap and let rise for 30 minutes at room temperature.

5 Turn the dough (see page 37).

6 Place the dough back in the mixing bowl, cover the bowl with plastic wrap, and let rise for an additional 30 minutes.

7 Preshape the dough into a round (see page 38). Let rest for 30 minutes at room temperature, covered with a towel. Shape the dough into a boule (see page 42) and place the dough seam side down onto a baking sheet lined with parchment paper. Brush the top of the dough with cold water using the pastry brush, then sprinkle it with the sunflower seeds.

8 Cover the loaf with a towel and let rise for 1½ hours in a warm place, 77 to 82°F (25 to 28°C), for the proofing.

9 Preheat the oven to 500°F (260°C) with a baking sheet and a bowl filled with water placed in the oven. Score a single cross into the dough (see page 51).

10 When the oven comes to temperature, slide everything onto the hot baking sheet. Spritz the bottom of the oven with water, and bake for 25 to 30 minutes. Slightly prop open the oven door 5 to 10 minutes before the end of the baking time.

WHOLE WHEAT
SOURDOUGH

Understanding

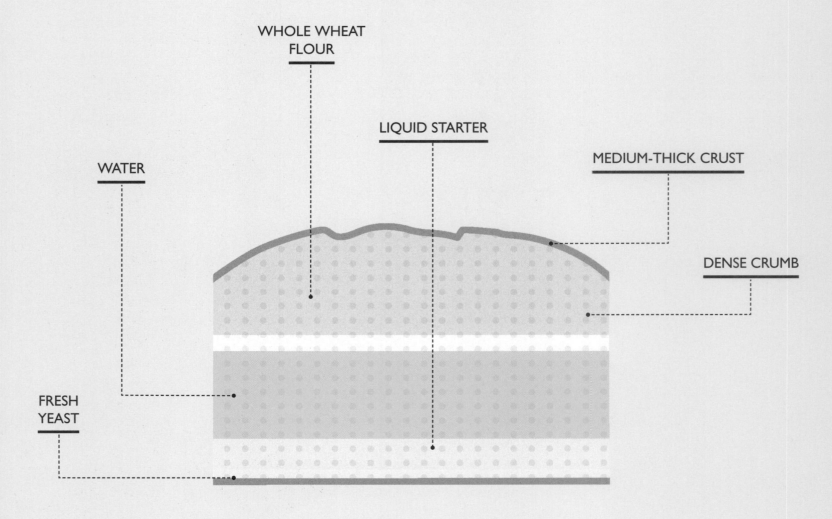

WHOLE WHEAT
FLOUR

LIQUID STARTER

MEDIUM-THICK CRUST

WATER

DENSE CRUMB

FRESH
YEAST

WHAT IT IS

A bread dough made with liquid starter and whole wheat flour, shaped into a bâtard.

CHARACTERISTICS

–Weight: 12¾ ounces (360 g)
–Size: 9¾ inches (25 cm)
–Crumb: dense
–Crust: medium
–Taste: rustic

COMPLETION TIME

–Preparation time: 15 minutes
–Fermentation time: 3 to 3½ hours
  (1 hour rising, 30 minutes resting,
  1½ to 2 hours proofing)
–Baking time: 25 to 30 minutes

EQUIPMENT

–Stand mixer fitted with the
  dough hook (optional)
–Lame

IT'S READY

When the bread is golden and sounds hollow when tapped.

SKILLS TO MASTER

–Kneading (pages 30 and 32)
–Preshaping a Round (page 38)
–Shaping a Bâtard (page 45)
–Scoring (page 50)

USEFUL TIP

At the end of the proofing, the dough has sufficiently risen when gently pressing into it with your fingertip leaves no mark.

SHELF LIFE

Two days.

MAKES 1 LOAF

DOUGH

1½ cups minus 1 tablespoon (180 g)
 whole wheat flour (or T150 flour)
½ cup plus 1 tablespoon (130 g) water
1½ ounces (45 g) Liquid Starter (page 20)
⅜ packed teaspoon (3 g) fresh yeast
⅔ teaspoon (4 g) salt

SIFTING

1½ tablespoons (15 g) high-protein all-purpose
 flour (or use bread flour or T65 flour)

1 Knead (see page 32) together the flour, water, starter, crumbled yeast, and salt in the bowl of a stand mixer fitted with the dough hook for 4 minutes on the lowest speed (speed 1), then for 6 minutes on medium speed. The dough should detach from the sides of the bowl. (For kneading by hand, see page 30.)

2 Place the dough in a mixing bowl, cover the bowl with a towel, and let rise for 1 hour in a warm place, 77 to 82°F (25 to 28°C).

3 Preshape the dough into a round (see page 38). Cover and let rest on a floured work surface for 30 minutes.

4 Shape the dough into a bâtard (see page 45). Place the dough seam side down onto a sheet of parchment paper. Sift the 1½ tablespoons (15 g) flour over the bread.

5 Score the dough in a diagonal (see page 51).

6 Cover the dough with a towel and let rise for 1½ to 2 hours in a warm place, 77 to 82°F (25 to 28°C), for the proofing.

7 Preheat the oven to 500°F (260°C) with a baking sheet and a bowl filled with water placed in the oven. When the oven comes to temperature, slide the parchment paper and dough onto the hot baking sheet. Spritz the bottom of the oven with water and bake 25 to 30 minutes (leaving the bowl of water in the oven). Slightly prop open the oven door 5 minutes before the end of the baking time.

SOURDOUGH RYE

Understanding

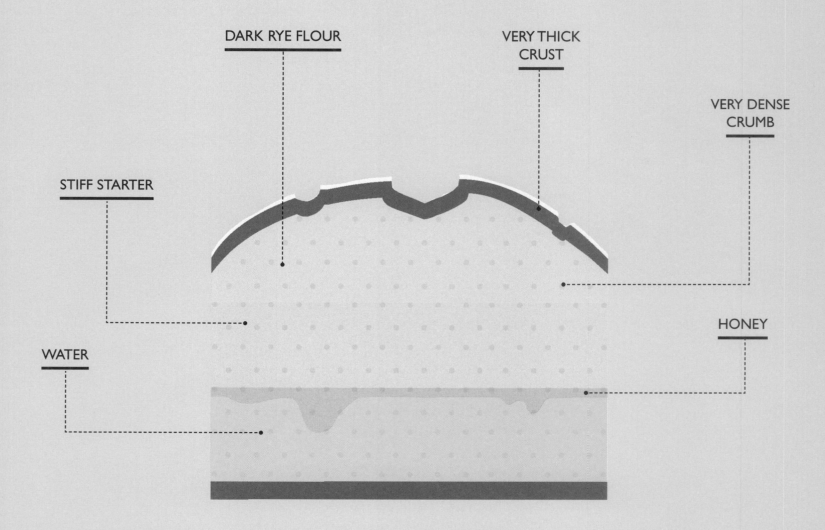

DARK RYE FLOUR

VERY THICK CRUST

VERY DENSE CRUMB

STIFF STARTER

HONEY

WATER

WHAT IT IS

A bread dough made with rye flour only and a stiff starter, flavored with honey, and shaped into a large boule.

CHARACTERISTICS

–Weight: 1⅛ pounds (500 g)
–Size: 8 inches (20 cm) in diameter
–Crumb: very dense
–Crust: very thick, cracked, and floured
–Taste: strong, sour, slight caramel taste

COMPLETION TIME

–Preparation time: 30 minutes
–Fermentation time: 3½ hours (2 hours rising, 1½ hours proofing)
–Baking time: 40 to 45 minutes

EQUIPMENT

Stand mixer fitted with the dough hook (optional)

SKILLS TO MASTER

–Kneading (pages 30 and 32)
–Shaping a Boule (page 42)

IT'S READY

When the bread is dark golden. The bread should sound hollow when the top is tapped.

SHELF LIFE

Four to five days, wrapped in a towel.

HOW DO YOU EXPLAIN THE DENSE CRUMB?

The acidity of the dough (provided by the stiff starter) and the low proportion of gluten (rye flour contains very little) make the formation of a gluten network difficult. Consequently, the gases created from fermentation escape, and the crumb has fewer holes and is therefore more dense.

MAKES I LOAF

1¼ cups plus 1 tablespoon (170 g) dark rye flour (or use T170 flour)

¾ cup minus 2 teaspoons (165 g) water at 140°F (60°C)

6 ounces (170 g) Stiff Starter (page 22)

¾ teaspoon (5 g) salt

1 teaspoon (7 g) honey

Making the sourdough rye

1. Knead (see page 32) together the flour, water, crumbled starter, salt, and honey in the bowl of a stand mixer fitted with the dough hook for 4 minutes on the lowest speed (speed 1), then for 6 minutes on medium speed. (For kneading by hand, see page 30.)

2. Cover the bottom of a mixing bowl with flour and place the dough on top of it.

3. Cover the bowl with plastic wrap and let rise for 2 hours.

4. Shape the dough into a boule (see page 42). Flour your hands and the work surface, if necessary.

5. Cover the bottom of a mixing bowl with a floured towel and place the ball of dough on top of it, seam side down.

6. Cover the bowl with another towel and let rest for 1½ hours in a warm place, 77 to 82°F (25 to 28°C), for the proofing.

7. Preheat the oven to 500°F (260°C) with a baking sheet and a bowl filled with water placed in the oven. Turn the bread over seam side up, dust off any excess flour with your hand, and place the dough onto parchment paper. When the oven comes to temperature, slide the parchment with the loaf onto the hot baking sheet. Spritz the bottom of the oven with water and bake for 40 to 45 minutes (keeping the bowl of water in the oven). Slightly prop open the oven door 5 to 10 minutes before the end of the baking time.

LEMON SOURDOUGH
RYE

Understanding

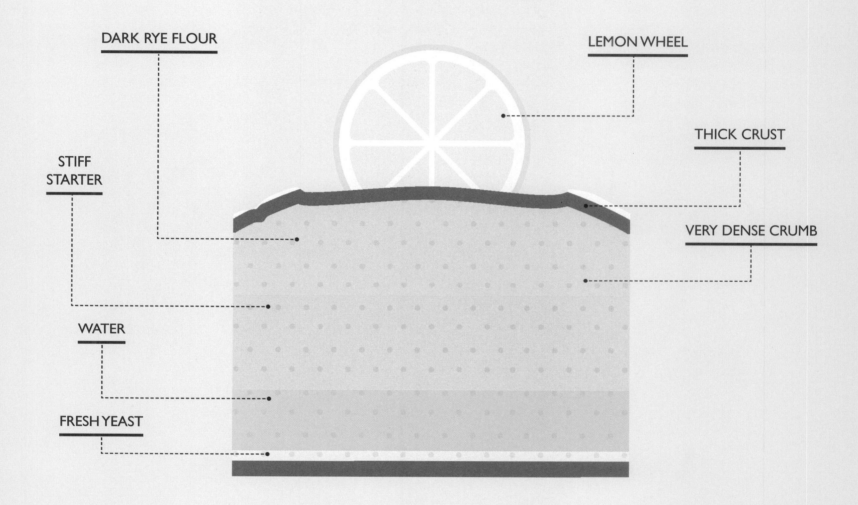

DARK RYE FLOUR

STIFF STARTER

WATER

FRESH YEAST

LEMON WHEEL

THICK CRUST

VERY DENSE CRUMB

WHAT IT IS

A bread dough made with rye flour only and a stiff starter, flavored with lemon juice and zest.

CHARACTERISTICS

– Weight: 9 ounces (250 g)
– Size: 6 inches (15 cm) in diameter
– Crumb: very dense
– Crust: thick
– Taste: sour and lemony

COMPLETION TIME

– Preparation time: 30 minutes

– Fermentation time: 1 hour and 45 minutes (45 minutes rising, 1 hour proofing)
– Baking time: 35 minutes

EQUIPMENT

– Stand mixer fitted with the dough hook (optional)
– Bench scraper

SKILLS TO MASTER

– Kneading (pages 30 and 32)
– Shaping a Boule (page 42)

USEFUL TIP

Add a few drops of essential oil of lemon to enhance the flavor.

SHELF LIFE

Two days.

IT'S READY

When the crust of the bread is well browned. The bread should sound hollow when the top is tapped.

HOW DO YOU EXPLAIN THE VERY DENSE CRUMB?

Rye flour contains little gluten, so the gluten network is weaker. The gases from fermentation escape so holes do not form in the crumb, leaving the crumb very dense once baked.

MAKES 2 LOAVES

1¼ cups (160 g) dark rye flour (or use T170 flour)

½ cup plus 1½ tablespoons (140 g) water

5½ ounces (160 g) Stiff Starter (page 22)

¼ packed teaspoon (2 g) fresh yeast

¾ teaspoon (5 g) salt

1 tablespoon (15 g) organic lemon juice

1½ tablespoons (10 g) organic lemon zest

FINISHING

1½ tablespoons (15 g) high-protein all-purpose flour (or use bread flour or T65 flour)

Water

2 slices organic lemon

1 Knead (see page 32) together the rye flour, water, crumbled starter and yeast, salt, and lemon juice and zest in the bowl of a stand mixer fitted with the dough hook for 4 minutes on the lowest speed (speed 1), then for 6 minutes on medium speed. The dough should detach from the sides of the bowl. (For kneading by hand, see page 30.)

2 Place the dough in a floured mixing bowl. Cover the bowl with a towel and let rise for 45 minutes.

3 Divide the dough into two pieces, 9 ounces (250 g) each, using the bench scraper. Shape the pieces into boules (see page 42).

4 Place the loaves seam side down onto a sheet of parchment paper. Cover them with a towel, and let rest for 1 hour in a warm place, 77 to 82°F (25 to 28°C), for the proofing.

5 Preheat the oven to 475°F (240°C) with a baking sheet placed in the oven. Sift the 1½ tablespoons (15 g) flour over the loaves. Lightly moisten the center of the loaves using the pastry brush and arrange a slice of lemon in the center, pressing it down lightly to adhere.

6 Once the oven comes to temperature, slide the parchment with the loaves onto the hot baking sheet. Spritz the bottom of the oven with water and bake for 35 minutes. Slightly prop open the oven door 5 minutes before the end of the baking time to dry the crumb.

MULTIGRAIN
BROWN LOAF
(PAIN NOIR)

Understanding

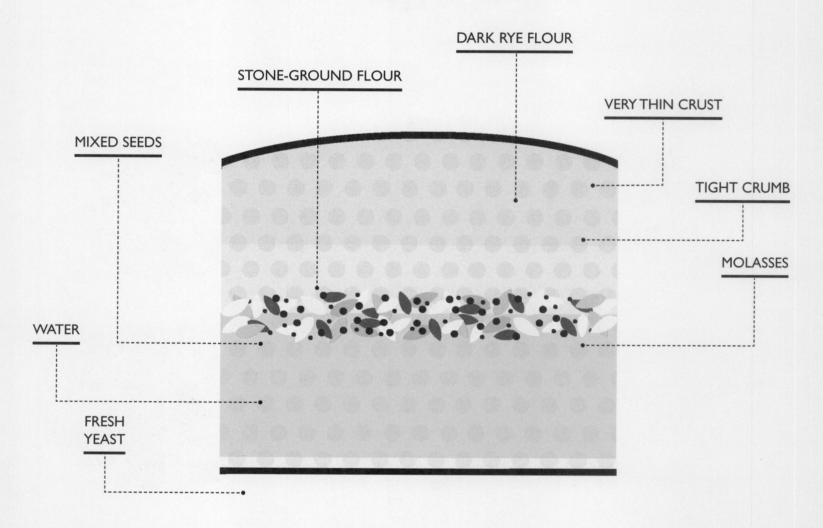

DARK RYE FLOUR

STONE-GROUND FLOUR

VERY THIN CRUST

MIXED SEEDS

TIGHT CRUMB

MOLASSES

WATER

FRESH YEAST

WHAT IT IS

A bread dough made from rye and stone-ground flours, enriched with molasses and seeds.

CHARACTERISTICS

–Weight: 1⅔ pounds (750 g)
–Size: 8 inches (20 cm)
–Crumb: tight
–Crust: very thin, tender
–Taste: rustic, pronounced

COMPLETION TIME

–Preparation time: 30 minutes
–Fermentation time: 1 hour
–Baking time: 45 minutes

EQUIPMENT

–Stand mixer fitted with the dough hook
–One 8-inch (20 cm) loaf pan
–Pastry brush
–Lame

SKILL TO MASTER

Kneading (pages 30 and 32)

IT'S READY

When the tip of a knife inserted into the center comes out dry. Otherwise, place the loaf back in the oven for a few minutes.

SHELF LIFE

Four to five days, when not exposed to air.

WHY IS THE CRUST NOT CRISP?

Baking in a loaf pan limits the development of the crust because the dough bakes in a humid environment inside the pan and cannot dry out.

MAKES I LOAF

SEEDS

¼ cup plus 2 tablespoons (50 g) mixed seeds (poppy, brown flax, sesame, sunflower)
2½ tablespoons (40 g) water

DOUGH

2 cups minus 1 tablespoon (250 g) dark rye flour (or use T170 flour)
1¼ cups (150 g) white whole wheat flour (or use stone-ground T110 flour)
1⅓ cups plus 1 teaspoon (320 g) water at 68 to 77°F (20 to 25°C)
1¼ packed teaspoons (10 g) fresh yeast
1⅔ teaspoons (10 g) salt
1 tablespoon (20 g) molasses

PAN

Olive oil

THE DAY BEFORE

1 Soak the seeds in the water (see page 94).

THE SAME DAY

2 Knead (see page 32) together the rye and whole wheat flours, water, crumbled yeast, salt, and molasses in the bowl of a stand mixer fitted with the dough hook for 4 minutes on the lowest speed (speed 1), then for 6 minutes on medium speed. The dough must detach from the sides of the bowl. (For kneading by hand, see page 30.)

3 Add the seeds and knead for several minutes on speed 1 until fully incorporated.

4 Scrape the dough into the loaf pan that has been lightly brushed on the bottom and sides with the oil.

5 Cover the pan with a towel and let rest for 1 hour in a warm place, 77 to 82°F (25 to 28°C), for the proofing.

6 Preheat the oven to 450°F (230°C) with a baking sheet and a bowl of water placed in the oven. When the oven comes to temperature, place the pan on the hot baking sheet. Spritz the bottom of the oven with water and bake for 45 minutes (keeping the bowl of water in the oven). Slightly prop open the oven door 5 to 10 minutes before the end of the baking time.

CHESTNUT
SOURDOUGH

Understanding

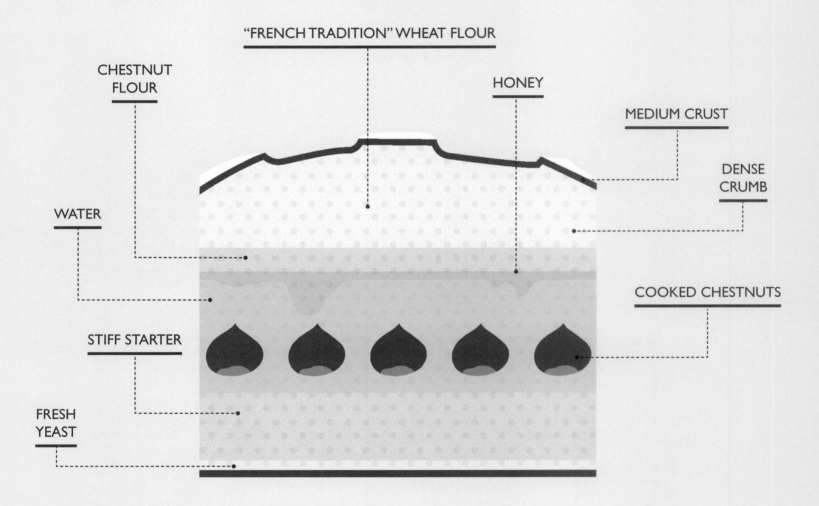

CHESTNUT
FLOUR

"FRENCH TRADITION" WHEAT FLOUR

HONEY

MEDIUM CRUST

WATER

DENSE
CRUMB

STIFF STARTER

COOKED CHESTNUTS

FRESH
YEAST

WHAT IT IS

A bread dough made from "French tradition" and chestnut flours, studded with chestnuts cooked in butter.

CHARACTERISTICS

–Weight: 10½ ounces (300 g)
–Size: 6 to 7 inches (16 to 18 cm) in diameter
–Crumb: dense
–Crust: medium
–Taste: very chestnut-y

COMPLETION TIME

–Preparation time: 40 minutes
–Fermentation time: 2 hours and 15 minutes (45 minutes rising, 1½ hours proofing)
–Baking time: 30 minutes

EQUIPMENT

–Stand mixer fitted with the dough hook (optional)
–Bench scraper
–Lame

SKILLS TO MASTER

–Kneading (pages 30 and 32)
–Preshaping a Round (page 38)
–Shaping a Boule (page 42)
–Scoring a Crisscross (page 51)

SHELF LIFE

Up to one week if stored unsliced, not exposed to air; two to three days if sliced.

IT'S READY

When the crust is golden brown and the diamond slashes have widened slightly.

MAKES 2 LOAVES

CHESTNUTS

3½ ounces (100 g) cooked chestnuts
(from a jar or cooked sous-vide)
2 teaspoons (10 g) unsalted butter

DOUGH

1½ cups (200 g) T65 "French tradition"
wheat flour (or use organic high-protein
all-purpose flour or bread flour)
¼ cup (25 g) chestnut flour
⅔ cup plus 1 teaspoon (160 g) water
3⅛ ounces (90 g) Stiff Starter (page 22)
⅜ packed teaspoon (3 g) fresh yeast
1 teaspoon (6 g) salt
1½ teaspoons (10 g) honey

SIFTING

1½ tablespoons (15 g) high-protein all-purpose
flour (or use bread flour or T65 flour)

1 Place the chestnuts in a saucepan with the butter
and cook for 10 minutes. Let cool for 5 minutes.
Cut them in half, or into quarters if they are large.

2 Knead (see page 32) together the wheat and
chestnut flours, water, starter, crumbled yeast,
and salt in the bowl of a stand mixer fitted with
the dough hook for 4 minutes on the lowest speed
(speed 1), then for 6 minutes on medium speed.
The dough should detach from the sides of the
bowl. (For kneading by hand, see page 30.)

3 Add the chestnuts and honey to the
dough and knead to distribute them well.

4 Place the dough in a mixing bowl, cover
the bowl with plastic wrap, and let rise
for 45 minutes at room temperature.

5 Divide the dough into two pieces, 10½ ounces
(300 g) each, using the bench scraper. Preshape
the pieces into rounds (see page 38) and let rest
for 20 minutes. Shape the rounds into boules
(see page 42). Place the loaves seam side down
onto a sheet of parchment paper. Cover them
with a towel and let rest for 1½ hours in a warm
place, 77 to 82°F (25 to 28°C), for the proofing.

6 Preheat the oven to 500°F (260°C) with
a baking sheet placed in the oven. Sift the
1½ tablespoons (15 g) flour over the dough and
score the boules in a large crisscross (see page
51). Slide the parchment paper with the loaves
onto the hot baking sheet. Spritz the bottom of
the oven with water and bake for 30 minutes.

CORNMEAL LOAF

Understanding

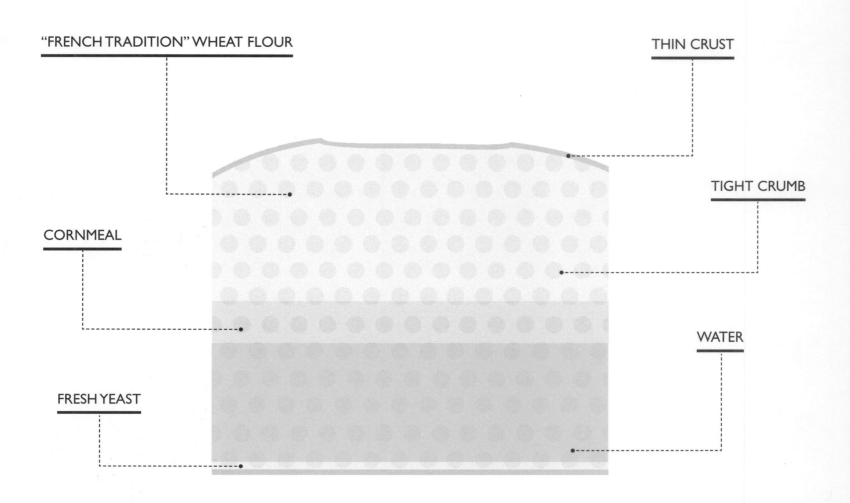

"FRENCH TRADITION" WHEAT FLOUR

THIN CRUST

CORNMEAL

TIGHT CRUMB

FRESH YEAST

WATER

WHAT IT IS

A bread dough made from "French tradition" wheat flour and cornmeal, shaped into a bâtard.

CHARACTERISTICS

–Weight: 9 ounces (250 g)
–Size: 8 inches (20 cm)
–Crumb: tight
–Crust: thin
–Taste: slightly sweet

COMPLETION TIME

–Preparation time: 30 minutes
–Fermentation time: 2 hours and 5 minutes
  (30 minutes rising, 20 minutes resting,
  1 hour and 15 minutes proofing)
–Baking time: 25 minutes

EQUIPMENT

–Stand mixer fitted with the
  dough hook (optional)
–Bench scraper
–Lame

SKILLS TO MASTER

–Kneading (pages 30 and 32)
–Preshaping a Round (page 38)
–Shaping a Bâtard (page 45)
–Scoring a Traditional Slash (page 51)

USEFUL TIP

At the end of the proofing, the dough has sufficiently risen when gently pressing into it with your fingertip leaves no mark.

IT'S READY

When the bread is golden and sounds hollow when tapped.

SHELF LIFE

Two to three days.

2A

2B

6

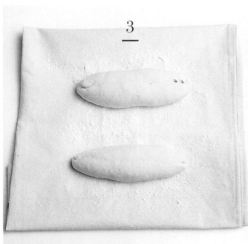

3

4

5

MAKES 2 LOAVES

2 cups plus 2 tablespoons (285 g) T65 "French tradition" wheat flour (or use organic high-protein all-purpose flour or bread flour)

⅓ cup plus 1 tablespoon (70 g) cornmeal

1 cup minus 2 teaspoons (225 g) water at 68 to 77°F (20 to 25°C)

⅛ packed teaspoon (1 g) fresh yeast

1⅓ teaspoons (8 g) salt

FINISHING

1 tablespoon (15 g) cornmeal

1 Knead (see page 32) together the flour, cornmeal, water, crumbled yeast, and salt in the bowl of a stand mixer fitted with the dough hook for 4 minutes on the lowest speed (speed 1), then for 6 minutes on medium speed. The dough should detach from the sides of the bowl. (For kneading by hand, see page 30.)

2 Place the dough in a mixing bowl, cover the bowl with plastic wrap, and let rise for 30 minutes at room temperature.

3 Divide the dough into two pieces, 10½ ounces (300 g) each, with the bench scraper, and shape them into rounds (see page 38). Cover and let rest on a floured work surface for 20 minutes.

4 Shape the rounds into bâtards (see page 45). Place them seam side up on a towel floured with cornmeal. Cover with a second towel and let rest for 1 hour and 15 minutes in a warm place, 77 to 82°F (25 to 28°C), for the proofing.

5 Preheat the oven to 500°F (260°C) with a baking sheet and a bowl filled with water placed in the oven. Place the loaves seam side down on parchment paper. Score a traditional slash (see page 51) down the entire length of the loaves. When the oven comes to temperature, transfer the parchment with the loaves onto the hot baking sheet.

6 Spritz the bottom of the oven with water, and bake for 25 minutes (leaving the bowl of water in the oven).

GLUTEN-FREE LOAF

Understanding

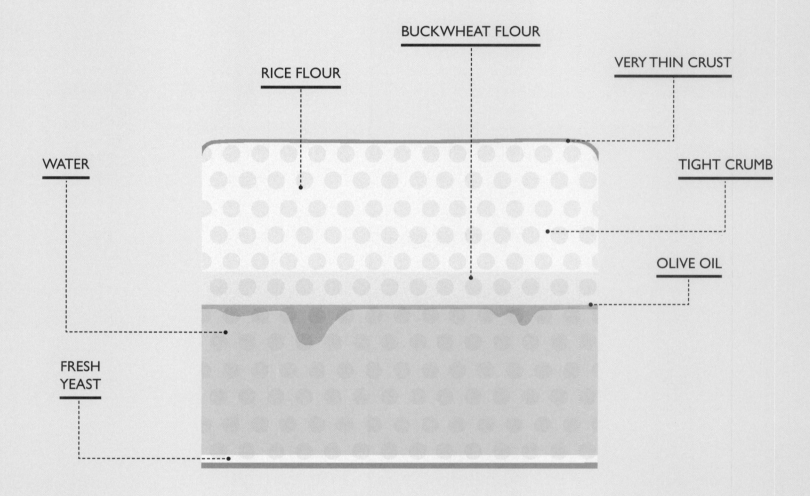

BUCKWHEAT FLOUR

RICE FLOUR

VERY THIN CRUST

WATER

TIGHT CRUMB

OLIVE OIL

FRESH
YEAST

WHAT IT IS

A gluten-free bread dough made from rice and buckwheat flours. This bread needs a great deal of water and has only one rise.

CHARACTERISTICS

– Weight: 10½ ounces (300 g)
– Size: 6 to 8 inches (15 to 20 cm), according to the pan size
– Crumb: tight
– Crust: very thin, tender
– Taste: very neutral

COMPLETION TIME

– Preparation time: 15 minutes
– Fermentation time: 1 hour and 15 minutes (proofing only)
– Baking time: 45 minutes

EQUIPMENT

– Stand mixer fitted with a paddle, or use a rubber spatula
– One 2-cup (500 ml) loaf pan

SKILL TO MASTER

Kneading (pages 30 and 32)

SHELF LIFE

Two to three days, not exposed to air.

USEFUL TIP

The dough has sufficiently risen when gently pressing into it with your fingertip leaves no mark.

IT'S READY

When the bread is golden and sounds hollow when tapped.

WHY IS A LOT OF WATER NECESSARY?

Gluten-free flours contain more starch than flours with gluten. Starch needs water to swell and gelatinize when baked. In order for the bread to take shape, a great deal of water is necessary.

MAKES 1 LOAF

DOUGH

1⅔ cups (260 g) rice flour
½ cup (60 g) buckwheat flour
1¼ cups plus 1 teaspoon (300 g) water
¾ packed teaspoon (6 g) fresh yeast
¾ teaspoon (5 g) salt
1 tablespoon (10 g) olive oil

LOAF PAN

1 tablespoon (15 g) Beurre en
   Pommade (page 284)

1 Combine the rice and buckwheat flours, water, crumbled yeast, salt, and olive oil for 5 minutes in a stand mixer fitted with the paddle.

2 Scrape the dough into the loaf pan greased with the beurre en pommade.

3 Cover the pan with a towel and let rise for 1 hour and 15 minutes at room temperature for the proofing.

4 Preheat the oven to 450°F (230°C) with a baking sheet placed in the oven. Place the pan on the hot baking sheet and bake for 45 minutes.

BEER BREAD

Understanding

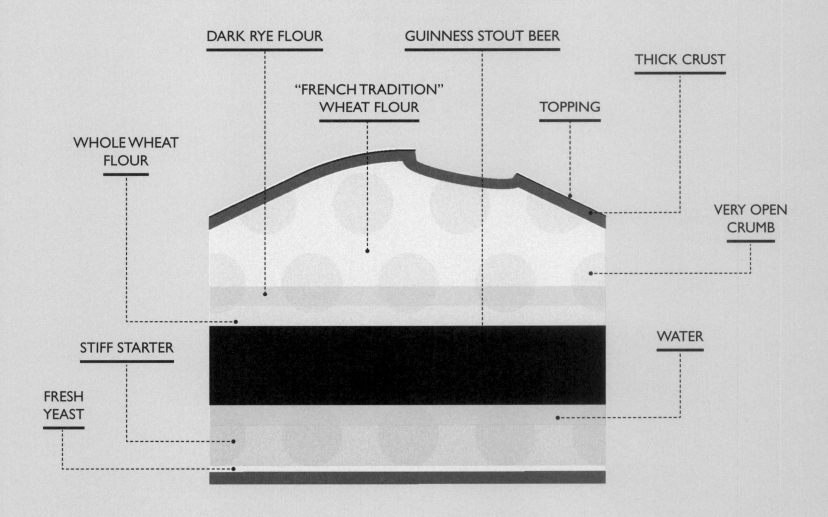

DARK RYE FLOUR

GUINNESS STOUT BEER

THICK CRUST

"FRENCH TRADITION"
WHEAT FLOUR

TOPPING

WHOLE WHEAT
FLOUR

VERY OPEN
CRUMB

STIFF STARTER

WATER

FRESH
YEAST

WHAT IT IS
A bread dough made from three flours ("French tradition," rye, and whole wheat) as well as with dark beer. It's shaped into a triangle and covered with a topping that cracks when baked.

CHARACTERISTICS
– Weight: 10½ ounces (300 g)
– Size: about 6 inches (15 cm)
– Crumb: very open, irregular
– Crust: thick
– Taste: malty

COMPLETION TIME
– Preparation time: 30 minutes
– Fermentation time: 3 hours (1 hour rising, 30 minutes resting, 1½ hours proofing)
– Resting time: 1½ hours (for the beer topping)
– Baking time: 25 to 30 minutes

EQUIPMENT
– Stand mixer fitted with the dough hook (optional)
– Offset or frosting spatula

CHALLENGE
The topping: the preparation must be smooth and evenly spread on the bread to obtain a nice tiger skin–like pattern to the crust.

SKILLS TO MASTER
– Kneading (pages 30 and 32)
– Turning (page 37)

IT'S READY
When the crust is deep brown and cracked.

SHELF LIFE
Three days, after slicing.

Learning

HOW DO YOU EXPLAIN THE TEXTURE OF THE CRUMB?

The acidity in the beer limits the bonds of the gluten network causing it to be less developed. As a result, the crumb is very delicate.

MAKES 2 LOAVES

1   DOUGH

1½ cups (200 g) T65 "French tradition" wheat flour (or use organic high-protein all-purpose flour or bread flour)
¼ cup plus 1 tablespoon (40 g) dark rye flour (or use T170 flour)
¼ cup plus 1 tablespoon (40 g) white whole wheat flour (or use T110 flour)
¾ cup (180 g) Guinness stout beer
3 ounces (80 g) Stiff Starter (page 22)
¼ packed teaspoon (2 g) fresh yeast
1 teaspoon (6 g) salt

2   SPRITZING

2½ tablespoons (40 g) water

3   TOPPING

⅛ packed teaspoon (1 g) fresh yeast
2 teaspoons (10 g) water
3 tablespoons (30 g) rice flour
1 teaspoon (5 g) melted butter
1¼ teaspoons (5 g) sugar
⅛ teaspoon (1 g) salt

4   SIFTING

1½ tablespoons (15 g) high-protein all-purpose flour (or use bread flour or T65 flour)

Making the beer bread

1 Knead (see page 32) together the wheat, rye, and whole wheat flours, the Guinness, the starter, the crumbled yeast, and the salt in the bowl of a stand mixer fitted with the dough hook for 4 minutes on the lowest speed (speed 1), then for 6 minutes on medium speed. (For kneading by hand, see page 30.)

2 Spritz the dough (see page 282) with water at the end of the kneading time to adjust the consistency of it. Knead until the additional water is fully incorporated into the dough. Place the dough into a mixing bowl, cover the bowl with a towel, and let rise for 30 minutes.

3 Turn the dough (see page 37).

4 Place the dough back in the mixing bowl, and let rise for an additional 30 minutes at room temperature, covered with a towel.

5 Shape the dough into a triangle using the edges of your hands.

6 Place the loaf seam side down onto a sheet of parchment paper.

7 Cover the loaf with a towel and let rest for 1½ hours in a warm place, 77 to 82°F (25 to 28°C), for the proofing.

8 Make the topping: Dilute the crumbled yeast in the water. Add the remaining ingredients. Whisk until the mixture is smooth. Let rest for 1½ hours.

9 Preheat the oven to 500°F (260°C) with a baking sheet placed in the oven. Spread the topping over the loaf using the spatula.

10 Slide the loaf onto the hot baking sheet with the parchment paper and sift the 1½ tablespoons (15 g) flour over the top. Spritz the bottom of the oven with water and bake for 25 minutes.

MIXED SEEDS RING

Understanding

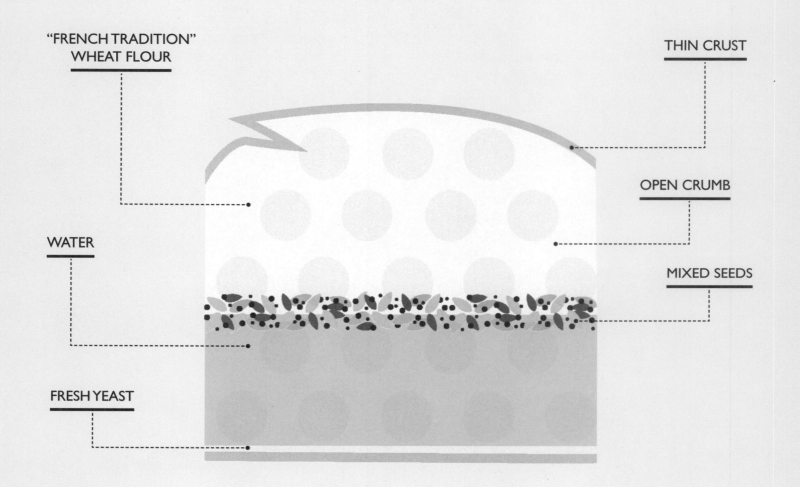

"FRENCH TRADITION" WHEAT FLOUR

WATER

FRESH YEAST

THIN CRUST

OPEN CRUMB

MIXED SEEDS

WHAT IT IS
A seed-filled straight dough shaped into a ring.

CHARACTERISTICS
–Weight: 5¼ ounces (150 g)
–Size: 7 inches (18 cm) in diameter
–Crumb: open crumb, irregular
–Crust: thin
–Taste: neutral, with the taste of seeds

EQUIPMENT
–Stand mixer fitted with the dough hook (optional)
–Bench scraper
–Lame

COMPLETION TIME
–Preparation time: 30 minutes
–Fermentation time: 3½ hours (1 hour rising, 30 minutes resting, 2 hours proofing)
–Baking time: 20 minutes

CHALLENGE
Properly shaping the ring.

SKILLS TO MASTER
–Kneading (pages 30 and 32)
–Preshaping a Round (page 38)
–Shaping a Couronne (page 46)
–Cutting an Épi (page 51)

IT'S READY
When the bread is golden brown and sounds hollow when tapped.

SHELF LIFE
Two to three days.

WHY SHOULD YOU LET THE DOUGH REST AFTER IT'S SHAPED INTO A RING?
To give the gluten network time to relax; the dough must be supple so that the shape of the ring stays uniform and rounded before and after baking.

MAKES 2 LOAVES

1 SEEDS

¼ cup (30 g) mixed seeds (sesame,
   linseed, millet, poppy, etc.)
2 tablespoons (30 g) water

2 DOUGH

1⅔ cups (220 g) T65 "French tradition"
   wheat flour (or use organic high-protein
   all-purpose flour or bread flour)
½ cup plus 2 tablespoons (145 g) water
   at 68 to 77°F (20 to 25°C)
½ packed teaspoon (4 g) fresh yeast
⅔ teaspoon (4 g) salt

3 SIFTING

1½ tablespoons (15 g) high-protein all-purpose
   flour (or use bread flour or T65 flour)

Making the mixed seeds ring

THE DAY BEFORE

1 Toast the seeds for 10 to 15 minutes in the oven preheated to 350°F (180°C). Let cool, then place the seeds with the water in a mixing bowl. Set aside at room temperature.

THE SAME DAY

2 Knead (see page 32) together the flour, water, crumbled yeast, and salt in the bowl of a stand mixer fitted with the dough hook for 4 minutes on the lowest speed (speed 1), then for 6 minutes on medium speed. The dough should detach from the sides of the bowl. (For kneading by hand, see page 30.)

3 Add the seed mixture and knead on speed 1 until the seeds are fully incorporated. Cover the bowl in plastic wrap and let rise for 1 hour at room temperature.

4 Divide the dough into two pieces, 7 ounces (200 g) each, using the bench scraper, and preshape them into rounds (see page 38). Cover and let rest on a floured work surface for 30 minutes.

5 Shape the pieces into couronnes (see page 46). Dip your index finger in flour and pierce the rounds with your finger all the way through to the work surface.

6 Place both thumbs inside the hole and move them side to side in a circular motion. When the dough no longer stretches, let it rest for 5 minutes. Begin these steps again until you have a diameter of 4 inches (10 cm) inside the ring.

7 Place the rings seam side down onto a baking sheet lined with parchment paper and let rest for 2 hours, covered with a towel, in a warm place, 77 to 82°F (25 to 28°C), for the proofing.

8 Sift the 1½ tablespoons (15 g) flour over the rings.

9 Preheat the oven to 500°F (260°C) with a bowl filled with water placed in the oven. Cut the rings as when cutting an épi (see page 51). Make cuts using scissors angled at forty-five degrees, following the curve of the rings. Pull the sliced pieces out slightly toward the outside.

10 Spritz the bottom of the oven with water and bake for 20 minutes (leaving the bowl of water in the oven).

WALNUT LOAF

Understanding

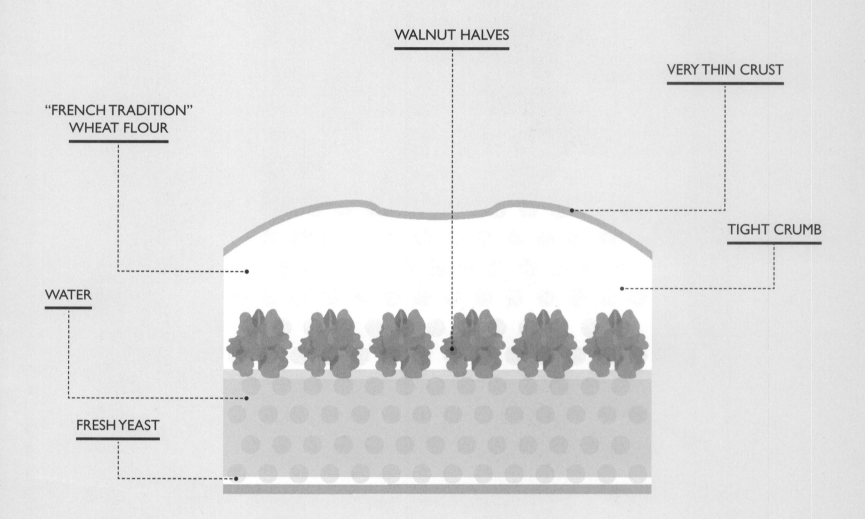

WALNUT HALVES

VERY THIN CRUST

"FRENCH TRADITION" WHEAT FLOUR

TIGHT CRUMB

WATER

FRESH YEAST

WHAT IT IS

A dough made with "French tradition" wheat flour, studded with walnuts, and shaped into a round.

CHARACTERISTICS

– Weight: 1¼ pounds (550 g)
– Size: 6 inches (15 cm) in diameter
– Crumb: tight
– Crust: thin and supple

COMPLETION TIME

– Preparation time: 45 minutes
– Fermentation time: 3 hours (1 hour rising, 30 minutes resting, 1½ hours proofing)
– Baking time: 20 to 25 minutes

EQUIPMENT

– Stand mixer fitted with the dough hook (optional)
– Bench scraper

VARIATIONS

– Walnuts, hazelnuts
– Walnuts, hazelnuts, and raisins

SKILLS TO MASTER

– Kneading (pages 30 and 32)
– Preshaping a Round (page 38)
– Shaping a Boule (page 42)
– Scoring a Single Cross (page 51)

IT'S READY

When the bottom of the loaf sounds hollow when tapped.

SHELF LIFE

Two days, wrapped in a dry cloth and not exposed to air.

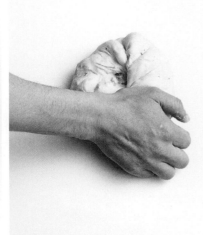

MAKES I LOAF

2 cups (270 g) T65 "French tradition" wheat
   flour (or use organic high-protein
   all-purpose flour or bread flour)
¾ cup plus 1 tablespoon (190 g) water
   at 68 to 77°F (20 to 25°C)
1 ounce (30 g) Liquid Starter (page 20)
⅜ packed teaspoon (3 g) fresh yeast
¾ teaspoon (5 g) salt
1 cup (100 g) walnuts halves

1 Knead (see page 32) together the flour, water,
starter, crumbled yeast, and salt in the bowl of a stand
mixer fitted with the dough hook for 4 minutes on
the lowest speed (speed 1), then for 6 minutes on
medium speed. The dough should detach from the
sides of the bowl. (For kneading by hand, see page 30.)

2 Add the walnuts. Knead on speed 1 until they are
fully incorporated.

3 Place the dough in a mixing bowl, cover the
bowl with plastic wrap, and let rest for 1 hour
in a warm place, 77 to 82°F (25 to 28°C). Turn
the dough (see page 37) after 30 minutes.

4 Preshape the dough into a round (see page 38) on
a floured work surface. Cover with a towel and let rest
for 30 minutes in a warm place, 77 to 82°F (25 to 28°C).

5 Shape the round into a boule (see page 42).

6 Let the dough rest seam side down for
1½ hours, covered with a towel, in a warm place,
77 to 82°F (25 to 28°C), for the proofing.

7 Preheat the oven to 475°F (240°C) with a baking
sheet and a bowl of water placed in the oven. Place
the dough seam side down onto parchment paper.
Score a single cross (see page 51) using a lame or razor
blade. When the oven comes to temperature, slide the
parchment with the loaf onto the hot baking sheet.

8 Spritz the bottom of the oven with water and
bake for 20 to 25 minutes (leaving the bowl of water
in the oven).

CHOCOLATE LOAF

Understanding

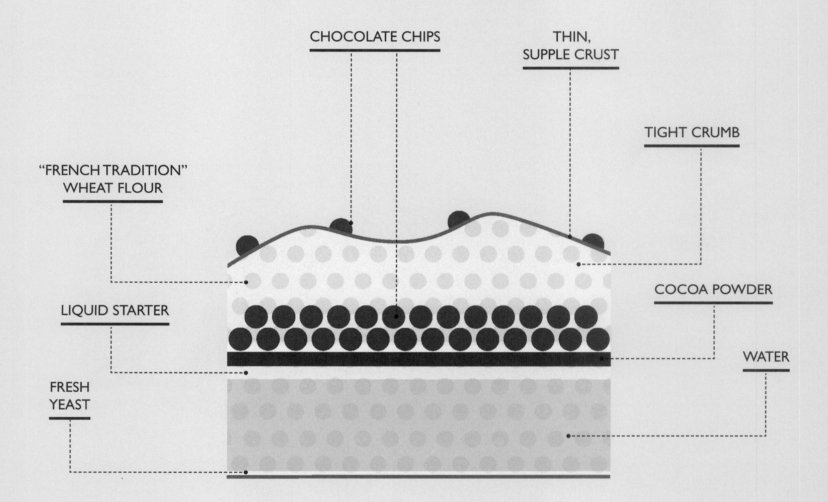

CHOCOLATE CHIPS

THIN, SUPPLE CRUST

TIGHT CRUMB

"FRENCH TRADITION" WHEAT FLOUR

COCOA POWDER

LIQUID STARTER

WATER

FRESH YEAST

WHAT IT IS

A "French tradition" straight dough enriched with unsweetened cocoa powder and pieces of dark chocolate, shaped into bâtards.

CHARACTERISTICS

−Weight: 5¼ ounces (150 g)
−Size: 4¾ inches (12 cm)
−Crumb: tight
−Crust: thin and supple

EQUIPMENT

−Stand mixer fitted with the dough hook (optional)
−Bench scraper

COMPLETION TIME

−Preparation time: 45 minutes
−Fermentation time: 3½ to 4 hours
 (2 hours rising, 30 minutes resting,
 1 to 1½ hours proofing)
−Baking time: 15 minutes

CHALLENGE

Working with the chocolate chips. To prevent the chips from melting, stop kneading the dough as soon as they are incorporated.

SKILLS TO MASTER

−Kneading (pages 30 and 32)
−Preshaping a Round (page 38)
−Turning (page 37)
−Shaping a Bâtard (page 45)
−Scoring a Traditional Slash (page 51)

IT'S READY

When the crust just starts to become firm.

SHELF LIFE

Three to four days.

Learning

1

2

3

WHAT IS THE PURPOSE OF SPRITZING THE DOUGH?

To soften the dough, which becomes firm after adding the cocoa powder. When added at the end of the kneading time, the water can be incorporated slowly to prevent adding too much at once.

MAKES 3 LOAVES

1 DOUGH

1¼ cups (170 g) T65 "French tradition" wheat flour (or use organic high-protein all-purpose flour or bread flour)

½ cup minus ¾ teaspoon (115 g) water at 68 to 77°F (20 to 25°C)

¾ ounce (20 g) Liquid Starter (page 20)

¼ packed teaspoon (2 g) fresh yeast

⅔ teaspoon (4 g) salt

2 CHOCOLATE

2½ teaspoons (10 g) sugar

¼ cup (20 g) unsweetened cocoa powder

1 tablespoon (15 g) water

¼ cup plus 2 tablespoons (70 g) chocolate chips

3 SPRITZING

1 tablespoon (15 g) water at 68 to 77°F (20 to 25°C)

<u>1</u>

<u>2</u>

<u>4</u>

<u>9</u>

<u>11</u>

1 Knead (see page 32) together the flour, ½ cup minus ¾ teaspoon (115 g) water, starter, crumbled yeast, and salt in the bowl of a stand mixer fitted with the dough hook for 4 minutes on the lowest speed (speed 1), then for 6 minutes on medium speed. The dough should detach from the sides of the bowl. (For kneading by hand, see page 30.)

2 Add the sugar, cocoa, and the 1 tablespoon (15 g) water. Knead on speed 1 until the dough is homogeneous.

3 Spritz the dough (see page 282) with water and continue kneading slowly until the water is fully incorporated.

4 Add the chocolate chips and knead on speed 1 until they are well incorporated.

5 Place the dough in a mixing bowl, cover the bowl with plastic wrap, and let rise for 30 minutes in a warm place 77 to 82°F (25 to 28°C). Turn the dough (see page 37). Place the dough back in the mixing bowl, cover the bowl with plastic wrap, and let rise for 30 minutes in a warm place, 77 to 82°F (25 to 28°C).

6 Turn the dough again. Place the dough back in the mixing bowl, cover the bowl with plastic wrap, and let rise for an additional 1 hour in a warm place, 77 to 82°F (25 to 28°C).

7 Divide the dough into three pieces, about 5¼ ounces (150 g) each, using the bench scraper. Preshape the pieces into rounds (see page 38) on a floured work surface.

8 Cover with a towel and let the loaves rest for 30 minutes in a warm place, 77 to 82°F (25 to 28°C).

9 Shape the loaves into bâtards (see page 45).

10 Place the loaves seam side down onto a sheet of parchment paper and let rest for 1 to 1½ hours, covered with a towel, in a warm place, 77 to 82°F (25 to 28°C), for the proofing.

11 Preheat the oven to 475°F (240°C) with a baking sheet and a bowl of water placed in the oven. Score a traditional slash (see page 51). When the oven comes to temperature, slide the parchment with the loaves onto the hot baking sheet.

12 Spritz the bottom of the oven with water and bake for 15 minutes (leaving the bowl of water in the oven).

SMALL
HAZELNUT-FIG LOAVES

Understanding

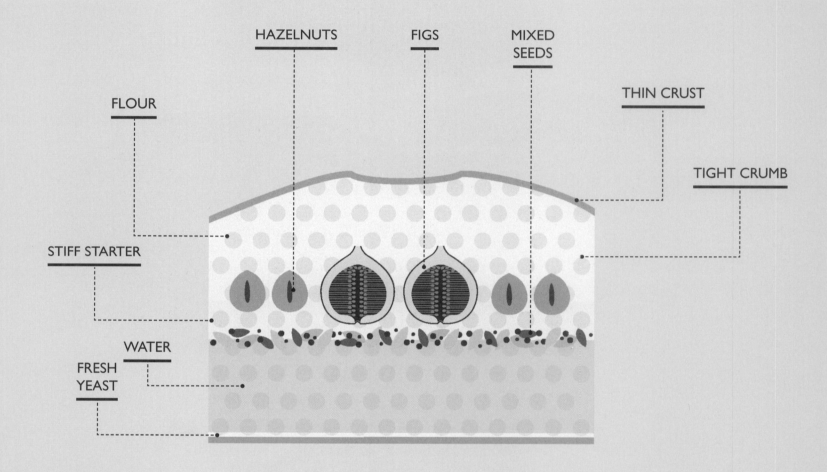

FLOUR

HAZELNUTS

FIGS

MIXED SEEDS

THIN CRUST

TIGHT CRUMB

STIFF STARTER

WATER

FRESH YEAST

WHAT IT IS

A bread dough made from wheat flour and a stiff starter, studded with roasted seeds, figs, and hazelnuts, and shaped into individual boules.

CHARACTERISTICS

–Weight: 2½ ounces (75 g)
–Size: 4 inches (10 cm) in diameter
–Crumb: tight
–Crust: thin

COMPLETION TIME

–Preparation time: 25 minutes
–Fermentation time: 3 to 3½ hours (1 hour rising, 30 minutes resting, 1½ to 2 hours proofing)
–Baking time: 15 minutes

EQUIPMENT

–Stand mixer fitted with the dough hook (optional)
–Bench scraper
–Lame

SKILLS TO MASTER

–Kneading (pages 30 and 32)
–Preshaping a Round (page 38)
–Shaping a Boule (page 42)
–Turning (page 37)
–Scoring a Single Cross (page 51)

USEFUL TIP

If the seeds have not absorbed all the water, drain them before adding them to the dough.

IT'S READY

When the crust is golden and the loaves sound hollow when tapped.

SHELF LIFE

Three days.

MAKES 6 LOAVES

MIX-INS

¼ cup (30 g) mixed seeds (sesame, yellow
    and brown flax, millet, and poppy)
2 tablespoons (15 g) hazelnuts
2 tablespoons (30 g) water
½ ounce (15 g) dried figs

DOUGH

1½ cups minus 1½ tablespoons (190 g)
    high-protein all-purpose flour (or
    use bread flour or T65 flour)
½ cup plus 1 tablespoon (130 g) water
2⅛ ounces (60 g) Stiff Starter (page 22)
¼ packed teaspoon (2 g) fresh yeast
⅔ teaspoon (4 g) salt

THE DAY BEFORE

1 Toast the seeds and hazelnuts for 10 minutes in
the oven at 350°F (180°C). Let cool. Transfer them to a
bowl with the water. Set aside at room temperature.

THE SAME DAY

2 Knead (see page 32) together the flour, water,
starter, crumbled yeast, and salt in the bowl of a stand
mixer fitted with the dough hook for 4 minutes on
the lowest speed (speed 1), then for 6 minutes on
medium speed. The dough should detach from the
sides of the bowl. (For kneading by hand, see page 30.)

3 Add the hazelnuts, seeds, and figs (cut into
quarters) and knead on speed 1 until fully incorporated.

4 Place the dough in a mixing bowl. Cover the
bowl with plastic wrap and let rise for 30 minutes

at room temperature. Turn the dough (see page 37),
place it back in the bowl, and cover the bowl with
plastic wrap. Let rise for an additional 30 minutes.

5 Divide the dough into six pieces, 2½ ounces (75 g)
each, using the bench scraper. Preshape the pieces
into rounds (see page 38) and let rest for 30 minutes
on a floured work surface, covered with a towel.

6 Shape the rounds into boules (see page 42). Place
them seam side down on a sheet of parchment paper
and let rest for 1½ to 2 hours covered with a towel in a
warm place, 77 to 82°F (25 to 28°C), for the proofing.

7 Score a single cross (see page 51) into each loaf.
Preheat the oven to 475°F (240°C) with a baking
sheet and a bowl of water placed in the oven. Slide
the parchment paper with the loaves onto the hot
baking sheet. Spritz oven floor with water and bake for
15 minutes (keeping the bowl of water in the oven).

SMALL MUESLI LOAVES

Understanding

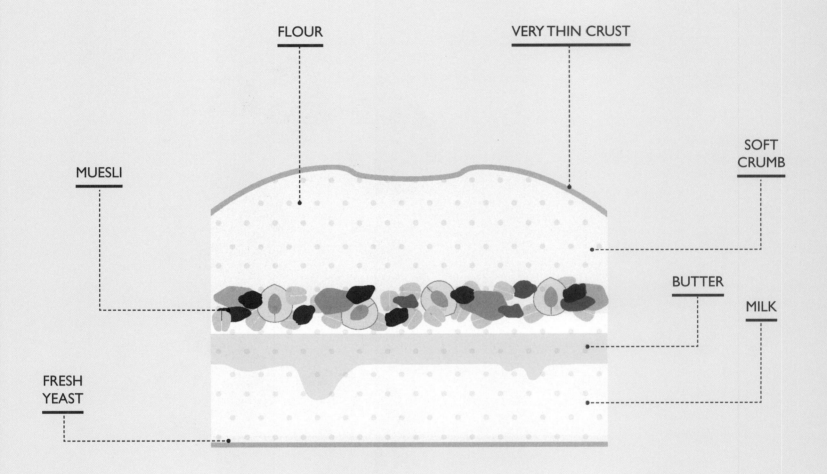

FLOUR

VERY THIN CRUST

SOFT CRUMB

MUESLI

BUTTER

MILK

FRESH YEAST

WHAT IT IS

A Vienna dough filled with muesli and shaped into individual boules.

CHARACTERISTICS

– Weight: 3 ounces (80 g)
– Size: 4 inches (10 cm) in diameter
– Crumb: moist
– Crust: very thin, supple

COMPLETION TIME

– Preparation time: 30 minutes
– Fermentation time: 8 hours (30 minutes rising, 5 hours chilling, 30 minutes resting, 2 hours proofing)
– Baking time: 15 minutes

EQUIPMENT

– Stand mixer fitted with the dough hook (optional)
– Bench scraper
– Strainer
– Pastry brush

SKILLS TO MASTER

– Kneading (pages 30 and 32)
– Turning (page 37)
– Preshaping a Round (page 38)
– Shaping a Boule (page 42)
– Glazing (page 48)
– Scoring a Crisscross (page 51)

USEFUL TIPS

– Use a muesli with oatmeal.
– Avoid fresh fruits that will create too much moisture in the dough.

IT'S READY

When the crust is golden brown.

SHELF LIFE

One to two days, maximum.

MAKES 6 LOAVES

VIENNA DOUGH

1¾ cups (240 g) high-protein all-purpose
    flour (or use bread flour or T65 flour)
½ cup plus 2 tablespoons (150 g) whole milk
⅝ packed teaspoon (5 g) fresh yeast
1½ tablespoons (20 g) sugar
¾ teaspoon (5 g) salt
2 tablespoons plus 2 teaspoons
    (40 g) unsalted butter

MIX-IN

½ cup (60 g) muesli (rolled oats, hazelnuts,
    raisins, and dried tropical fruits)

GLAZE

1 large (50 g) egg
½ teaspoon (3 g) whole milk
Pinch of salt

1 Using the technique on page 61, make the Vienna dough.

2 Add the muesli. Knead the dough slowly until the muesli is evenly incorporated.

3 Place the dough in a mixing bowl, cover the bowl with plastic wrap, and let rise for 30 minutes.

4 Turn the dough (see page 37), cover it by pressing plastic wrap onto its surface (see page 285) in the mixing bowl, and let rise for an additional 5 hours in the refrigerator.

5 Divide the dough into six pieces, about 3 ounces (80 g) each, using the bench scraper. Preshape the pieces into rounds (see page 38), and let rest for 30 minutes on a floured work surface, covered with a towel.

6 Shape rounds into boules (see page 42), then place them seam side down onto a sheet of parchment paper.

7 Make the glaze (see page 49) and glaze the loaves using the pastry brush. Score them in a crisscross (see page 51). Let rest for 2 hours, covered with a towel, in a warm place, 77 to 82°F (25 to 28°C), for the proofing.

8 Preheat the oven to 400°F (200°C) with a baking sheet placed in the oven. Slide the loaves onto the hot baking sheet with the parchment paper, glaze the loaves again, if necessary, and bake for 15 minutes.

CHEESE BREAD

Understanding

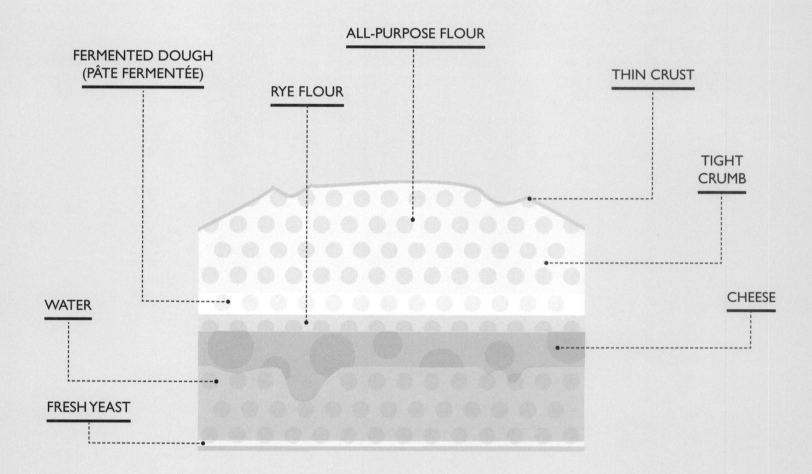

FERMENTED DOUGH
(PÂTE FERMENTÉE)

ALL-PURPOSE FLOUR

RYE FLOUR

THIN CRUST

TIGHT
CRUMB

WATER

CHEESE

FRESH YEAST

WHAT IT IS

A fermented dough (see variation on page 54) made with wheat and rye flours, topped with cheese, shaped into individual bâtards.

CHARACTERISTICS

– Weight: 7 ounces (200 g)
– Size: 6 inches (15 cm)
– Crumb: tight
– Crust: thin

COMPLETION TIME

– Preparation time: 30 minutes
– Fermentation time: 2½ hours (1 hour rising, 30 minutes resting, 1 hour proofing)
– Baking time: 20 to 25 minutes

EQUIPMENT

– Stand mixer fitted with the dough hook (optional)
– Bench scraper
– Lame

CHALLENGE

Baking: the bread must be fully baked yet remain soft.

SKILLS TO MASTER

– Kneading (pages 30 and 32)
– Preshaping a Round (page 38)
– Shaping a Bâtard (page 45)
– Scoring a Diagonal (page 51)

USEFUL TIP

At the end of the proofing time, the dough has sufficiently risen when gently pressing into it with your fingertip leaves no mark.

IT'S READY

When the bread is golden brown and sounds hollow when tapped.

SHELF LIFE

Two to three days.

MAKES 3 LOAVES

DOUGH

2 cups minus 2½ tablespoons (250 g)
    high-protein all-purpose flour (or
    use bread flour or T65 flour)
¼ cup (30 g) dark rye flour (or use T170 flour)
¾ cup plus 1½ tablespoons (200 g)
    water at 68 to 77°F (20 to 25°C)
⅜ packed teaspoon (3 g) fresh yeast
2⅛ ounces (60 g) Fermented Dough
    (see variation on page 54)
¾ teaspoon (5 g) salt

MIX-IN

4¼ ounces (120 g) Comté or Cantal cheese

SIFTING

1½ tablespoons (15 g) high-protein all-purpose
    flour (or use bread flour or T65 flour)

1 Knead (see page 32) together the wheat and rye flours, water, crumbled yeast, fermented dough, and salt in the bowl of a stand mixer fitted with the dough hook for 4 minutes on the lowest speed (speed 1), then for 6 minutes on medium speed. The dough should detach from the sides of the bowl. (For kneading by hand, see page 30.)

2 Cut the cheese into ⅓-inch (1 cm) cubes. Add them to the dough and knead until they are well incorporated.

3 Place the dough in a mixing bowl and let the dough rise for 1 hour, covered with a towel, in a warm place, 77 to 82°F (25 to 28°C).

4 Divide the dough into three pieces, 7 ounces (200 g) each, using the bench scraper and preshape them into rounds (see page 38). Cover and let rest on a floured work surface for 30 minutes.

5 Shape the rounds into bâtards (see page 45).

6 Place the loaves seam side down on a sheet of parchment paper. Cover them with a towel and let rise for 1 hour in a warm place, 77 to 82°F (25 to 28°C), for the proofing.

7 Preheat the oven to 475°F (250°C) with a baking sheet and bowl of water placed in the oven. Sift the 1½ tablespoons (15 g) flour over the dough and score the loaves in a diagonal (see page 51). Transfer the parchment onto the hot baking sheet. Spritz the bottom of the oven with water and bake for 20 to 25 minutes (leaving the bowl of water in the oven).

SMALL ITALIAN LOAVES

Understanding

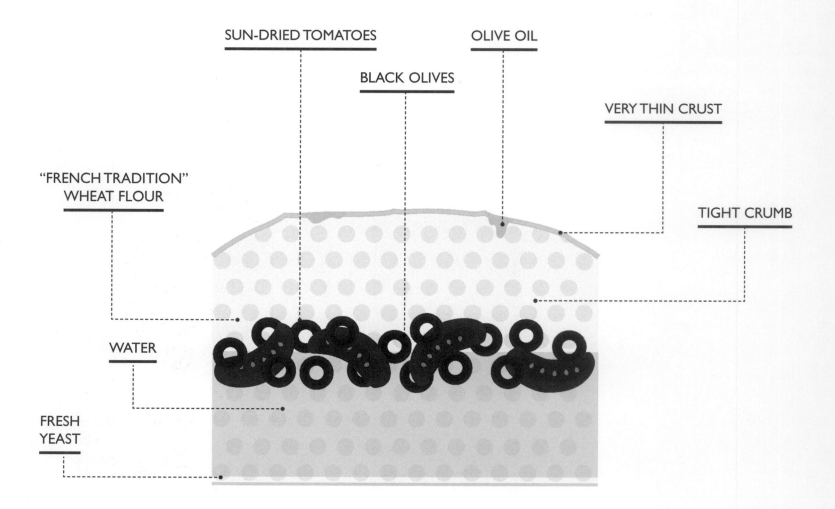

SUN-DRIED TOMATOES

BLACK OLIVES

OLIVE OIL

VERY THIN CRUST

"FRENCH TRADITION"
WHEAT FLOUR

TIGHT CRUMB

WATER

FRESH
YEAST

WHAT IT IS
A dough made with "French tradition" wheat flour, studded with olives, sun-dried tomatoes, and herbes de Provence, shaped into ficelles (long, thin loaves).

CHARACTERISTICS
–Weight: 3 ounces (85 g)
–Size: 8 inches (20 cm)
–Crumb: tight
–Crust: very thin, tender

COMPLETION TIME
–Preparation time: 25 minutes
–Fermentation time: 3½ hours
 (1½ hours rising, 30 minutes
 resting, 1½ hours proofing)
–Baking time: 10 minutes

EQUIPMENT
–Stand mixer fitted with the
 dough hook (optional)
–Bench scraper
–Lame
–Pastry brush

SKILLS TO MASTER
–Kneading (pages 30 and 32)
–Turning (page 37)
–Preshaping an Oblong (page 38)
–Shaping a Ficelle (page 44)

IT'S READY
When the crust just begins to brown.

SHELF LIFE
One day.

MAKES 6 LOAVES

"FRENCH TRADITION" STRAIGHT DOUGH

1¾ cups plus 1 tablespoon (245 g) T65 "French tradition" wheat flour (or use organic high-protein all-purpose flour or bread flour)

⅔ cup plus 1 teaspoon (160 g) water

½ packed teaspoon (4 g) fresh yeast

⅔ teaspoon (4 g) salt

FINISHING

⅓ cup (60 g) sliced black olives

⅓ cup (40 g) sun-dried tomatoes

Pinch of herbes de Provence

Olive oil

1 Drain the olives and sun-dried tomatoes well. Using the technique on page 57, make "French tradition" straight dough. Add the tomatoes, olives, and herbes de Provence and knead on low speed (speed 1) until the ingredients are fully incorporated.

2 Place the dough in a mixing bowl, cover the bowl with plastic wrap, and let rise for 30 minutes at room temperature.

3 Turn the dough (see page 37). Place the dough back in the mixing bowl, cover the bowl with plastic wrap, and let rise for an additional 1 hour at room temperature.

4 Divide the dough into six pieces, about 3 ounces (85 g) each, using the bench scraper. Preshape each piece into an oblong (see page 38).

5 Let the dough rest for 30 minutes on a floured work surface, covered with a towel.

6 Shape the dough into ficelles (see page 44). Place them seam side down onto a piece of parchment paper and let rest for 1½ hours, covered with a towel, in a warm place, 77 to 82°F (25 to 28°C), for the proofing.

7 Preheat the oven to 475°F (240°C) with a baking sheet and a bowl of water placed in the oven. Slide the sheet of parchment paper with the loaves onto the hot baking sheet. Spritz the bottom of the oven with water and bake for 10 minutes (keeping the bowl of water in the oven).

8 Using a pastry brush, brush the loaves with a little olive oil as soon as they come out of the oven.

CHEESE FICELLES
WITH SEEDS

Understanding

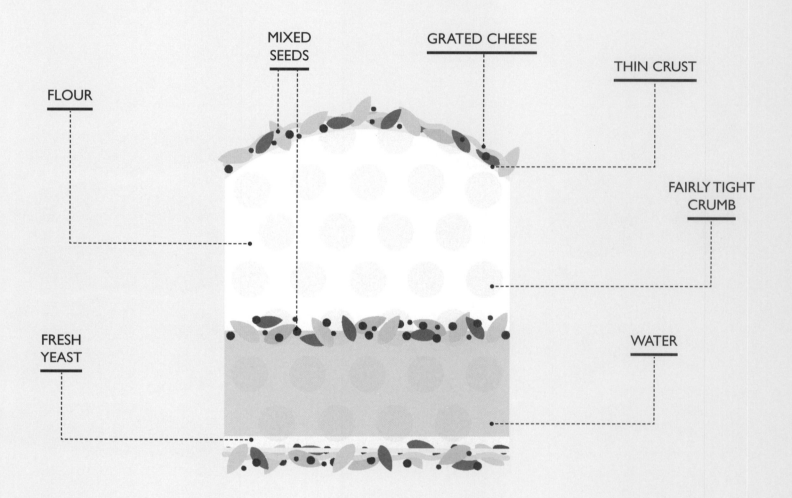

FLOUR

MIXED SEEDS

GRATED CHEESE

THIN CRUST

FAIRLY TIGHT CRUMB

FRESH YEAST

WATER

WHAT IT IS

A straight dough enriched with cream, shaped into ficelles (long, thin loaves), then rolled in a mixture of grated cheese, fleur de sel sea salt, and seeds before baking.

CHARACTERISTICS

–Weight: 4¼ ounces (120 g)
–Size: 9¾ inches (25 cm)
–Crumb: fairly tight, uniform
–Crust: thin

COMPLETION TIME

–Preparation time: 40 minutes over 2 days (20 minutes per day)
–Fermentation time: 1 hour and 20 minutes (20 minutes rising, 1 hour proofing)
–Baking time: 15 to 20 minutes

EQUIPMENT

–Stand mixer fitted with the dough hook (optional)
–Bench scraper
–Pastry brush

CHALLENGE

Coating the loaves with the seeds and cheese.

SKILLS TO MASTER

–Kneading (pages 30 and 32)
–Shaping a Baguette (page 43)

IT'S READY

When the loaves are pale golden.

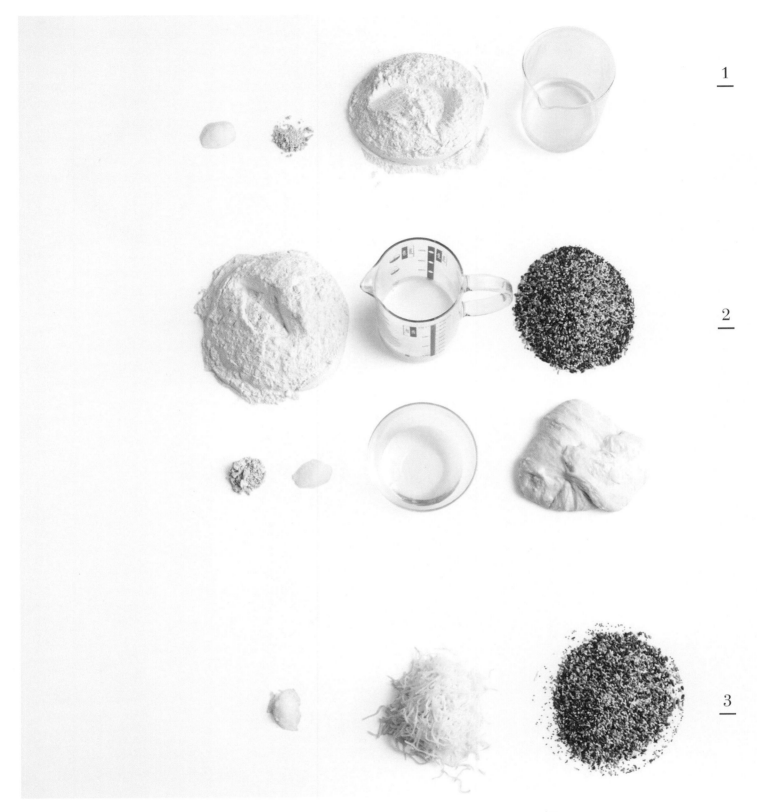

1

2

3

MAKES 4 LOAVES

1 FERMENTED DOUGH (PÂTE FERMENTÉE)

1 cup minus 1 tablespoon (125 g) high-protein all-purpose flour (or use bread flour or T65 flour)

¼ cup plus 1 teaspoon (65 g) water

⅓ teaspoon (2 g) salt

⅛ packed teaspoon (1 g) fresh yeast

2 FICELLE DOUGH

1½ cups minus 1½ tablespoons (190 g) high-protein all-purpose flour (or use bread flour or T65 flour)

2½ tablespoons (40 g) water

6⅔ ounces (190 g) Fermented Dough (see variation on page 54)

⅜ packed teaspoon (3 g) fresh yeast

⅓ cup plus 1½ tablespoons (100 g) cream

⅔ teaspoon (4 g) salt

½ cup plus 1 tablespoon (70 g) mixed seeds (flax, poppy, sesame, etc.)

3 FINISHING

½ cup (60 g) mixed seeds (flax, poppy, sesame, etc.)

½ cup (50 g) shredded cheese

½ teaspoon (2 g) fleur de sel sea salt

Making the cheese ficelles with seeds

THE DAY BEFORE

1 Make the fermented dough (see variation on page 54 and technique on page 55, but use ingredient amounts on page 151).

THE SAME DAY

2 Knead (see page 32) together the flour, water, fermented dough, crumbled yeast, cream, and salt in the bowl of a stand mixer fitted with the dough hook for 4 minutes on the lowest speed (speed 1), then for 6 minutes on medium speed. (For kneading by hand, see page 30.)

3 Add the seeds and continue kneading on speed 1 until fully incorporated.

4 Place the dough in a mixing bowl. Cover the bowl with a towel and let rise for 20 minutes.

5 Divide the dough into four pieces, 5 ounces (145 g) each, using the bench scraper. Shape each piece into a ficelle (see page 44).

6 Moisten the loaves with a little water on the seam side using the pastry brush. Place them in a dish containing the seeds, shredded cheese, and salt and coat them with this mixture.

7 Place the loaves seam side up on a baking sheet lined with parchment paper and let rest for 1 hour, covered with a towel, in a warm place, 77 to 82°F (25 to 28°C), for the proofing.

8 Preheat the oven to 475°F (240°C) with a baking sheet and a bowl of water placed in the oven. Slide the loaves onto the hot baking sheet with the parchment paper. Spritz the bottom of the oven with water and bake for 15 to 20 minutes (leaving the bowl of water in the oven).

"SURPRISE" LOAF

Understanding

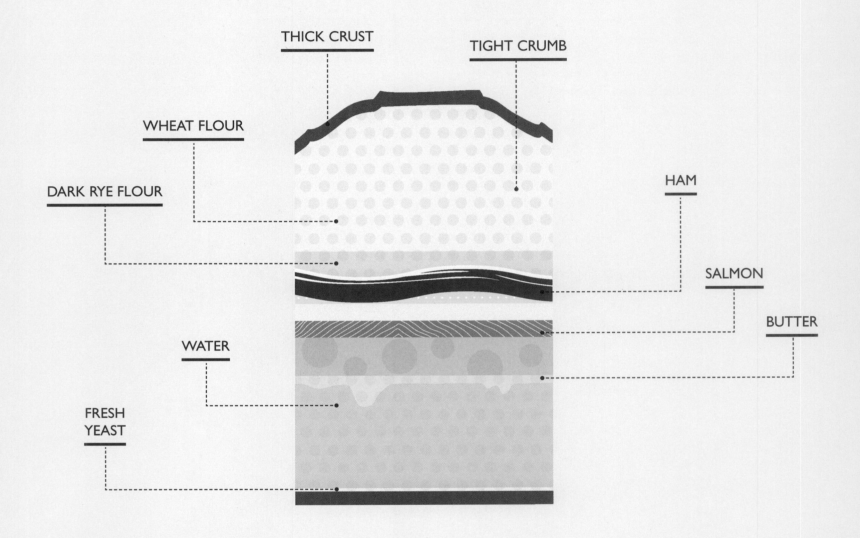

THICK CRUST

TIGHT CRUMB

WHEAT FLOUR

DARK RYE FLOUR

HAM

SALMON

BUTTER

WATER

FRESH
YEAST

WHAT IT IS

A bread dough made with wheat and rye flours, baked in a deep pastry ring. After baking, the loaf is filled and cut into sandwiches.

CHARACTERISTICS

–Size: 14 inches (35 cm) high
–Weight: 4½ pounds (2 kg)
–Crumb: tight
–Crust: thick

COMPLETION TIME

–Preparation time: 40 minutes
–Fermentation time: 2 hours (30 minutes rising, 1½ hours proofing)
–Baking time: 1 hour and 20 minutes

EQUIPMENT

–Stand mixer fitted with the dough hook (optional)
–Lame
–Serrated knife
–Pastry ring 6 inches (16 cm) in diameter and 4¾ inches (12 cm) deep
–Pastry brush

CHALLENGE

Removing the crumb from the center of the loaf without damaging it.

SKILLS TO MASTER

–Kneading (pages 30 and 32)
–Turning (page 37)
–Shaping a Boule (page 42)
–Scoring a Crisscross (page 51)

USEFUL TIP

Cover the loaf with a piece of greased parchment paper after 30 minutes of baking to prevent the crust from browning too much.

IT'S READY

When the top of the loaf is golden brown and the slashes have widened.

SHELF LIFE

Four to five days, when not exposed to air.

MAKES 1 "SURPRISE" LOAF; 60 TO 70 SANDWICHES

1 DOUGH

5⅓ cups (725 g) high-protein all-purpose
    flour (or use bread flour or T65 flour)
⅔ cup (80 g) dark rye flour (or use T170 flour)
2¼ cups (525 g) cold water
¼ packed teaspoon (2 g) fresh yeast
2½ teaspoons (15 g) salt

2 SIFTING

2½ tablespoons (20 g) high-protein all-purpose
    flour (or use bread flour or T65 flour)

3 PASTRY RING

2 tablespoons plus 2 teaspoons (40 g)
    Beurre en Pommade (page 284),
    made with unsalted butter

4 FILLING

1 tablespoon plus 2 teaspoons (25 g)
    Beurre en Pommade (page 284),
    made with unsalted butter
6 slices Bayonne ham or other similar cured ham
1 tablespoon plus 2 teaspoons (25 g)
    Beurre en Pommade (page 284),
    made with salted butter
5¼ ounces (150 g) Comté cheese
3½ ounces (100 g) fromage frais or
    light cream cheese spread
4 slices smoked salmon

1   Knead (see page 32) together the wheat and rye flours, water, crumbled yeast, and salt in the bowl of a stand mixer fitted with the dough hook for 4 minutes on the lowest speed (speed 1), then for 6 minutes on medium speed. The dough should detach from the sides of the bowl. (For kneading by hand, see page 30.)

2   Let the dough rise on a floured work surface, covered with a towel, for 30 minutes at room temperature. Turn the dough (see page 37) after 15 minutes by folding it in half.

3   Shape the dough into a boule (see page 42), and place it in the pastry ring previously greased with the beurre en pommade using the pastry brush.

4   Allow the dough to rest, covered with a towel, for 1½ hours in a warm place, 77 to 82°F (25 to 28°C), for the proofing; the dough should rise slightly above the rim of the ring.

5   Preheat the oven to 475°F (240°C) with a bowl of water placed in the oven. Sift the 2½ tablespoons (20 g) flour over the dough, then score a crisscross (see page 51) into the top.

6   Spritz the bottom of the oven with water, and bake for 40 minutes (keeping the bowl of water in the oven), then reduce the oven to temperature to 350°F (180°C) and bake for an additional 40 minutes. Slightly prop open the oven door 5 to 10 minutes before the end of the baking time. Unmold the bread onto a rack and let cool.

7   Cut off the top of the bread using a serrated knife. Slice off a ⅓-inch (1 cm) section from the bottom of the bread. Push the point of a sharp knife vertically down into the bread between the crust and the crumb and cut all around the edge in an up and down motion to separate the crust completely from the crumb. Carefully detach the crustless center by placing light pressure on it and lifting it out. Set the crust and the bread top aside (these will be replaced during the last step).

8   Lay the crumb cylinder on its side and slice about twenty ¼-inch (5 mm) portions.

9   Spread unsalted butter on 4 slices and top with ham. Spread salted butter over 3 more slices and top with Comté. Spread fromage frais over 3 slices and top with smoked salmon.

10   Top each slice with another slice of bread to form a large sandwich, then cut each into 6 small wedges.

11   Place the crust circle on a serving platter for presentation. Place the sandwiches back inside the crust, alternating the flavors, to reform the loaf. Replace the top.

CIABATTA

Understanding

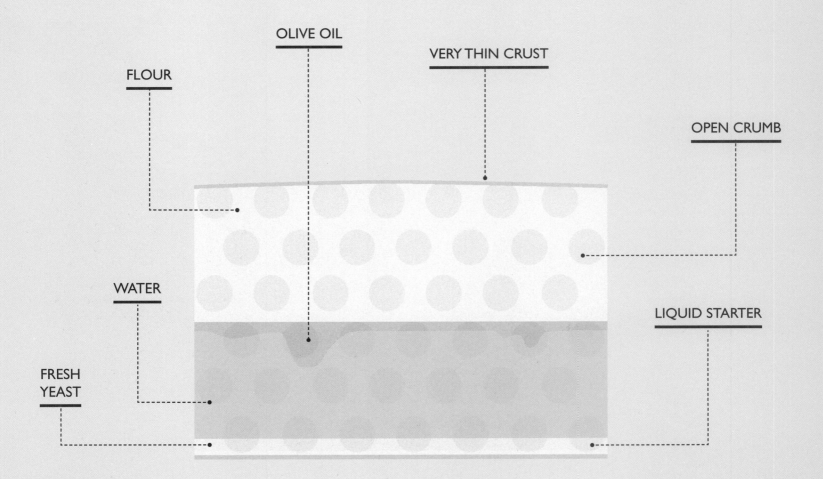

FLOUR

OLIVE OIL

VERY THIN CRUST

OPEN CRUMB

WATER

LIQUID STARTER

FRESH YEAST

WHAT IT IS

A dough made from flour, liquid starter, and olive oil, and shaped into a rectangle.

CHARACTERISTICS

–Weight: 7 ounces (200 g)
–Size: 6 inches (15 cm)
–Crumb: open
–Crust: very thin, tender
–Flavor: of olive oil, and very slightly tart

COMPLETION TIME

–Preparation time: 30 minutes
–Fermentation time: 3 hours (1 hour rising, 2 hours proofing)
–Baking time: 15 minutes

EQUIPMENT

Stand mixer fitted with the dough hook (optional)

SKILLS TO MASTER

–Kneading (pages 30 and 32)
–Turning (page 37)
–Final Shaping (page 40)

SHELF LIFE

Two days, wrapped airtight.

IT'S READY

When the loaf begins to color slightly.

MAKES 2 LOAVES

DOUGH

1½ cups (205 g) high-protein all-purpose
    flour (or use bread flour or T65 flour)
½ cup plus 2 tablespoons (145 g) water
1 ounce (25 g) Liquid Starter (page 20)
⅛ packed teaspoon (1 g) fresh yeast
⅔ teaspoon (4 g) salt
2 tablespoons (20 g) olive oil

OR DOUGH WITHOUT A STARTER

1¾ cups (220 g) all-purpose (or T55) flour
⅔ cup (155 g) water, at room temperature
½ packed teaspoon (4 g) fresh yeast
⅔ teaspoon (4 g) salt
2 tablespoons (18 g) olive oil

SIFTING

1 tablespoon (10 g) flour

1   Place the flour, water, starter (if using the dough
with the starter), crumbled yeast, and salt in the
bowl of a stand mixer fitted with the dough hook.

2   Knead (see page 32) for 4 minutes on the lowest
speed (speed 1), then for 6 minutes on medium
speed. (For kneading by hand, see page 30.)

3   Drizzle in the olive oil, and continue kneading
slowly until the oil is fully incorporated.

4   Place the dough in a mixing bowl. Cover the
bowl with a towel, and let rise for 30 minutes
in a warm place, 77 to 82°F (25 to 28°C).

5   Turn the dough (see page 37). Let rise for
an additional 30 minutes, covered with a towel,
in a warm place, 77 to 82°F (25 to 28°C).

6   Divide the dough into two pieces, 7 ounces
(200 g) each. Shape the pieces into rectangles.

7   Place the loaves seam side down onto
a sheet of parchment paper and let rise for
2 hours, covered with a towel, in a warm place,
77 to 82°F (25 to 28°C), for the proofing.

8   Preheat the oven to 500°F (260°C) with a
baking sheet and a bowl of water placed in the
oven. Lightly sift the 1 tablespoon (10 g) flour
over the loaves. Slide the loaves onto the hot
baking sheet with the parchment paper. Spritz
the bottom of the oven with water, reduce the
temperature to 475°F (240°C), and bake for
15 minutes (keeping the bowl of water in the oven).

FOCACCIA

Understanding

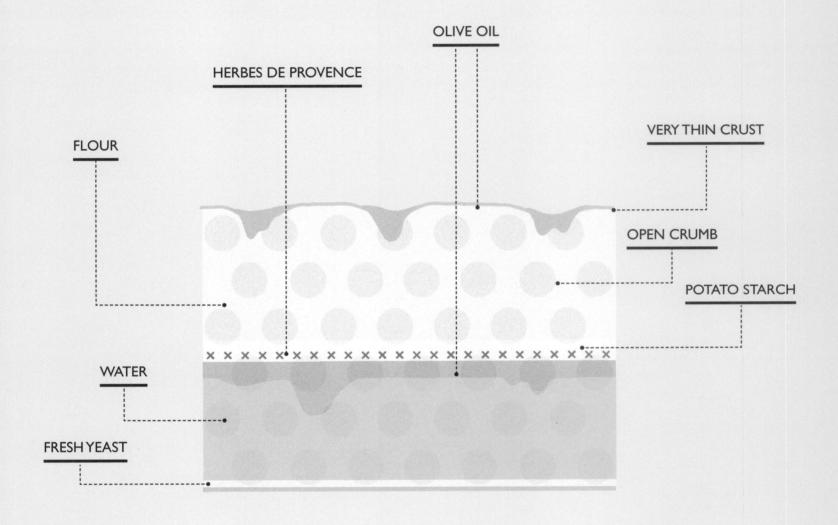

OLIVE OIL

HERBES DE PROVENCE

VERY THIN CRUST

FLOUR

OPEN CRUMB

POTATO STARCH

WATER

FRESH YEAST

WHAT IT IS
A bread dough made with olive oil and shaped into a flat rectangle.

CHARACTERISTICS
–Weight: 7 ounces (200 g)
–Size: approximately 8 × 6 inches (20 × 15 cm)
–Crumb: open
–Crust: very thin, tender

COMPLETION TIME
–Preparation time: 20 minutes
–Fermentation time: 2½ hours
  (1½ hours rising, 1 hour proofing)
–Baking time: 10 minutes

EQUIPMENT
–Stand mixer fitted with the
  dough hook (optional)
–Bench scraper
–Pastry brush
–Rolling pin

VARIATION
Focaccia used as the crust for a pizza.

CHALLENGE
Not piercing through the dough when making the dimples.

SKILLS TO MASTER
–Kneading (pages 30 and 32)
–Turning (page 37)
–Preshaping a Round (page 38)

IT'S READY
When the loaves are slightly golden and still very soft.

SHELF LIFE
Twenty-four hours in the refrigerator, wrapped in plastic wrap.

Learning

1

2

WHAT IS THE DIFFERENCE BETWEEN FOCACCIA AND CIABATTA?

Focaccia does not contain a starter; its aromatic notes are therefore less acidic. Additionally, the fermentation of focaccia is shorter, which gives it a less airy texture.

MAKES 2 FOCACCIAS

1 DOUGH

1½ cups minus 1½ tablespoons (190 g) high-protein all-purpose flour (or use bread flour or T65 flour)
½ cup plus 1½ tablespoons (140 g) water
¾ packed teaspoon (6 g) fresh yeast
¼ cup (35 g) potato starch
1 tablespoon (2 g) herbes de Provence
⅔ teaspoon (4 g) salt
2½ tablespoons (25 g) olive oil

2 FINISHING

1½ teaspoons (5 g) olive oil

Making the focaccia

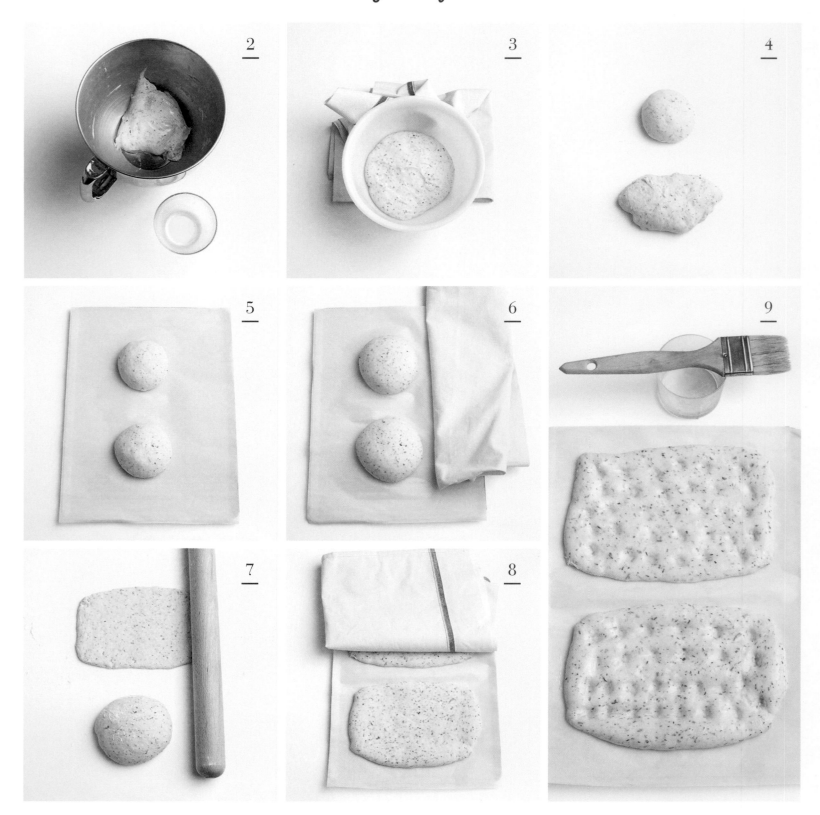

1 Knead (see page 32) together the flour, water, crumbled yeast, potato starch, herbes de Provence, and salt in the bowl of a stand mixer fitted with the dough hook for 4 minutes on the lowest speed (speed 1), then for 6 minutes on medium speed. The dough should detach from the sides of the bowl. (For kneading by hand, see page 30.)

2 Drizzle in the olive oil and continue to knead on speed 1 until the oil is fully incorporated.

3 Place the dough in a mixing bowl. Cover the bowl with a towel and let rise for 30 minutes in a warm place, 77 to 82°F (25 to 28°C).

4 Turn the dough (see page 37). Let rise again for 30 minutes in the mixing bowl, covered with a towel, in a warm place, 77 to 82°F (25 to 28°C).

5 Divide the dough into two pieces, 7 ounces (200 g) each, using the bench scraper. Preshape the pieces into rounds (see page 38) by squeezing tightly.

6 Place the loaves onto a sheet of parchment paper and let rest for 30 minutes, covered with a towel, in a warm place, 77 to 82°F (25 to 28°C).

7 Roll out (see page 283) each loaf with a rolling pin into an 8 × 6-inch (20 × 15 cm) rectangle about ¾ inch (2 cm) thick.

8 Return loaves to parchment paper. Cover with a towel and let rise for about 1 hour in a warm place, 77 to 82°F (25 to 28°C), for the proofing.

9 Preheat the oven to 500°F (260°C) with a baking sheet and a bowl of water placed in the oven. Make about thirty dimples in the dough using your fingertips (do not pierce through the dough), and fill the dimples with olive oil using the pastry brush.

10 Transfer the parchment with the loaves onto the hot baking sheet. Spritz the bottom of the oven with water and bake for 10 minutes (leaving the bowl of water in the oven).

FOUGASSE

Understanding

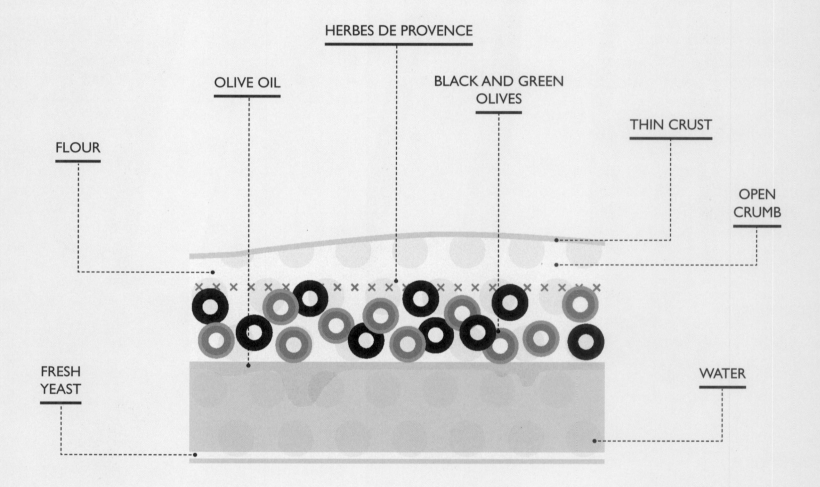

HERBES DE PROVENCE

OLIVE OIL

BLACK AND GREEN
OLIVES

THIN CRUST

FLOUR

OPEN
CRUMB

FRESH
YEAST

WATER

WHAT IT IS

A bread dough made with fresh yeast
and olive oil, flavored with herbes de
Provence and studded with olives. It
is shaped into a flat rectangle, with
cuts all the way through the loaf.

CHARACTERISTICS

–Weight: 10½ ounces (300 g)
–Size: 6 × 12 inches (15 × 30 cm)
–Crumb: open
–Crust: thin

COMPLETION TIME

–Preparation time: 45 minutes
–Fermentation time: 45 minutes (rising)
–Baking time: 12 minutes

EQUIPMENT

–Stand mixer fitted with the
  dough hook (optional)
–Rolling pin
–Lame

CHALLENGE

Making the cuts in the dough.

SKILLS TO MASTER

–Kneading (pages 30 and 32)
–Scoring (page 50)

WHAT IS THE PURPOSE OF
THE CUTS?

*They increase the surface area of the
crust and therefore the crispness of the
bread. In this way, the distribution of
crumb and crust is more balanced.*

Learning

1

2

MAKES 1 FOUGASSE

1 DOUGH

1 cup (140 g) high-protein all-purpose flour
  (or use bread flour or T65 flour)
⅓ cup plus 1 tablespoon (95 g) water
⅜ packed teaspoon (3 g) fresh yeast
2 tablespoons (5 g) herbes de Provence
½ teaspoon (3 g) salt
1 tablespoon (10 g) olive oil

2 MIX-IN

⅓ cup (60 g) sliced olives (black and green)

Making the fougasse

2A

2B

3

4

5

6

1   Knead (see page 32) together the flour, water, crumbled yeast, herbes de Provence, and salt in the bowl of a stand mixer fitted with the dough hook for 4 minutes on the lowest speed (speed 1), then for 6 minutes on medium speed. The dough should detach from the sides of the bowl. (For kneading by hand, see page 30.)

2   Drizzle in the olive oil and continue kneading slowly until the oil is fully incorporated. Add the olives and knead again lightly to incorporate them into the dough.

3   Place the dough in a mixing bowl, cover the bowl with plastic wrap, and let rise for 45 minutes in a warm place, 77 to 82°F (25 to 28°C).

4   Shape the dough into a large rectangle and place it on a sheet of parchment paper.

5   Position the dough with a short side facing you and roll it out (see page 283) to about ¾ inch (2 cm) thick. Make four cuts using the bench scraper and spread the holes open wide using your fingers.

6   Preheat the oven to 500°F (260°C) with a baking sheet placed inside the oven. Slide the loaf onto the hot baking sheet with the parchment paper, and bake for 12 minutes.

CRUNCHY
BREADSTICKS
(GRISSINI)

Understanding

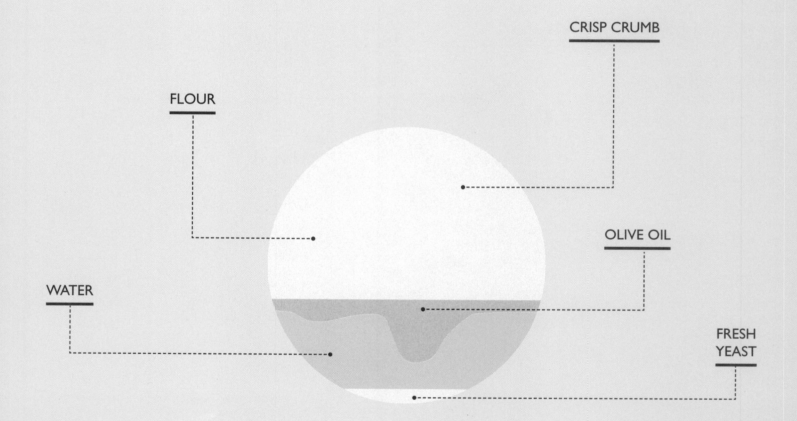

CRISP CRUMB

FLOUR

OLIVE OIL

WATER

FRESH YEAST

WHAT IT IS

A bread dough shaped into long, thin sticks, brushed with olive oil. Originally from Turin, they can be plain, flavored with herbs or spices, or covered with seeds.

CHARACTERISTICS

−Weight: ¾ ounce (20 g)
−Size: about 19½ inches (50 cm) long
−Crumb: crunchy
−Crust: no crust

COMPLETION TIME

−Preparation time: 30 minutes
−Fermentation time: 30 minutes (rising)
−Baking time: 10 to 15 minutes

EQUIPMENT

−Stand mixer fitted with the dough hook (optional)
−Rolling pin
−Pastry brush

SKILL TO MASTER

Kneading (pages 30 and 32)

USEFUL TIP

Pinch the ends of the breadsticks closed using wet fingers so that they do not spread open while baking.

IT'S READY

When the breadsticks are golden brown and dry.

SHELF LIFE

Four to five days.

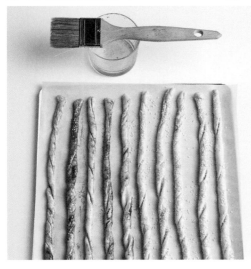

MAKES 15 TO 20 BREADSTICKS

DOUGH

1⅔ cups (225 g) high-protein all-purpose
     flour (or use bread flour or T65 flour)
⅞ packed teaspoon (7 g) fresh yeast
½ cup plus 1⅓ tablespoons (135 g) water
     at 68 to 77°F (20 to 25°C)
¾ teaspoon (5 g) salt

FINISHING

1½ ounces (40 g) each fleur de sel sea salt, chile
     powder, garlic powder, sesame seeds, black
     pepper, tomato sauce, and tandoori spices
2 tablespoons (20 g) olive oil

1   Place the flour, crumbled yeast, water, and salt in
the bowl of a stand mixer fitted with the dough hook.

2   Knead (see page 32) together for 4 minutes on
the lowest speed (speed 1) until the dough is smooth,
then on medium speed for 6 minutes. The dough
should detach from the sides of the bowl. (For
kneading by hand, see page 30.)

3   Place the dough in a mixing bowl. Press plastic
wrap onto its surface (see page 285) and let rise for
30 minutes at room temperature.

4   Preheat the oven to 525°F (270°C) or as high as
your oven will go. Roll out (see page 283) the dough to
about ⅓ inch (1 cm) thick using a rolling pin. Cut strips
⅓ inch (1 cm) wide down the length of the dough.

5   Sprinkle the strips with any of the selected
seasonings. Holding the dough strips at each
end, twist them while stretching them so that
they are between 19½ and 24 inches (50 and
60 cm) long. Place the breadsticks onto a
baking sheet lined with parchment paper.

6   Lightly brush the breadsticks with olive oil
using the pastry brush. Bake for 10 to 15 minutes.

PULLMAN LOAF
SANDWICH BREAD (PAIN DE MIE)

Understanding

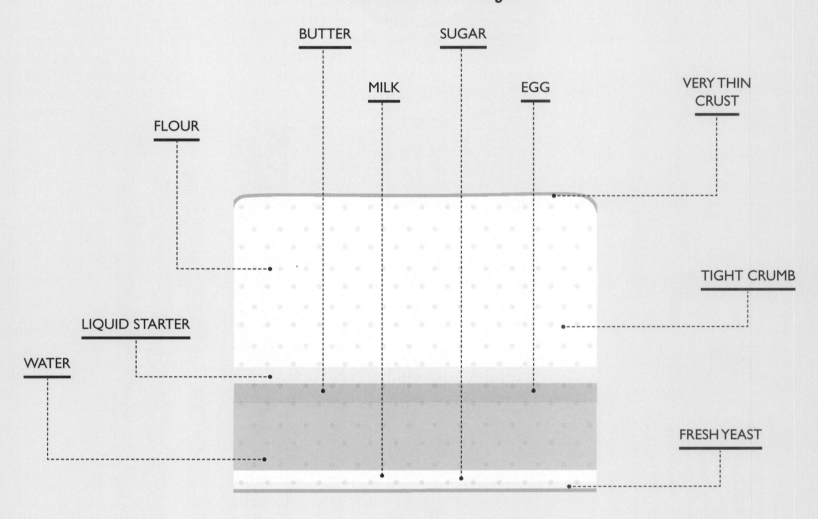

BUTTER

SUGAR

MILK

EGG

VERY THIN CRUST

FLOUR

LIQUID STARTER

TIGHT CRUMB

WATER

FRESH YEAST

WHAT IT IS
A slightly sweet white bread dough, baked in a rectangular mold.

CHARACTERISTICS
–Weight: 1 pound (450 g)
–Size: 18 inches (45 cm)
–Crumb: tight, soft
–Crust: very thin, tender

COMPLETION TIME
–Preparation time: 25 minutes
–Fermentation time: 2½ to 3 hours
  (1½ hours rising, 1 to 1½ hours proofing)
–Baking time: 25 minutes

EQUIPMENT
–Stand mixer with the dough hook (optional)
–Pullman loaf pan with a lid 7 inches
  (18 cm) long and 3 inches (8 cm) deep
–Rolling pin
–Pastry brush

CHALLENGES
– Preparing for baking: the loaf should neither be too small in the pan nor have risen too much.
– Baking: the loaf must remain soft and moist.

SKILLS TO MASTER
–Kneading (pages 30 and 32)
–Turning (page 37)

–Preshaping a Round (page 38)
–Final Shaping (page 40)

USEFUL TIP
In the absence of a bread mold with a lid, place a baking sheet on the mold with a small weight on top.

IT'S READY
When the bread has a beautifully colored crust.

SHELF LIFE
Three days in the refrigerator (to prevent mold).

MAKES I LOAF

1¼ cups (170 g) high-protein all-purpose
    flour (or use bread flour or T65 flour)
⅓ cup plus ¾ teaspoon (80 g) cold water
¾ ounce (20 g) Liquid Starter (page 20)
⅜ packed teaspoon (3 g) fresh yeast
1 tablespoon plus ½ teaspoon (15 g) sugar
2 teaspoons (10 g) whole milk
½ teaspoon (3 g) salt
2 tablespoons (10 g) whole egg (lightly
    blended and then measured)
1 tablespoon plus 2 teaspoons (25 g)
    unsalted butter, softened
1 tablespoon (15 g) Beurre en Pommade
    (page 284), for greasing the pan

1 Knead (see page 32) together the flour, water, starter, crumbled yeast, sugar, milk, salt, and egg in the bowl of a stand mixer fitted with the dough hook for 6 minutes on the lowest speed (speed 1), then for 5 minutes on medium-low speed (speed 2). The dough should detach from the sides of the bowl. (For kneading by hand, see page 30.) Add the unsalted butter and knead on speed 1 until the butter is fully incorporated into the dough.

2 Cover the dough with a towel and let rise for 1½ hours in a warm place, 77 to 82°F (25 to 28°C). After 45 minutes, turn the dough (see page 37).

3 Preshape the dough into a round (see page 38), then shape it into an elongated form (see page 41) the length of the pan.

4 Grease the pan using the beurre en pommade. Place the dough seam side down into the pan.

5 Close the lid and let rest for 1 to 1½ hours in a warm place, 77 to 82°F (25 to 28°C), for the proofing. At the end of the proofing time, the dough should have risen to about ¼ inch (5 mm) from the rim of the pan.

6 Preheat the oven to 400°F (200°C). Bake for 25 minutes, with the lid closed.

BAGEL

Understanding

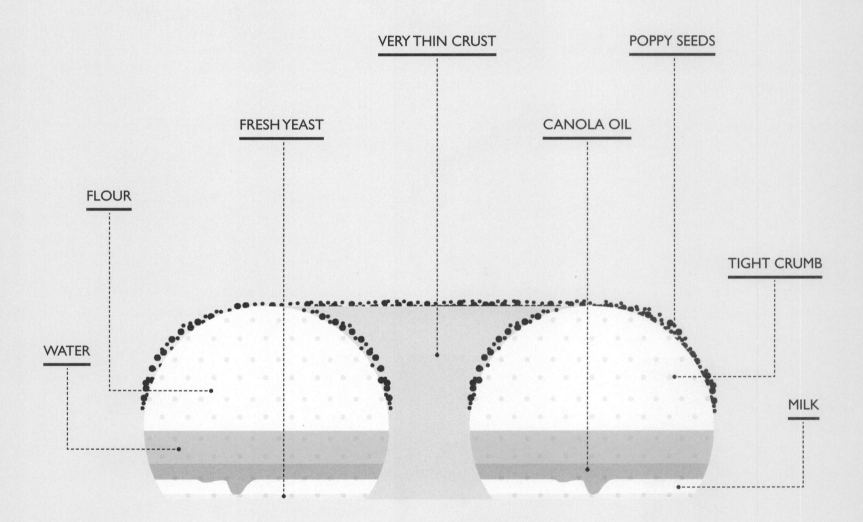

FLOUR

WATER

FRESH YEAST

VERY THIN CRUST

CANOLA OIL

POPPY SEEDS

TIGHT CRUMB

MILK

WHAT IT IS

A slightly sweet bread dough made with milk, shaped into a small ring, poached, then baked.

CHARACTERISTICS

– Weight: 5¼ ounces (150 g)
– Size: 6 inches (15 cm) in diameter
– Crumb: tight, soft
– Crust: very thin, tender

COMPLETION TIME

– Preparation time: 1 hour
– Fermentation time: 1½ to 2 hours
– Baking time: 12 to 13 minutes

EQUIPMENT

– Stand mixer fitted with the dough hook (optional)
– Bench scraper

CHALLENGES

– Final shaping.
– Poaching.

SKILLS TO MASTER

– Kneading (pages 30 and 32)
– Preshaping a Round (page 38)
– Shaping a Couronne (page 46)

IT'S READY

When the bagel is lightly browned.

SHELF LIFE

Two days.

WHY IS THE BAGEL POACHED BEFORE BAKING IT?

To ensure the crust is smooth after baking: boiling water allows the starches to gelatinize on the surface. To achieve the very soft texture: during poaching, water vapor forms in the dough and inflates it.

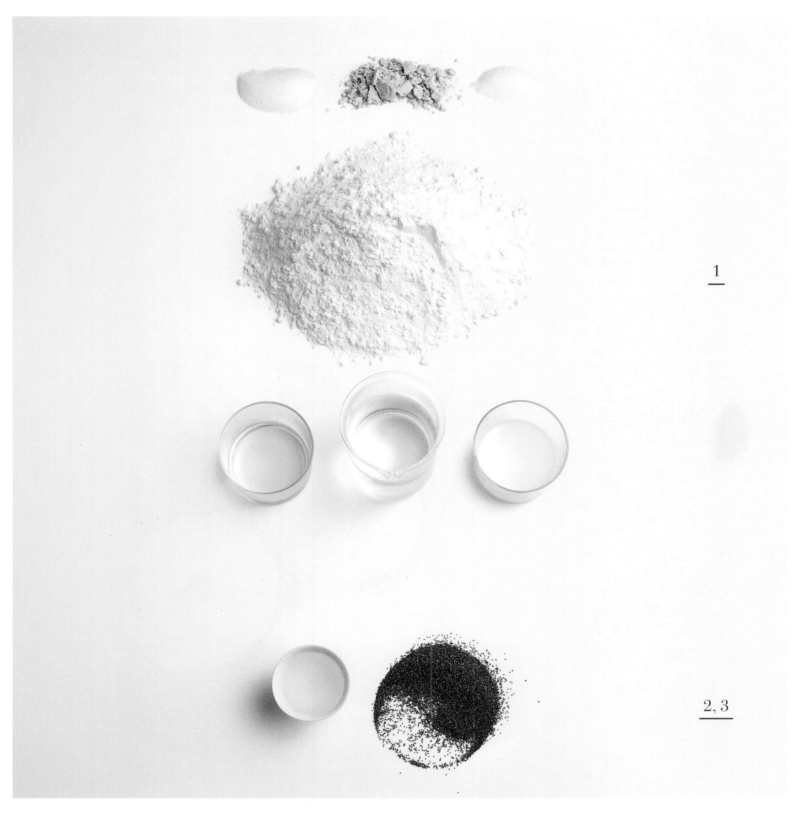

1

2, 3

MAKES 8 BAGELS

1 DOUGH

5¾ cups plus 1 tablespoon (700 g)
      pastry flour (or use T45 flour)
1¼ cups plus 1 teaspoon (300 g) water
⅝ packed teaspoon (5 g) fresh yeast
3 tablespoons plus 1 teaspoon (50 g) whole milk
1 tablespoon plus ½ teaspoon (15 g) sugar
2½ teaspoons (15 g) salt
¼ cup (50 g) canola oil

2 BOILING

1 tablespoon (15 g) white vinegar

3 FINISHING

3 tablespoons (30 g) poppy seeds

Making bagels

1 Knead (see page 32) together the flour, water, crumbled yeast, milk, sugar, and salt in the bowl of a stand mixer fitted with the dough hook on the lowest speed (speed 1) until the mixture is smooth, then for 6 minutes at the highest speed. (For kneading by hand, see page 30.)

2 Add the oil and knead for a few more minutes on speed 1 until fully incorporated.

3 Let rest for 15 minutes, covered with a towel, at room temperature.

4 Cut the dough into eight pieces, 5¼ ounces (150 g) each, using the bench scraper. Preshape the doughs into rounds (see page 38), and let rest for 30 minutes, covered with a towel.

5 Pierce the rounds all the way through the center using your thumb, then dip your fingers lightly into flour.

6 Shape each piece of dough into a couronne (see page 46) measuring 6 inches (15 cm) in diameter from outer edge to outer edge.

7 Place the rings onto a sheet of parchment paper, four on a sheet, cover with a towel, and let rise in a warm place, 77 to 82°F (25 to 28°C), until they have almost doubled in size (1 to 1½ hours).

8 Preheat the oven to 475°F (240°C). Bring a large saucepan of water with the white vinegar to a boil. Boil the bagels (two at a time) for 30 seconds on each side. Remove them with a skimmer and place them on a rack.

9 Dredge one side of the bagels in the poppy seeds to coat them, then place the bagels on a baking sheet lined with parchment paper.

10 Bake for 12 to 13 minutes.

SESAME SEED BUN

Understanding

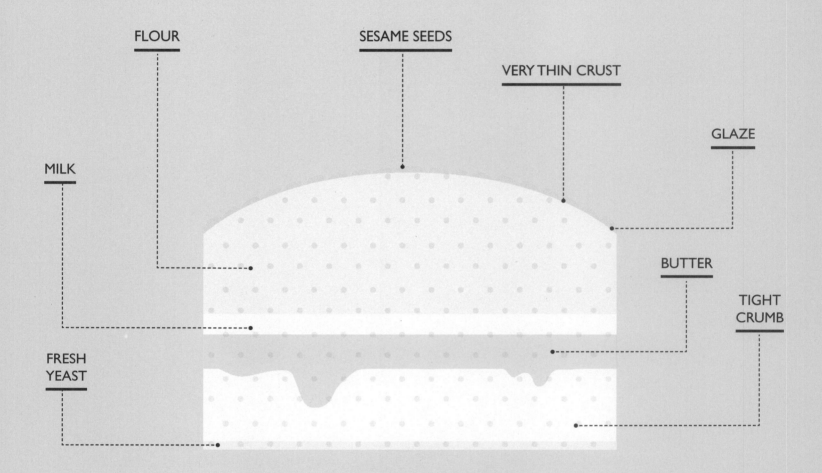

FLOUR

SESAME SEEDS

VERY THIN CRUST

GLAZE

MILK

BUTTER

TIGHT CRUMB

FRESH YEAST

WHAT IT IS

A Vienna dough shaped into boules and covered with sesame seeds.

CHARACTERISTICS

–Weight: 3 ounces (80 g)
–Size: 4 inches (10 cm) in diameter
–Crumb: tight
–Crust: very thin, tender

COMPLETION TIME

–Preparation time: 3 hours
–Fermentation time: 6 hours
–Baking time: 10 to 15 minutes

EQUIPMENT

–Stand mixer fitted with the
 dough hook (optional)
–Bench scraper
–Sieve
–Pastry brush

CHALLENGE

The final shaping: if the rounds are too flat, they will lose their gas and the buns will be flat after baking.

SKILLS TO MASTER

–Kneading (pages 30 and 32)
–Shaping a Boule (page 42)
–Glazing (page 48)

IT'S READY

When the buns are golden brown.

SHELF LIFE

Two days maximum, at room temperature. A few weeks in the freezer.

1

2

3

HOW DO YOU EXPLAIN THE SOFTNESS OF THE BUN?

The bun is made using a Vienna dough, which is enriched with milk and butter, lending softness to the bun. However, it contains less butter than a pain au lait or brioche, and no egg—two ingredients that promote incorporation of air into a dough and therefore soft textures.

MAKES 4 BUNS

1 VIENNA DOUGH

1¾ cups (240 g) high-protein all-purpose
    flour (or use bread flour or T65 flour)
½ cup plus 1½ tablespoons (145 g) whole milk
½ packed teaspoon (4 g) fresh yeast
1½ tablespoons (20 g) sugar
⅔ teaspoon (4 g) salt
2 tablespoons plus 1 teaspoon (35 g) unsalted
    butter, at room temperature

2 GLAZE

1 large (50 g) egg
½ teaspoon (3 g) whole milk
Pinch of salt

3 FINISHING

2 tablespoons (20 g) white sesame seeds (or
    black sesame seeds or poppy seeds)

Making sesame seed buns

1   Knead (see page 32) together the flour, milk, crumbled yeast, sugar, and salt in the bowl of a stand mixer fitted with the dough hook for 4 minutes on the lowest speed (speed 1), then for 6 minutes on medium speed. The dough should detach from the sides of the bowl. (For kneading by hand, see page 30.)

2   Add the butter and knead on speed 1 until fully incorporated.

3   Place the dough in a mixing bowl. Cover the bowl with plastic wrap and let rest for 4 hours in the refrigerator.

4   Divide the dough into four pieces, 3½ ounces (100 g) each, using the bench scraper. Preshape the pieces into rounds (see page 38). Place the rounds seam side down onto a baking sheet lined with parchment paper and let rest for an additional 30 minutes in the refrigerator.

5   Gently flatten the rounds by pressing them with the palm of your hand.

6   Make the glaze (see page 49) and glaze the buns using the pastry brush. Sprinkle with the sesame seeds. Let rest for 1½ hours in a warm place, 77 to 82°F (25 to 28°C), protected from air, for the proofing.

7   Preheat the oven to 500°F (260°C) with a baking sheet and a bowl of water placed in the oven. Slide the buns onto the hot baking sheet with the parchment paper. Spritz the bottom of the oven with water and bake 10 to 15 minutes (leaving the bowl of water in the oven).

CROISSANT

Understanding

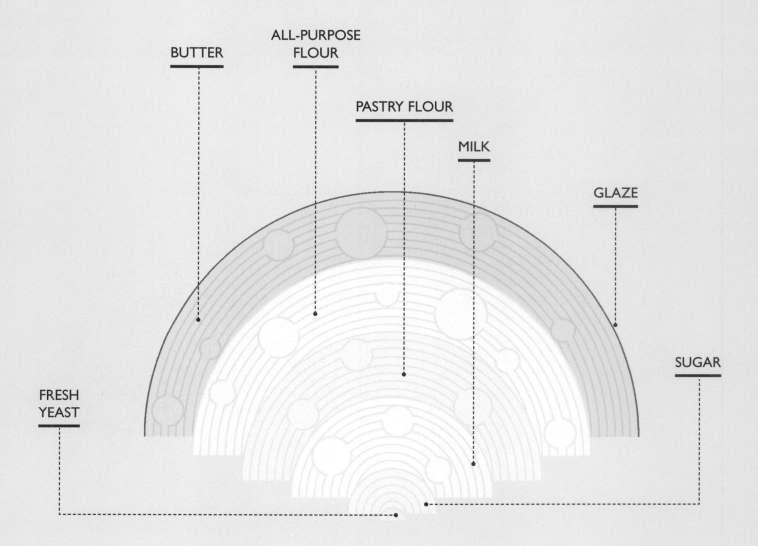

BUTTER

ALL-PURPOSE
FLOUR

PASTRY FLOUR

MILK

GLAZE

SUGAR

FRESH
YEAST

WHAT IT IS
A leavened puff pastry cut into triangles then rolled.

CHARACTERISTICS
–Weight: 3 to 3⅛ ounces (80 to 90 g)
–Size: 4¾ inches (12 cm)
–Layering: very open

COMPLETION TIME
–Preparation time: 1½ hours
–Resting time: 6 hours (3 hours refrigerated, 3 hours at 77°F/25°C)
–Baking time: 15 minutes

EQUIPMENT
–Stand mixer fitted with the dough hook (optional)
–Rolling pin
–Sieve
–Pastry brush

CHALLENGE
Rolling out the dough. Do not press down too firmly. There must be distinctive layers of butter and dough, otherwise the flaky layers will not develop.

SKILLS TO MASTER
–Kneading (pages 30 and 32)
–Shaping a Boule (page 42)
–Glazing (page 48)

IT'S READY
When the croissants are golden and flaky.

Learning

1

2

3

HOW DO YOU ACHIEVE LIGHT, FLAKY LAYERS?

From the balance of the alternating layers of dough and butter. When baking, the outer layers of dough separate and dry out (due to the butter, which waterproofs them) to form the flaky layers, while the inner layers remain moist and develop like thin layers of bread.

MAKES 6 CROISSANTS

1 DOUGH LAYER (DÉTREMPE)

¾ cup plus 1 tablespoon (110 g) high-protein all-purpose flour (or use bread flour or T65 flour)

1 cup minus 1 tablespoon (110 g) pastry flour (or use T45 flour)

2½ tablespoons (30 g) sugar

⅓ cup plus 1½ tablespoons (105 g) cold whole milk

⅞ packed teaspoon (7 g) fresh yeast

⅔ teaspoon (4 g) salt

2 ROLL-IN BUTTER

8½ tablespoons (120 g) unsalted butter, chilled

3 GLAZE

1 large (50 g) egg

½ teaspoon (3 g) whole milk

Pinch of salt

Making croissants

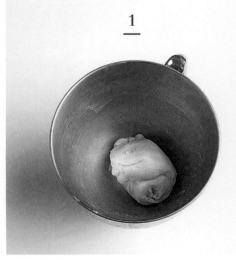

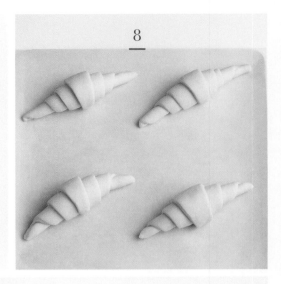

1 Make the dough layer: Knead (see page 32) together the wheat flours, sugar, milk, crumbled yeast, and salt for 5 minutes on the lowest speed (speed 1), then for 5 minutes on medium speed. (For kneading by hand, see page 30.) Shape the dough into a very tight boule (see page 42), cover the bowl with plastic wrap, and let rest for 1 hour in the refrigerator.

2 Tamp down the roll-in butter with a rolling pin to soften it. Roll it out to a uniform square measuring ⅓ inch (1 cm) thick and 3 inches (8 cm) on each side.

3 Roll out (see page 283) the dough to the same width as the butter block but twice the length (6 inches/16 cm).

4 Place the butter block in the center of the dough and fold both ends of the dough over the butter to create a seam in the center. Turn the dough a quarter of a turn so that the seam is vertical to you.

5 Make a single turn: Roll out the dough in front of you with the seam vertical to you using the rolling pin to make a strip of dough measuring 9½ inches (24 cm) long. Fold it over into thirds (like a wallet) to form a rectangle. Wrap the dough in plastic wrap and place it in the freezer for 10 minutes, then in the refrigerator for 30 minutes. Repeat this step twice more.

6 Roll out the dough to ½ inch (12 mm) thick and 9½ inches (24 cm) wide. Cut out triangles, with the ends measuring 3½ inches (9 cm) wide and the sides measuring 9½ inches (24 cm) long.

7 Cut out a small notch (about ¼ inch/5 mm wide) from the center of the wide end of each triangle. Gently spread the two sections slightly apart and roll up the triangle without tightening it too much; the tip must be positioned under the roll.

8 Place the croissants on a baking sheet lined with parchment paper, spaced 1⅛ to 1½ inches (3 to 4 cm) apart. Make the glaze (see page 49) and glaze the croissants using the pastry brush.

9 Let rest for 3 hours in a warm place, 77 to 82°F (25 to 28°C), without covering them.

10 Preheat the oven to 375°F (190°C). Glaze the croissants again and bake for about 15 minutes.

CHOCOLATE-FILLED
CROISSANT ROLLS
(PAIN AU CHOCOLAT)

Understanding

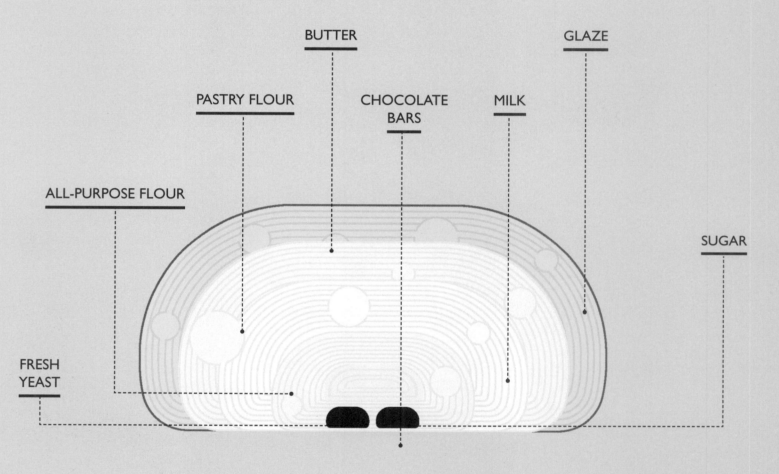

BUTTER

GLAZE

PASTRY FLOUR

CHOCOLATE
BARS

MILK

ALL-PURPOSE FLOUR

SUGAR

FRESH
YEAST

WHAT IT IS
A leavened puff pastry, cut into rectangles, filled with two bars of chocolate, then rolled.

CHARACTERISTICS
– Weight: 3 to 3⅛ ounces (80 to 90 g)
– Size: 4 inches (10 cm)
– Layering: very open

COMPLETION TIME
– Preparation time: 1 hour
– Fermentation time: 5½ hours (3 hours refrigerated, 2½ hours proofing)
– Baking time: 15 minutes

EQUIPMENT
– Stand mixer fitted with the dough hook (optional)
– Rolling pin
– Bench scraper
– Sieve
– Pastry brush

CHALLENGE
Rolling out the dough. Do not press down too firmly. There must be distinctive layers of butter and dough, otherwise the flaky layers will not develop.

SKILLS TO MASTER
– Kneading (pages 30 and 32)
– Shaping a Boule (page 42)
– Glazing (page 48)

USEFUL TIP
If chocolate bars specifically designed for use in pastries are not available, use a row of chocolate squares instead.

IT'S READY
When the pastries are golden and well risen.

MAKES ABOUT 6 PASTRIES

LEAVENED PUFF PASTRY

¾ cup plus 1 tablespoon (110 g) high-
protein all-purpose flour (or use
bread flour or T65 flour)

1 cup minus 1 tablespoon (110 g) pastry
flour (or use T45 flour)

2½ tablespoons (30 g) sugar

⅔ teaspoon (4 g) salt

⅓ cup plus 1½ tablespoons (105 g) whole milk

⅞ packed teaspoon (7 g) fresh yeast

8½ tablespoons (120 g) unsalted
butter (for rolling in), chilled

FILLING

12 small bars of chocolate (those made
for pastries)

GLAZE

1 large (50 g) egg

½ teaspoon (3 g) whole milk

Pinch of salt

1   Make the leavened puff pastry (see page 62).

2   Roll out (see page 283) the dough to ½ inch
(12 mm) thick and 5 inches (13 cm) wide.

3   Cut out rectangles measuring 5 inches (13
cm) long and 4 inches (10 cm) wide. Place 2
bars of chocolate on top of each rectangle, one
placed ¾ inch (2 cm) from one end and the other
placed 1 inch (3 cm) from the opposite end.

4   Roll up the rectangles, starting at the end with
the bar of chocolate closest to the end, folding the
end of the dough over the bar of chocolate. Continue
rolling to the end; the seam must be under the roll.

5   Make the glaze (see page 49) and glaze the pastries
using the pastry brush. Let rest for 2½ hours in a
warm place, 77 to 82°F (25 to 28°C), uncovered.

6   Preheat the oven to 350°F (180°C). Brush the
pastries again with the glaze and bake for 15 minutes
on a baking sheet lined with parchment paper.

RAISIN AND CREAM
CROISSANT SPIRALS
(PAIN AUX RAISINS)

Understanding

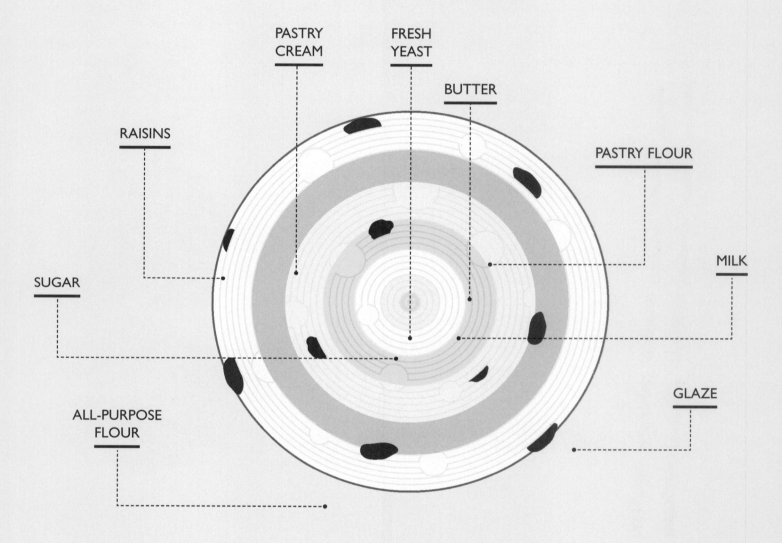

PASTRY CREAM

FRESH YEAST

BUTTER

PASTRY FLOUR

RAISINS

MILK

SUGAR

GLAZE

ALL-PURPOSE FLOUR

WHAT IT IS

A leavened puff pastry filled with pastry cream and raisins, then rolled into a spiral.

CHARACTERISTICS

–Weight: 4¼ ounces (120 g)
–Size: 8 inches (20 cm) in diameter
–Layering: open

COMPLETION TIME

–Preparation time: 1½ hours
–Fermentation time: 5½ hours (3 hours refrigeration, 2½ hours proofing)
–Resting time: 1 night (for the raisins)
–Baking time: 15 minutes

EQUIPMENT

–Stand mixer fitted with the dough hook (optional)
–Rolling pin
–Bench scraper
–Sieve
–Pastry brush

CHALLENGE

Rolling out the dough. Do not press down too firmly. There must be distinctive layers of butter and dough, otherwise the flaky layers will not develop. Roll tightly.

SKILLS TO MASTER

–Whisking until Lightened (page 284)
–Kneading (pages 30 and 32)
–Shaping a Boule (page 42)
–Glazing (page 48)

IT'S READY

When the pastries are golden brown and puffed.

SHELF LIFE

One or two days, maximum.

Learning

2

1

3, 4, 5

MAKES ABOUT 6 PASTRIES

1 PASTRY CREAM (CRÈME PATISSIÈRE)

1 cup plus 1 teaspoon (250 g) whole milk
½ cup (100 g) sugar
2 large (100 g) eggs
¼ cup (25 g) cornstarch

2 LEAVENED PUFF PASTRY

1 cup minus 2 tablespoons (120 g) high-protein all-purpose flour (or use bread flour or T65 flour)
1 cup (120 g) pastry flour (or use T45 flour)
⅓ cup plus 2 tablespoons (115 g) whole milk
2½ tablespoons (30 g) sugar
¾ teaspoon (5 g) salt
⅞ packed teaspoon (7 g) fresh yeast
8½ tablespoons (120 g) unsalted butter (for rolling in), chilled

3 FILLING

1⅓ cups (200 g) raisins

4 GLAZE

1 large (50 g) egg
½ teaspoon (3 g) whole milk
Pinch of salt

5 SYRUP

1 tablespoon plus 2 teaspoons (25 g) water
2 tablespoons (25 g) sugar

Making raisin and cream croissant spirals (pain aux raisins)

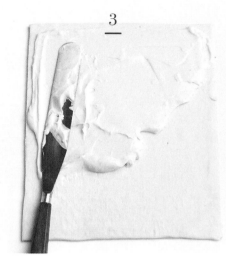

THE DAY BEFORE

1 Soak the raisins in tepid water.

THE SAME DAY

2 Make the pastry cream (see page 76). Scrape it onto a baking sheet, press plastic wrap onto its surface (see page 285), and refrigerate it for 1 hour to set.

3 Make the leavened puff pastry (see page 62). Roll out (see page 283) the dough to 9¾ inches (25 cm) wide and 12 inches (30 cm) long. Spread the pastry cream over the top of the dough.

4 Drain the raisins and distribute them over the cream, placing more on the lower end (the outside of the pastry once it is rolled).

5 Roll up tightly, starting on a short side.

6 Cut the roll into 1½-inch (4 cm) slices.

7 Tuck the ends under each roll and place the rolls on a baking sheet lined with parchment paper. Make the glaze (see page 49) and glaze the pastries using the pastry brush.

8 Let rest for 2½ hours in a warm place, 77 to 82°F (25 to 28°C), for the proofing.

9 Preheat the oven to 350°F (180°C). Brush the pastries again with the glaze. Bake for 15 minutes.

10 Make the syrup: bring the water and sugar to a boil in a saucepan and remove it from the heat. Brush the syrup over the pastries as soon as they come out of the oven.

PAIN SUISSE

Understanding

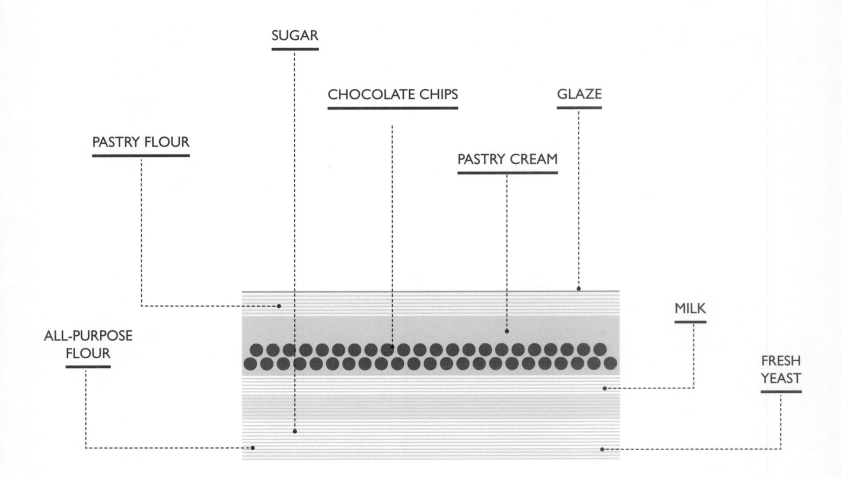

SUGAR

CHOCOLATE CHIPS

GLAZE

PASTRY FLOUR

PASTRY CREAM

ALL-PURPOSE FLOUR

MILK

FRESH YEAST

WHAT IT IS
Two layers of puff pastry sandwiching pastry cream and chocolate chips.

CHARACTERISTICS
– Weight: 4¼ ounces (120 g)
– Size: 4 inches (10 cm)
– Layering: open

COMPLETION TIME
– Preparation time: 2 hours
– Fermentation time: 4 hours (3 hours refrigeration, 1 hour proofing)
– Baking time: 30 minutes

EQUIPMENT
– Stand mixer fitted with the dough hook (optional)
– Pastry brush
– Sieve
– Bench scraper

SKILLS TO MASTER
– Kneading (pages 30 and 32)
– Glazing (page 48)

IT'S READY
When the pastries are golden brown and have risen slightly.

SHELF LIFE
One to two days, at room temperature.

1

2

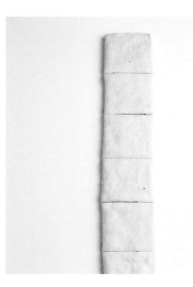

3

4, 5

6

MAKES 6 PASTRIES

PASTRY CREAM (CRÈME PATISSIÈRE)

1 cup plus 1 teaspoon (250 g) whole milk
¼ cup (50 g) sugar
¼ vanilla bean
¼ cup (25 g) cornstarch
2 large (100 g) eggs

LEAVENED PUFF PASTRY

1 cup minus 2 tablespoons (120 g) high-
  protein all-purpose flour (or use
  bread flour or T65 flour)
1 cup (120 g) pastry flour (or use T45 flour)
⅓ cup plus 2 tablespoons (115 g) whole milk
⅞ packed teaspoon (7 g) fresh yeast

2½ tablespoons (30 g) sugar
¾ teaspoon (5 g) salt
8½ tablespoons (120 g) unsalted butter, chilled

FILLING

⅓ cup (60 g) chocolate chips

GLAZE

1 large (50 g) egg
½ teaspoon (3 g) whole milk or cream
Pinch of salt

1 Using the technique on page 77, make the pastry cream. Using the technique on page 63, make the leavened puff pastry. Cut the dough into two halves using the bench scraper, and roll out each half to 9¾ inches (25 cm) long and 4 inches (10 cm) wide.

2 Spread the pastry cream over the top of one of the two strips of dough to ¼ inch (5 mm) from the edges; distribute the chocolate chips over the cream.

3 Top with the other strip of dough.

4 Cut the dough every 4 inches (10 cm) to make 4-inch (10 cm) squares.

5 Place the squares on a sheet of parchment paper. Make the glaze (see page 49) and glaze the squares using the pastry brush. Let rest for 1 hour, covered with a towel, in a warm place, 77 to 82°F (25 to 28°C), for the proofing.

6 Preheat the oven to 350°F (180°C) with a baking sheet placed in the oven. Slide the squares onto the hot baking sheet with the parchment paper. Brush them again with the glaze and bake for 30 minutes.

ALMOND CROISSANT

Understanding

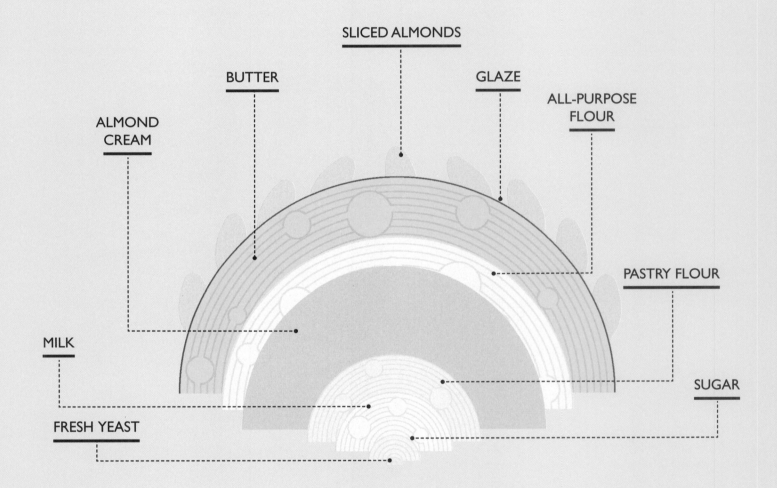

ALMOND
CREAM

BUTTER

SLICED ALMONDS

GLAZE

ALL-PURPOSE
FLOUR

PASTRY FLOUR

MILK

SUGAR

FRESH YEAST

WHAT IT IS
A previously baked croissant filled with almond cream and sprinkled with sliced almonds and baked again.

CHARACTERISTICS
–Weight: about 3½ ounces (100 g)
–Size: 4¾ inches (12 cm)
–Layering: open

COMPLETION TIME
–Preparation time: 30 minutes
–Baking time: 30 minutes

EQUIPMENT
–Sieve
–Pastry bag + ribbon pastry tip (or a knife)
–Pastry brush
–Serrated knife

SKILLS TO MASTER
–Whisking until Lightened (page 284)
–Making a Beurre en Pommade (page 284)

SHELF LIFE
One or two days maximum, when exposed to air.

IT'S READY
When the almond cream and the sliced almonds are golden brown.

MAKES 6 PASTRIES

SYRUP

½ cup minus 1 tablespoon (100 g) water
½ cup (100 g) sugar

ALMOND CREAM

3½ tablespoons (50 g) Beurre en
   Pommade (page 284)
½ cup minus 1 tablespoon (50 g) almond flour
2 teaspoons (5 g) cornstarch
1 large (50 g) egg
¼ cup (50 g) sugar

PASTRIES

6 previously baked Croissants (page 180)
   or Chocolate-Filled Croissant Rolls
   (Pain au Chocolat; page 184)

FINISHING

⅔ cup (60 g) sliced almonds
Confectioners' sugar

1   Make the syrup: bring the water and sugar to a
boil in a saucepan and remove it from the heat.

2   Preheat the oven to 350°F (180°C). Using the
technique on page 79, make the almond cream.

3   Slice the pastries open horizontally using the
serrated knife; do not slice all the way through them.
Brush the pastries generously with the syrup inside
and out using the pastry brush. Place the pastries
on a baking sheet lined with parchment paper.

4   Scrape the almond cream into a pastry bag fitted
with the ribbon pastry tip. Pipe the almond cream
inside the pastries to fill them, then replace the tops.

5   Pipe a little of the cream on top of the pastries
and sprinkle them with sliced almonds; press with
your fingers to make the almonds stick to the cream.

6   Bake for 30 minutes. Let cool, then sift
the confectioners' sugar over the top.

APPLE TURNOVER
(CHAUSSON AUX POMMES)

Understanding

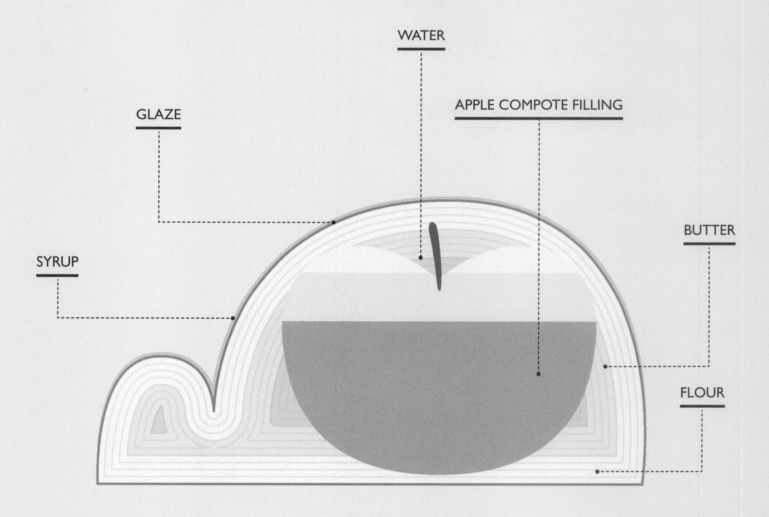

WATER

GLAZE

APPLE COMPOTE FILLING

SYRUP

BUTTER

FLOUR

WHAT IT IS

An inverse puff pastry dough filled with an apple compote filling. The pastry is folded in half to form a turnover.

CHARACTERISTICS

– Weight: 3½ ounces (100 g)
– Size: 3 inches (8 cm)
– Layering: airy, crispy

COMPLETION TIME

– Preparation time: 1½ hours
– Refrigeration time: 12 hours
– Cooking/Baking time: 1 hour for cooking the compote, 30 minutes for baking the pastry

EQUIPMENT

– Fluted cookie cutter 5 inches (13 cm) in diameter
– Stand mixer fitted with the dough hook and paddle
– Rolling pin
– Pastry brush

SKILLS TO MASTER

– Kneading (pages 30 and 32)
– Glazing (page 48)
– Scoring a Diagonal (page 51)

USEFUL TIP

Turn the pastries over before baking to achieve a more uniform shape.

IT'S READY

When the pastries are golden brown.

SHELF LIFE

One to two days, maximum.

WHAT MAKES THE PASTRIES
SHINE?

The syrup applied after cooking. When a sugar solution boils, the water evaporates. Upon cooling, the sugar crystals bind to each other and form a glossy glaze.

Learning

<table>
<tr><td></td><td>2</td></tr>
<tr><td></td><td>1</td></tr>
<tr><td></td><td>4</td></tr>
<tr><td></td><td>3</td></tr>
</table>

MAKES 8 PASTRIES

1 APPLE COMPOTE FILLING

1⅛ pounds (530 g) apples
2 tablespoons plus 2 teaspoons
    (40 g) unsalted butter
2½ tablespoons (30 g) sugar
1 vanilla bean

2 INVERSE PUFF PASTRY DOUGH

BEURRE MANIÉ
7 tablespoons (100 g) unsalted butter,
    cut into cubes, softened
¼ cup plus 1 tablespoon (40 g) high-
    protein all-purpose flour (or use
    bread flour or T65 flour)

DOUGH LAYER (DÉTREMPE)
⅔ cup (90 g) high-protein all-purpose flour
    (or use bread flour or T65 flour)
¾ teaspoon (5 g) salt
2½ tablespoons (40 g) cold water
2 tablespoons (30 g) Beurre en
    Pommade (page 284)
¼ teaspoon (1 g) white vinegar

3 GLAZE

1 large (50 g) egg
½ teaspoon (3 g) whole milk
Pinch of salt

4 SYRUP

1 tablespoon plus 2 teaspoons (25 g) water
2 tablespoons (25 g) sugar

1 Using the technique on page 81, make the apple compote filling.

2 Using the technique on page 69, make the inverse puff pastry. Preheat the oven to 350°F (180°C). Roll out (see page 283) the dough to a thickness of ½ inch (12 mm) using the rolling pin. Cut out 8 rounds of dough using the cookie cutter.

3 Stretch each dough round out slightly to form an oval.

4 Make the glaze (see page 49) and glaze the edges of each dough round.

5 Spoon some of the apple compote onto one side of each oval, leaving a ⅓-inch (1 cm) border all around. Fold the other half of the oval over onto the compote and seal the edges by pressing lightly with your fingers.

6 Turn the pastry over. Glaze the pastries with the remaining glaze using the pastry brush. Score parallel diagonal cuts (see page 51) across the top using a small paring knife.

7 Place the pastries on a baking sheet lined with parchment paper. Bake for 30 minutes.

8 Make the syrup: bring the water and sugar to a boil in a saucepan and remove it from heat. Brush the syrup over the turnovers as soon as they come out of the oven.

APPLE TART
WITH LATTICE

Understanding

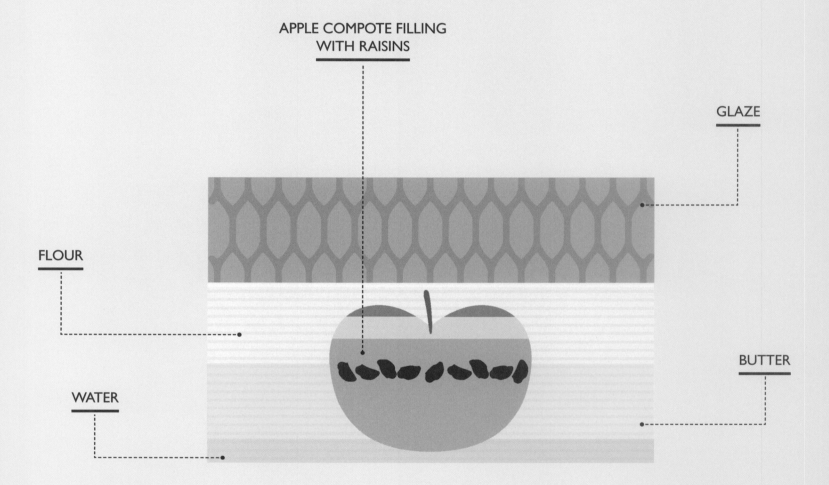

APPLE COMPOTE FILLING
WITH RAISINS

GLAZE

FLOUR

BUTTER

WATER

WHAT IT IS

An inverse puff pastry dough filled with apple compote, topped with a layer of inverse puff pastry that has been cut into a lattice.

COMPLETION TIME

- Preparation time: 30 minutes
- Refrigeration time: 12 hours
- Cooking/Baking time: 45 minutes for cooking the compote, 45 minutes for baking the pastry

EQUIPMENT

- Stand mixer fitted with the paddle and dough hook
- Baking sheet 16 × 24 inches (40 × 60 cm)
- Rolling pin
- Lattice dough cutter
- Bench scraper
- Pastry brush

CHALLENGE

Forming the lattice.

SKILLS TO MASTER

- Kneading (pages 30 and 32)
- Lining a Pan or Pastry Ring (page 283)
- Glazing (page 48)

USEFUL TIPS

- Place the dough sheet that will be used for the lattice in the refrigerator before working with it to assist with shaping a more uniform pattern.
- If you do not have a lattice dough cutter, cut out strips of puff pastry dough (about ½ inch/1.5 cm wide), arrange them in a diamond-shape pattern, then trim off the excess around the edges.

IT'S READY

When the pastry is golden brown.

SHELF LIFE

Two to three days.

Learning

MAKES 8 PASTRIES

1 INVERSE PUFF PASTRY

BEURRE MANIÉ
7 tablespoons (100 g) unsalted butter,
    cut into cubes, softened
¼ cup plus 1 tablespoon (40 g) high-
    protein all-purpose flour (or use
    bread flour or T65 flour)

DOUGH LAYER (DÉTREMPE)
⅔ cup (90 g) high-protein all-purpose flour
    (or use bread flour or T65 flour)
¾ teaspoon (5 g) salt
2½ tablespoons (40 g) cold water
2 tablespoons (30 g) Beurre en
    Pommade (page 284)
¼ teaspoon (1 g) white vinegar

2 APPLE COMPOTE FILLING

2¼ pounds (1 kg) Golden Delicious apples
¼ cup (50 g) cane sugar
⅔ cup minus 1 teaspoon (150 g) water
⅓ cup (50 g) raisins
1 vanilla bean
1 teaspoon (2 g) ground cinnamon

3 GLAZE

1 large (50 g) egg
½ teaspoon (3 g) whole milk or cream
Pinch of salt

Making the apple tart with lattice

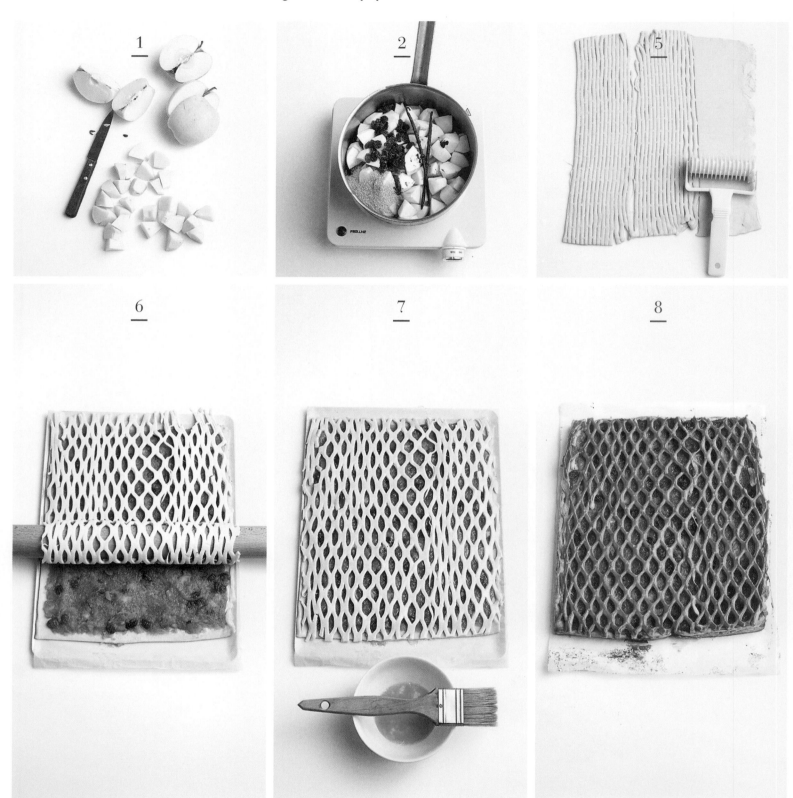

1 Using the technique on page 69, make the inverse puff pastry. Peel and core the apples, then cut them into large pieces.

2 Place the apple pieces in a saucepan with the sugar, water, raisins, and vanilla bean that has been split lengthwise in half and its seeds scraped out into the pan along with the empty pod. Bring the mixture to a boil, then reduce the heat and simmer for about 30 minutes, stirring occasionally. Add the cinnamon, stir to combine, and continue cooking for an additional 15 minutes over very low heat. Transfer the mixture to a container and let cool; remove the empty vanilla pod.

3 Cut the dough in half. Roll one half of the dough out to ⅛ inch (3 mm) thick.

4 Line a baking sheet with parchment paper, and place the dough on the paper. Scrape the compote over the top of the rolled-out strip of dough and spread it up to ⅓ inch (1 cm) from the edge, mounding it slightly.

5 Roll out (see page 283) the second half of the dough to ¹⁄₁₀ inch (2 mm) thick. Pass the lattice dough cutter over the strip of dough to cut slits, then carefully pull the slits apart slightly to form a lattice.

6 Wrap the lattice dough around the rolling pin, then unroll it over the compote.

7 Make the glaze (see page 49) and glaze the lattice using the pastry brush.

8 Preheat the oven to 325°F (160°C). Bake for 45 minutes. Slice into eight pastries when cool.

FLAKY APPLE TART

Understanding

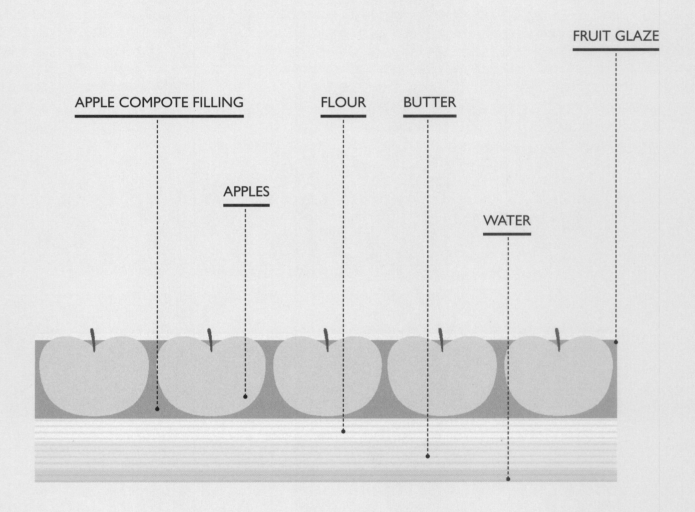

FRUIT GLAZE

APPLE COMPOTE FILLING   FLOUR   BUTTER

APPLES

WATER

WHAT IT IS

A base of inverse puff pastry filled with an apple compote then topped with thin apple slices.

COMPLETION TIME

– Preparation time: 1 hour and 15 minutes
– Refrigeration time: 12 hours
– Cooking/Baking time: 1 hour for cooking the compote; 25 minutes for baking the pastry

EQUIPMENT

– Stand mixer fitted with the paddle and dough hook
– Rolling pin
– Fluted cookie cutter 4 inches (10 cm) in diameter
– Pastry brush

VARIATIONS

– Apricots
– Mirabelle plums
– Pears/fresh figs

CHALLENGE

Slicing the apples.

SKILL TO MASTER

Kneading (pages 30 and 32)

USEFUL TIP

Add apple pieces to the compote to achieve a good volume of filling.

IT'S READY

When the apples turn golden and the dough is pale golden with a browned bottom.

SHELF LIFE

Up to three days, refrigerated.

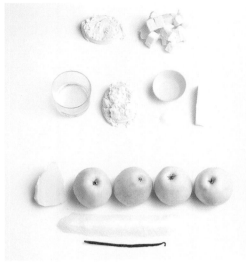

MAKES 4 PASTRIES

APPLE COMPOTE FILLING

6⅓ ounces (180 g) apples
1 tablespoon (15 g) unsalted butter
2½ teaspoons (10 g) sugar
½ vanilla bean

INVERSE PUFF PASTRY SHEET

BEURRE MANIÉ

7 tablespoons (100 g) unsalted butter,
    cut into cubes, softened
¼ cup plus 1 tablespoon (40 g) high-protein
    all-purpose flour (or use bread flour
    or T65 flour)

DOUGH LAYER (DÉTREMPE)

⅔ cup (90 g) high-protein all-purpose flour
    (or use bread flour or T65 flour)
¾ teaspoon (5 g) salt
2½ tablespoons (40 g) cold water
2 tablespoons (30 g) Beurre en
    Pommade (page 284)
¼ teaspoon (1 g) white vinegar

FILLING

2 or 3 apples
1½ teaspoons (10 g) apple or
    apricot jelly, warmed

1   Using the technique on page 81, make the apple compote filling.

2   Using the technique on page 69, make the inverse puff pastry (see page 68). Roll out the dough to ¹⁄₁₀ inch (2 mm) thick. Preheat the oven to 325°F (160°C).

3   Cut out 4 rounds using the cookie cutter and, using a fork, lightly dock the pastry. Place the disks on a baking sheet lined with parchment paper. Spread a generous layer of the apple compote onto each dough round so that the compote is slightly mounded in the center.

4   Peel and core the apples. Cut them in half, then slice them very thinly. Arrange the apples over the top of the compote in a rosette pattern, starting from the outside edge and moving in toward the center.

5   Bake for 25 minutes. Brush the pastries with the warm jelly as soon as they come out of the oven.

203

KING CAKE
(GALETTE DES ROIS)

Understanding

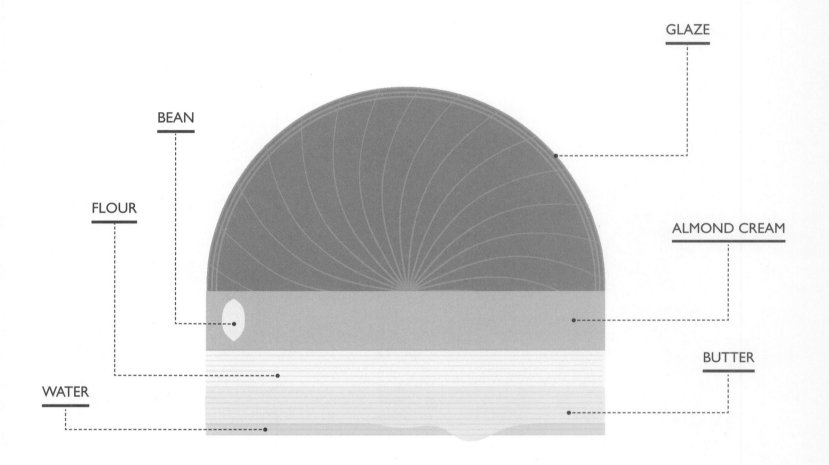

GLAZE

BEAN

ALMOND CREAM

FLOUR

BUTTER

WATER

WHAT IT IS
Two large rounds of puff pastry sandwiching almond cream.

COMPLETION TIME
- Preparation time: 30 minutes
- Refrigeration time: 12 hours
- Baking time: 40 to 45 minutes

EQUIPMENT
- Stand mixer fitted with the paddle and dough hook
- Rolling pin
- Pastry ring 12½ inches (32 cm) in diameter
- Pastry brush

- Pastry bag + number 8 plain tip
- Paring knife

VARIATION
Frangipane King Cake: ⅔ almond cream + ⅓ pastry cream

CHALLENGE
Positioning the top dough round.

SKILLS TO MASTER
- Kneading (pages 30 and 32)
- Glazing (page 48)
- Whisking until Lightened (page 284)
- Notching a Border (page 283)

USEFUL TIPS
- Make the almond cream the day before so that it will be thickened and facilitate piping.
- Place the dough rounds in the refrigerator for 1 hour before assembling the cake; this will make it easier to compose the cake.

IT'S READY
When the cake is golden brown in color.

SHELF LIFE
One to two days, maximum (to prevent the cream from drying out).

1

2

3

MAKES 1 CAKE (SERVES 8)

1 INVERSE PUFF PASTRY SHEET

BEURRE MANIÉ

14 tablespoons (200 g) unsalted butter, cut into cubes, softened

½ cup plus 2 tablespoons (80 g) high-protein all-purpose flour (or use bread flour or T65 flour)

DOUGH LAYER (DÉTREMPE)

1⅓ cups (180 g) high-protein all-purpose flour (or use bread flour or T65 flour)

1⅔ teaspoons (10 g) salt

⅓ cup plus ¾ teaspoon (80 g) cold water

4 tablespoons (60 g) Beurre en Pommade (page 284)

½ teaspoon (2 g) white vinegar

2 ALMOND CREAM

7 tablespoons (100 g) unsalted butter

1 cup minus 2 tablespoons (100 g) almond flour

1 tablespoon (10 g) cornstarch

2 large (100 g) eggs

½ cup (100 g) sugar

1 raw almond or precooked bean (if you get the piece of cake with the almond or bean, you're crowned king)

3 GLAZE

1 large (50 g) egg

½ teaspoon (3 g) whole milk

Pinch of salt

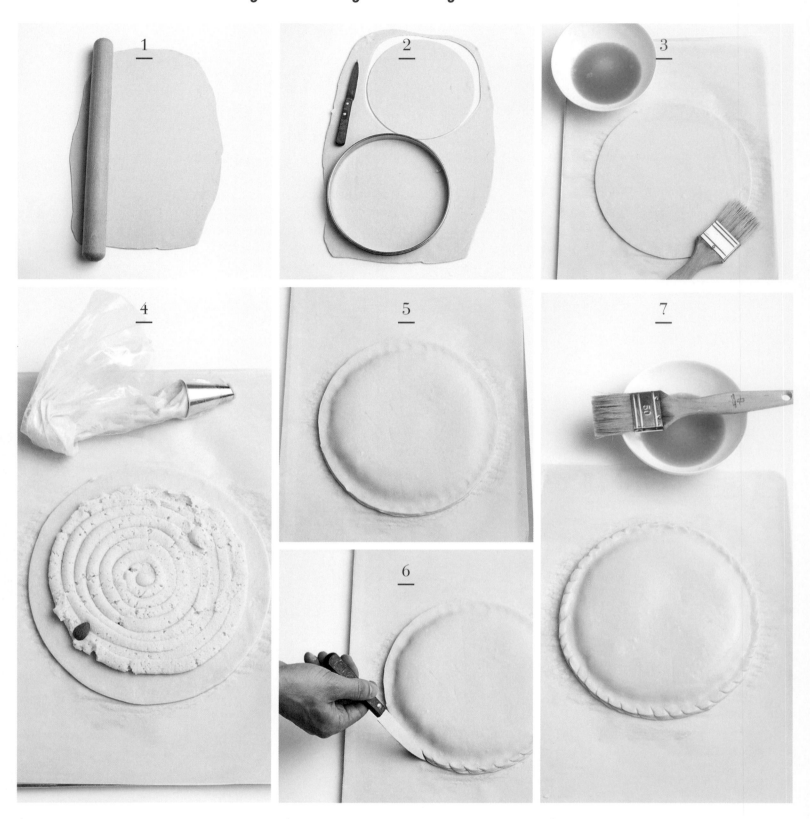

1 Using the technique on page 69, make the inverse puff pastry. Roll out (see page 283) the dough to ⅛ inch (4 mm) thick.

2 Cut out two dough rounds using the pastry ring.

3 Place one of the circles on a baking sheet lined with parchment paper. Make the glaze (see page 49). Brush the glaze in a ¾-inch (2 cm) border around the edge of the dough round using the pastry brush.

4 Using the technique on page 79, make the almond cream. Fill the pastry bag fitted with the plain pastry tip with the cream. Pipe the cream on the dough round in a spiral starting from the center, maintaining the border. Randomly place the almond or bean on top of the cream.

5 Flour the rolling pin and the second dough round, then wrap the round around the rolling pin and unroll it so that it is centered over the bottom dough round. Seal the top and bottom circles together by lightly pressing the edges together using your fingers.

6 Notch a border (see page 283) by making small nicks all around the outer edge of the round using the dull side of the paring knife.

7 Glaze the entire top with the remaining glaze.

8 Preheat the oven to 350°F (180°C). Score the top of the pastry multiple times by dragging the dull side of the paring knife across the dough starting from the center and moving out to the edge in a slight arc (see photo opposite).

9 Bake for 40 to 45 minutes.

SWEET LOAVES

Understanding

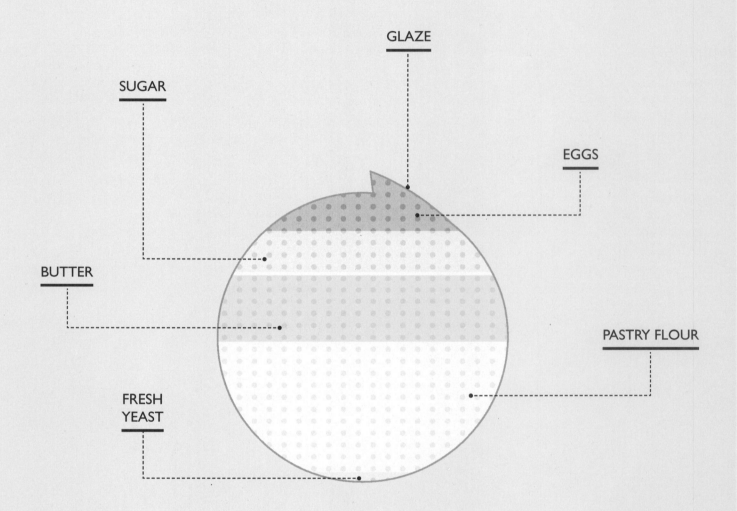

GLAZE

SUGAR

EGGS

BUTTER

PASTRY FLOUR

FRESH
YEAST

WHAT IT IS
A sweet yeast-raised dough shaped
into an individual loaf.

CHARACTERISTICS
– Weight: 1¾ ounces (50 g)
– Size: 7 inches (18 cm)
– Crumb: tight, soft

COMPLETION TIME
– Preparation time: 45 minutes
– Fermentation time: 30 minutes first day,
  then 1 night; 15 minutes refrigerated,
  1½ hours proofing same day
– Baking time: 10 minutes

EQUIPMENT
– Stand mixer and dough hook (optional)
– Pastry brush
– Bench scraper
– Scissors

CHALLENGE
Incorporating the butter without melting it
so that the dough maintains its consistency.

SKILLS TO MASTER
– Kneading (pages 30 and 32)
– Turning (page 37)
– Preshaping a Round (page 38)
– Shaping a Bâtard (page 45)
– Shaping an Elongated Form (page 41)
– Glazing (page 48)

IT'S READY
When the loaf is golden brown.

SHELF LIFE
Two to three days.

MAKES 16 LOAVES

YEAST-RAISED DOUGH

3¾ cups (450 g) pastry flour (or use T45 flour)
6 large (300 g) eggs
½ packed teaspoon (4 g) fresh yeast
¼ cup plus 2½ teaspoons (60 g) sugar
1⅓ teaspoons (8 g) salt
14 tablespoons (200 g) unsalted butter,
   cut into cubes, softened

GLAZE

1 large (50 g) egg
½ teaspoon (3 g) whole milk
Pinch of salt

1   Refrigerate all the ingredients the day before making the dough. Knead (see page 32) together the flour, eggs, crumbled yeast, sugar, and salt for 4 minutes on the lowest speed (speed 1), then for 6 minutes on medium speed. The dough should detach from the sides of the bowl. (For kneading by hand, see page 30.) Reduce the speed to speed 1 and add the butter. Mix slowly until all of the butter is incorporated.

2   Transfer the dough to a mixing bowl, cover the bowl with plastic wrap, and let stand for 30 minutes at room temperature. Turn the dough (see page 37), place it back in the mixing bowl, and cover the bowl with plastic wrap. Refrigerate overnight.

3   Divide the dough into sixteen pieces, 2⅛ ounces (60 g) each, and shape them into rounds (see page 38). Shape them into bâtards (see page 45), cover them with plastic wrap, and refrigerate for 15 minutes.

4   Roll each piece of dough with your hands, moving from the center toward the ends until each one measures 7 inches (18 cm).

5   Transfer to a sheet of parchment paper. Make the glaze (see page 49); glaze the loaves with a pastry brush. Let rest for 1½ hours, uncovered, in a warm place, 77 to 82°F (25 to 28°C), for the proofing.

6   Dip the scissors into the glaze (to prevent sticking), angle them 45 degrees above the work surface, and snip several V-shaped slits about ⅓ inch (1 cm) long evenly spaced along the top of the loaves.

7   Preheat the oven to 350°F (180°C) with a baking sheet placed in the oven. Slide the loaves onto the hot baking sheet with the parchment paper. Glaze, and bake for 10 minutes.

VIENNA BAGUETTE

Understanding

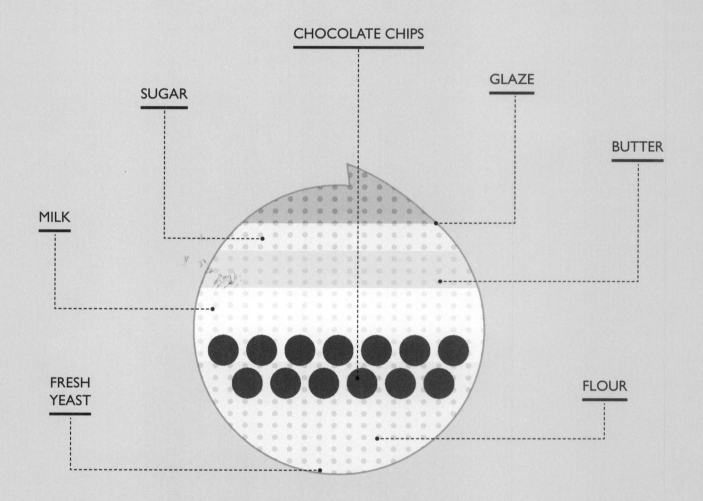

CHOCOLATE CHIPS

GLAZE

SUGAR

BUTTER

MILK

FRESH
YEAST

FLOUR

WHAT IT IS

A Vienna dough shaped into a
small baguette. They can be plain
or filled with chocolate chips.

CHARACTERISTICS

–Weight: 4¼ ounces (120 g)
–Size: 9¾ inches (25 cm)
–Crumb: tight, soft
–Crust: very thin, tender

COMPLETION TIME

–Preparation time: 40 minutes
–Fermentation time: 5½ hours
  (4 hours and 15 minutes refrigerated,
  1 hour and 15 minutes proofing)
–Baking time: 15 to 20 minutes

EQUIPMENT

–Stand mixer fitted with the
  dough hook (optional)
–Serrated knife
–Bench scraper
–Sieve
–Pastry brush

SKILLS TO MASTER

–Kneading (pages 30 and 32)
–Shaping a Baguette (page 43)
–Glazing (page 48)
–Scoring a Diagonal (page 51)

IT'S READY

As soon as the loaf is golden brown.

SHELF LIFE

Two days.

2, 3

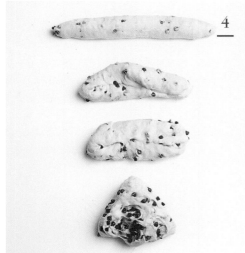

4

5

8

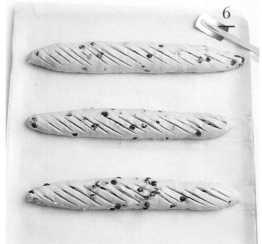

6

7

MAKES 2 LOAVES

VIENNA DOUGH

2½ cups (340 g) high-protein all-purpose
    flour (or use bread flour or T65 flour)
¾ cup plus 1½ tablespoons (210 g) whole milk
⅞ packed teaspoon (7 g) fresh yeast
2½ tablespoons (30 g) sugar
1⅛ teaspoons (7 g) salt
4 tablespoons (55 g) unsalted butter

MIX-IN (OPTIONAL)

½ cup (90 g) chocolate chips

GLAZE

1 large (50 g) egg
½ teaspoon (3 g) whole milk
Pinch of salt

1   Using the technique on page 61, make the Vienna dough.

2   If making the chocolate Vienna loaf, add the chocolate chips after incorporating the butter. Knead only for a short time, just until the chips are evenly distributed in the dough.

3   Place the dough in a mixing bowl, cover the bowl with plastic wrap, and refrigerate for 4 hours.

4   Divide the dough into four equal pieces using the bench scraper. Shape the pieces into baguettes (see page 43). Wrap them in plastic wrap and refrigerate for 15 minutes.

5   Place the loaves on parchment paper. Make the glaze (see page 49) and glaze the loaves using the pastry brush.

6   Score diagonals into the loaves (see page 51) using a lame. Let rest, uncovered, for 1 hour and 15 minutes in a warm place, 77 to 82°F (25 to 28°C), for the proofing.

7   Preheat the oven to 350°F (180°C) with a baking sheet placed in the oven. Brush them again with the glaze.

8   Slide the loaves onto the hot baking sheet with the parchment paper. Bake for 15 to 20 minutes.

FILLED DOUGHNUTS

Understanding

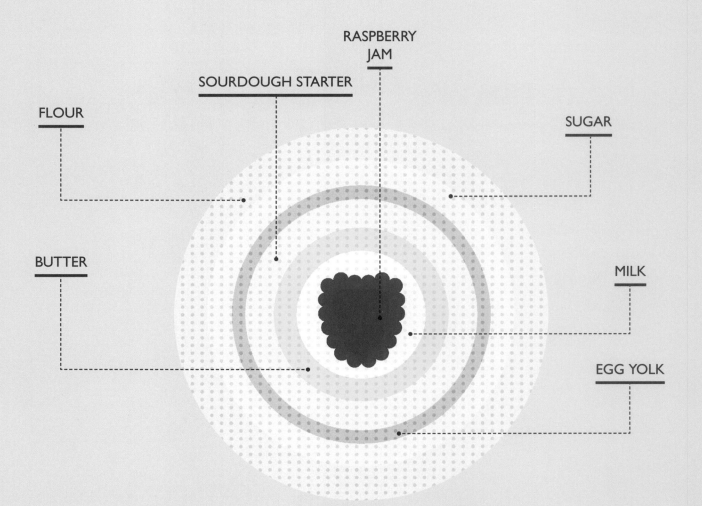

RASPBERRY JAM

SOURDOUGH STARTER

FLOUR

SUGAR

BUTTER

MILK

EGG YOLK

WHAT IT IS

A sweet yeast-raised dough made with a sourdough starter, shaped into individual boules. They are fried, rolled in a mixture of sugar and cinnamon, then filled with raspberry jam.

CHARACTERISTICS

–Weight: 3½ ounces (100 g)
–Size: 4 inches (10 cm) in diameter
–Crumb: tight and soft

COMPLETION TIME

–Preparation time: 1 hour
–Fermentation time: 5 hours
–Baking time: 20 minutes

EQUIPMENT

–Stand mixer fitted with the dough hook
–Bench scraper
–Pastry bag
–Number 6 plain pastry tip

FILLING VARIATIONS

–Apple Compote Filling (page 80)
–Pastry Cream (page 76)
–Sweetened chocolate-hazelnut spread

CHALLENGES

– Frying: controlling the temperature of the oil.
– Filling them.

SKILLS TO MASTER

–Kneading (pages 30 and 32)
–Shaping a Boule (page 42)

USEFUL TIP

The proofing is complete when gently pressing into it with your fingertip leaves no mark.

IT'S READY

When the doughnuts are golden brown.

SHELF LIFE

Two days, at room temperature.

3

1

2

4, 5

HOW DO YOU EXPLAIN THE WHITE LINE THAT EXTENDS AROUND THE CENTER OF A DOUGHNUT?

Doughnuts float on the surface of the oil while cooking. You have to turn them to cook them on both sides. This white line is the "floating" line.

MAKES 12 DOUGHNUTS

1 LEAVENED DOUGH

1 cup minus 1 tablespoon (125 g) high-protein all-purpose flour (or use bread flour or T65 flour)
3¾ packed teaspoons (30 g) fresh yeast
3 large (54 g) egg yolks
2 tablespoons plus 2½ teaspoons (35 g) sugar
1 tablespoon plus 1 teaspoon (20 g) whole milk
1 teaspoon (6 g) salt
2 tablespoons plus 1 teaspoon (35 g) unsalted butter, cut into cubes

2 STARTER

1 cup (140 g) high-protein all-purpose flour (or use bread flour or T65 flour)

⅜ packed teaspoon (3 g) fresh yeast
⅓ cup plus 2½ teaspoons (90 g) water

3 FRYING

4 cups (1 liter) canola oil

4 RASPBERRY JAM FILLING

2 cups (250 g) raspberries
½ cup plus 1½ tablespoons (120 g) sugar
1 teaspoon (3 g) pectin

5 COATING

½ cup (100 g) sugar
2 teaspoons (10 g) ground cinnamon

213

Making the filled doughnuts

1 Make the starter: Combine the flour, crumbled yeast, and water. Let stand for 1 hour at 75°F (24°C). Knead (see page 32) together all the ingredients (except the butter) for the dough along with the starter in the bowl of a stand mixer fitted with the dough hook for 6 to 8 minutes on the lowest speed (speed 1), then for 6 to 8 minutes on medium-low speed (speed 2). Add the butter and knead on speed 1 to incorporate.

2 When the dough detaches from the sides of the bowl, cover the bowl with plastic wrap, and place it in the refrigerator until it is completely cool (about 3 hours).

3 Divide the dough into twelve pieces, 1½ ounces (40 g) each, and preshape into rounds (see page 38). Shape them into boules (see page 42), then place them on a large floured towel.

4 Cover the boules with another towel and let rise for 1½ to 2 hours in a warm place, 77 to 82°F (25 to 28°C); the dough should double in volume.

5 In a saucepan, heat the oil to 284 to 300°F (140 to 150°C). Lower the doughnuts into the hot oil and cook for 30 seconds on each side. Remove them with a skimmer and place them on a sheet of absorbent paper.

6 Once cooled, roll them in the sugar mixed with the cinnamon.

7 Follow the directions for raspberry jam in Raspberry Strips (see page 268), but use the ingredient quantities here. Let cool, then transfer the jam to the pastry bag fitted with the plain pastry tip. Make a hole in the side of each doughnut and fill them with the jam.

PARISIAN BRIOCHE

Understanding

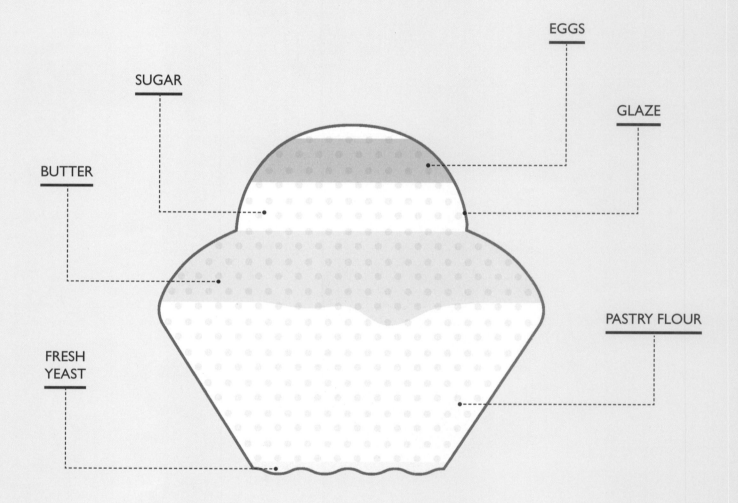

SUGAR

EGGS

GLAZE

BUTTER

PASTRY FLOUR

FRESH
YEAST

WHAT IT IS

A brioche dough shaped into two
pieces: a small round head and
a large round, fluted body.

CHARACTERISTICS

–Small brioche weight: 1¾ ounces (50 g)
–Large brioche weight: 12 ounces (350 g)
–Crumb: tight, silky

COMPLETION TIME

–Preparation time: 1 hour and 20 minutes
–Fermentation time: 13¼ hours
  (1 night rising, 15 minutes additional
  rising, 2½ hours proofing)
–Baking time: 10 to 15 minutes

EQUIPMENT

–4 fluted brioche molds 3 inches
  (8 cm) in diameter
–1 fluted brioche mold 7 inches
  (18 cm) in diameter
–Stand mixer and dough hook (optional)
–Bench scraper
–Sieve
–Pastry brush

CHALLENGE

Making the head of the brioche.

SKILLS TO MASTER

–Kneading (pages 30 and 32)
–Shaping a Boule (page 42)

–Glazing (page 48)
–Turning (page 37)

USEFUL TIP

To help the heads of the brioche
rise, gently press their sides into the
body using your fingers, otherwise
the heads will flatten after baking.

IT'S READY

When the head of the brioche is nicely
risen and the brioche is golden.

SHELF LIFE

Two to three days.

1
2
3

MAKES FOUR 1¾-OUNCE (50 G) LOAVES AND ONE 12-OUNCE (350 G) LOAF

1 BRIOCHE DOUGH

2 cups (240 g) pastry flour (or use T45 flour)
3 large (150 g) eggs
1 packed teaspoon (8 g) fresh yeast
3 tablespoons plus ½ teaspoon (40 g) sugar
¾ teaspoon (5 g) salt
9 tablespoons plus 1 teaspoon (130 g)
      unsalted butter, cut into pieces

2 GLAZE

1 large (50 g) egg
½ teaspoon (3 g) whole milk
Pinch of salt

3 MOLDS

3½ tablespoons (50 g) Beurre en
      Pommade (page 284)

Making a Parisian brioche

1   Refrigerate all of the ingredients the day before making the brioche. Before kneading, allow the cubes of butter to come to cool room temperature (see page 66). Knead (see page 32) together the flour, eggs, crumbled yeast, sugar, and salt for 4 minutes on the lowest speed (speed 1), then for 6 minutes on medium speed. The dough should detach from the sides of the bowl. (For kneading by hand, see page 30.)

2   Add the butter, then continue kneading at speed 1 until the butter is completely incorporated into the dough.

3   Transfer the dough to a mixing bowl. Press plastic wrap onto its surface (see page 285) and let rise for 30 minutes. Turn the dough (see page 37). Place the dough back in the mixing bowl, press plastic wrap onto its surface, and refrigerate it overnight.

4   Divide the dough into four 1¾-ounce (50 g) pieces, one 10½-ounce (300 g) piece, and another 3½-ounce (100 g) piece, using the bench scraper. Shape the dough pieces into boules (see page 42), cover them with plastic wrap, and refrigerate for 15 minutes.

5   Grease the molds with the beurre en pommade using the pastry brush. Pinch the four small pieces of dough into a bowling pin shape (be careful that the dough stays in one piece) to form the heads of the small brioche. Shape the 10½-ounce (300 g) boule into a couronne (see page 46) and roll the 3½-ounce (100 g) boule into a pear shape.

6   Place the four small "bowling pin" pieces in the molds with the smaller portion (the "head") on top. To make the larger brioche, place the smaller section of the pear-shaped piece of dough down into

the hole of the ring, seal the pieces together under the ring, then place the entire loaf into the mold. Using your fingers, gently press the edges of the five heads (of the smaller and larger brioches) down onto the bodies to seal the heads to the bodies.

7   Make the glaze (see page 49) and glaze the loaves using the pastry brush. Let rest for 2½ hours in a warm place, 77 to 82°F (25 to 28°C), for the proofing.

8   Preheat the oven to 500°F (260°C) with a baking sheet placed in the oven. Place the brioches on the hot baking sheet. Brush again with the glaze, then bake for 10 to 15 minutes. Let the brioches rest at least 5 minutes before unmolding.

PINK PRALINE BRIOCHE

Understanding

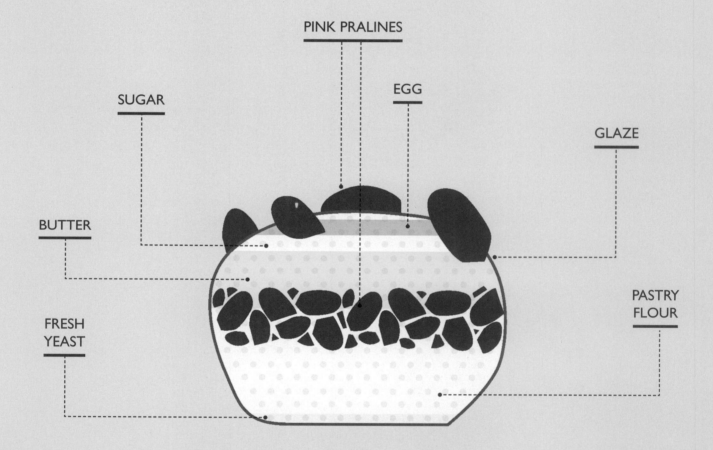

PINK PRALINES

EGG

SUGAR

GLAZE

BUTTER

PASTRY
FLOUR

FRESH
YEAST

WHAT IT IS

A brioche dough filled with pink pralines and shaped into a boule.

CHARACTERISTICS

–Weight: 1½ ounces (40 g)
–Size: individual
–Crumb: dense, silky

COMPLETION TIME

–Preparation time: 1 hour and 10 minutes
–Fermentation time: 14 hours (1 night rising, 2½ hours proofing)
–Baking time: 10 minutes

EQUIPMENT

–Stand mixer fitted with the dough hook
–Pastry brush
–Bench scraper
–Sieve

CHALLENGE

Shaping the dough properly to contain the pralines during baking.

SKILLS TO MASTER

–Kneading (pages 30 and 32)
–Turning (page 37)
–Shaping a Boule (page 42)
–Glazing (page 48)

VARIATION

Brioche with chocolate chips: using the stand mixer, incorporate the chips after adding the butter.

SHELF LIFE

Two to three days.

IT'S READY

When the brioche is golden brown.

1

2

3

MAKES 4 LOAVES

1 BRIOCHE DOUGH

⅔ cup (80 g) pastry flour (or use T45 flour)
1 large (50 g) egg
⅜ packed teaspoon (3 g) fresh yeast
1 tablespoon plus ½ teaspoon (15 g) sugar
⅓ teaspoon (2 g) salt
2 tablespoons plus 2 teaspoons (40 g)
    unsalted butter, cut into cubes

2 GLAZE

1 large (50 g) egg
½ teaspoon (3 g) whole milk or cream
Pinch of salt

3 FILLING

½ cup (60 g) pink pralines

1 Refrigerate all of the ingredients the day before making the brioche. Before kneading, allow the cubes of butter to come to cool room temperature (see page 66). Knead (see page 32) together the flour, egg, crumbled yeast, sugar, and salt for 4 minutes on the lowest speed (speed 1), then for 6 minutes on medium speed.

2 Reduce the mixer to speed 1 and knead in the butter, kneading slowly until the butter is fully incorporated.

3 Let rise for 30 minutes at room temperature, then turn the dough (see page 37). Cover the bowl with plastic wrap, then refrigerate it overnight.

4 Divide the dough into four pieces, 2⅛ ounces (60 g) each. Shape the pieces into boules (see page 42). Place the boules in the refrigerator for 15 minutes if the dough becomes too warm.

5 Roll out (see page 283) each boule to form rounds measuring 4 inches (10 cm) in diameter. Sprinkle the rounds with pralines on one side, pressing them into the dough using your fingers.

6 Fold the dough over onto the pralines and shape the dough into a boule again; the pralines must be fully contained inside the dough.

7 Place the brioches seam side down onto a sheet of parchment paper. Make the glaze (see page 49) and glaze the brioches using the pastry brush. Let rest for 2½ hours in a warm place, 77 to 82°F (25 to 28°C), for the proofing.

8 Preheat the oven to 350°F (180°C) with a baking sheet placed in the oven. Glaze the brioches again, and lightly press some pralines on top. Place parchment with brioches onto hot baking sheet and bake for 10 minutes.

BRAIDED BRIOCHE
(CHALLAH)

Understanding

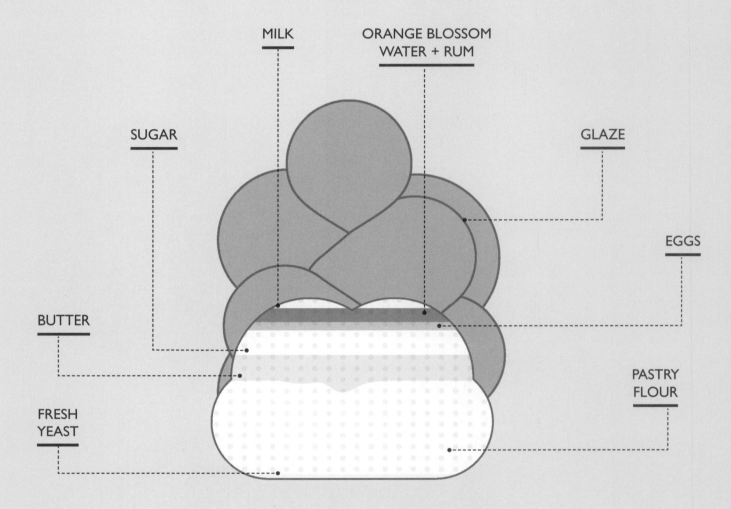

MILK

ORANGE BLOSSOM
WATER + RUM

SUGAR

GLAZE

EGGS

BUTTER

FRESH
YEAST

PASTRY
FLOUR

WHAT IT IS
A brioche dough flavored with orange blossom water and rum, and braided.

CHARACTERISTICS
−Weight: 12 ounces (350 g)
−Size: 15¾ inches (40 cm)
−Crumb: stringy

COMPLETION TIME
−Preparation time: 1 hour + 1 hour
−Fermentation time: 1 hour rising, 1 night rising, 4 hours proofing
−Baking time: 25 to 30 minutes

EQUIPMENT
−Stand mixer and dough hook (optional)
−Plastic dough scraper
−Bench scraper
−Sieve
−Pastry brush

CHALLENGE
Making the braid wide enough to facilitate the development of the bread while baking.

SKILLS TO MASTER
−Kneading (pages 30 and 32)
−Scraping (page 282)
−Turning (page 37)
−Glazing (page 48)

SHELF LIFE
Two to three days.

IT'S READY
When the crust is light golden and the crumb is a little pale and still moist.

HOW DO YOU EXPLAIN THE STRINGY TEXTURE OF THE CRUMB?
Braiding changes the "form" of the gluten network because the glutinous netting stretches inside each strand when braided.

Learning

MAKES 1 LOAF

1 BRIOCHE DOUGH

1½ cups minus 1 tablespoon (170 g)
    pastry flour (or use T45 flour)
2 large (100 g) eggs
3 tablespoons plus ½ teaspoon (40 g) sugar
2 teaspoons (10 g) whole milk
½ teaspoon (2 g) orange blossom water
2 teaspoons (10 g) rum
1¼ packed teaspoons (10 g) fresh yeast
½ teaspoon (3 g) salt
3½ tablespoons (50 g) unsalted butter, cut
    into cubes, at cool room temperature

2 GLAZE

1 large (50 g) egg
½ teaspoon (3 g) whole milk
Pinch of salt

225

Making the braided brioche (challah)

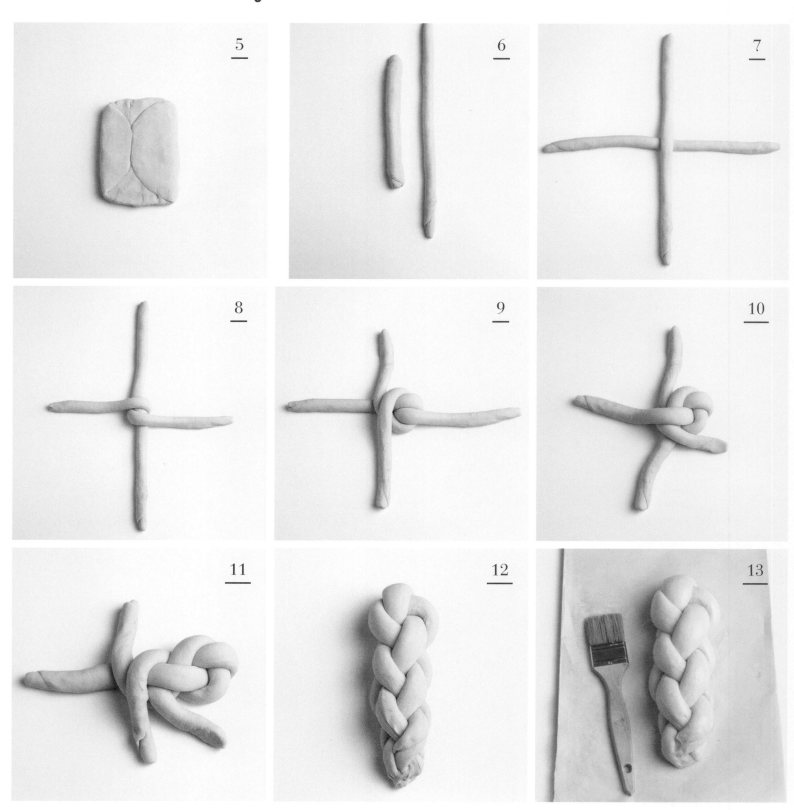

THE DAY BEFORE

1 Place the flour, eggs, sugar, milk, orange blossom water, rum, crumbled yeast, and salt in the bowl of a stand mixer fitted with the dough hook.

2 Knead (see page 32) together the ingredients for 4 minutes on the lowest speed (speed 1), then for at least 8 minutes on medium speed until the dough detaches from the sides of the bowl. (For kneading by hand, see page 30.) During kneading, regularly scrape the dough (see page 282) off the edges of the bowl.

3 Reduce the speed to speed 1 and add the butter, kneading slowly until all of the butter is fully incorporated.

4 Transfer the dough to a floured mixing bowl, cover the bowl with plastic wrap, and let rise for 1 hour at room temperature.

5 Turn the dough (see page 37). Place it back in the mixing bowl, press plastic wrap onto its surface (see page 285), and refrigerate it overnight.

THE SAME DAY

6 Divide the dough into two equal parts using the bench scraper. Roll each piece of dough under the palms of your hands to obtain two uniformly sized elongated strips measuring 24 inches (60 cm) long.

7 Place one piece of dough on top of the center of the second piece and perpendicular to it (forming a "+" sign).

8 Bring the left and right horizontal strands across each other from the center to switch positions.

9 Bring the upper and lower vertical strands across each other from the center to switch positions.

10 Repeat these steps, bringing the left and right strands across and overlapping through the center.

11 Bring the upper and lower vertical strands across again through the center in switched positions.

12 Continue these steps until you reach the ends of the strands. Press the ends of the strands together to seal them.

13 Make the glaze (see page 49) and glaze the loaf using the pastry brush. Let rest for 4 hours on parchment paper in a warm place, 77 to 82°F (25 to 28°C), for the proofing.

14 Preheat the oven to 375°F (190°C) with a baking sheet placed in the oven. Brush again, then slide the brioche onto the hot baking sheet with the parchment paper. Bake for 25 to 30 minutes.

FLAKY BRIOCHE

Understanding

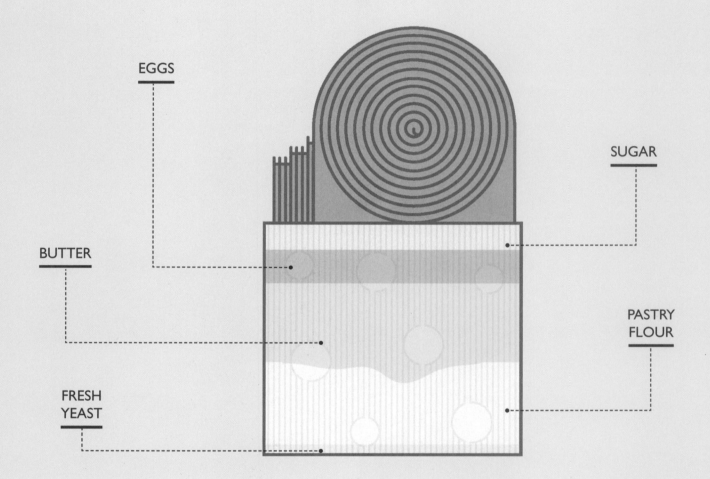

EGGS

SUGAR

BUTTER

PASTRY
FLOUR

FRESH
YEAST

WHAT IT IS

A rolled brioche dough containing a layer of butter that puffs into flaky layers when baked.

CHARACTERISTICS

- Weight: 14 ounces (400 g)
- Size: 4 inches (10 cm)
- Crumb: open
- Crust: flaky

COMPLETION TIME

- Preparation time: 45 minutes
- Fermentation time: 16 hours (30 minutes rising, 12 hours of overnight refrigeration, 1 hour refrigeration, 2½ hours proofing)
- Baking time: 35 minutes

EQUIPMENT

- Stand mixer fitted with the dough hook (optional)
- Rolling pin
- 1 round baking paper mold 6 inches (15 cm) in diameter
- Sieve
- Pastry brush

CHALLENGE

Rolling out the dough. Do not press down too firmly. There must be distinctive layers of butter and dough, otherwise the flaky layers will not develop.

SKILLS TO MASTER

- Kneading (pages 30 and 32)
- Turning (page 37)
- Glazing (page 48)

IT'S READY

When the brioche is well risen and golden.

MAKES 1 BRIOCHE

1 BRIOCHE DOUGH

1½ cups (180 g) pastry flour (or use T45 flour)
2 large (100 g) eggs
¾ packed teaspoon (6 g) fresh yeast
2½ tablespoons (30 g) sugar
½ teaspoon (3 g) salt
6 tablespoons (90 g) unsalted butter, cut
   into cubes, at cool room temperature

2 ROLL-IN BUTTER

7 tablespoons (100 g) unsalted butter, chilled

3 FINISHING

Confectioners' sugar

Making the flaky brioche

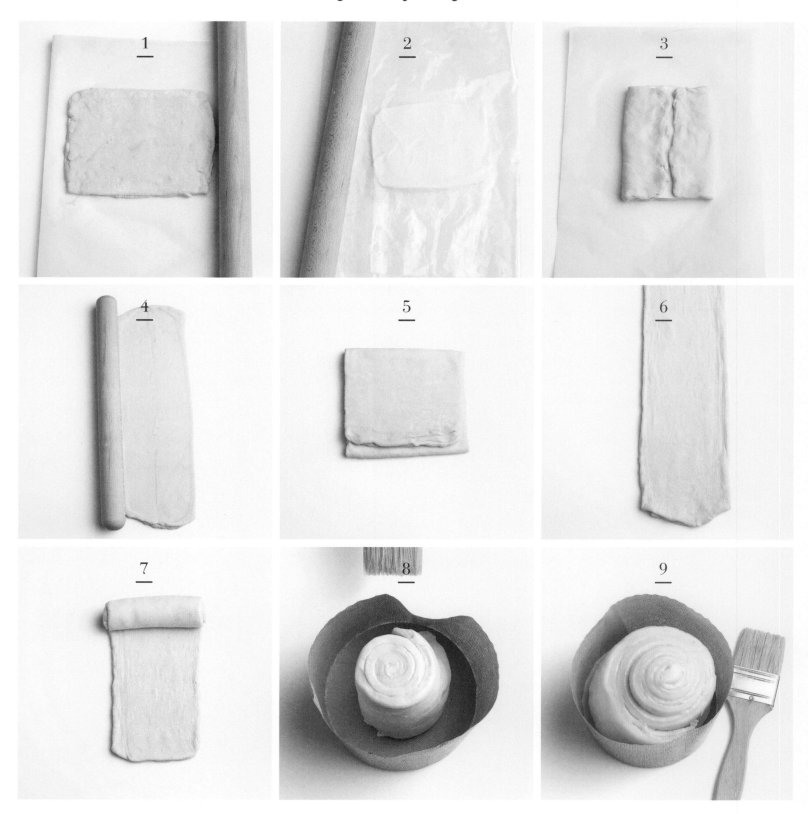

1 Using the technique on page 67, make the brioche dough. Roll out (see page 283) the dough into a 12 × 8-inch (30 × 20 cm) rectangle using the rolling pin.

2 Tamp the roll-in butter with the rolling pin to soften it, and roll it into a 6 × 8-inch (15 × 20 cm) rectangle.

3 Place the butter in the center of the dough. Fold both sides of the dough over onto the butter square so that the seam is in the center and vertical to you.

4 Make a single turn: roll out (see page 283) the dough in front of you with the seam vertical to you using the rolling pin to make a dough that is three times longer than it is wide.

5 Fold the dough over onto itself in thirds (like a wallet), wrap it in plastic wrap, and refrigerate it for 20 minutes. Make another single turn. Roll out the dough vertically with the folded edge vertical to you, fold the dough over onto itself again in thirds, wrap it in plastic wrap, and refrigerate it for an additional 20 minutes. Make one last single turn, wrap the dough in plastic wrap, and refrigerate it for 20 minutes.

6 Roll out (see page 283) the dough vertically using the rolling pin to a width of 4 inches (10 cm) and a thickness of ¼ inch (5 mm) to ⅓ inch (1 cm).

7 Roll up the dough, tightening it well.

8 Place the dough into the mold on its end. Make the glaze (see page 49) and glaze the dough using the pastry brush. Cover the dough with a towel and let rise in a warm place, 77 to 82°F (25 to 28°C), for 2½ hours for the proofing.

9 Preheat the oven to 350°F (180°C). Glaze the dough again and bake for 35 minutes. Let cool, then dust with the confectioners' sugar.

SUGAR TART
(TARTE AU SUCRE)

Understanding

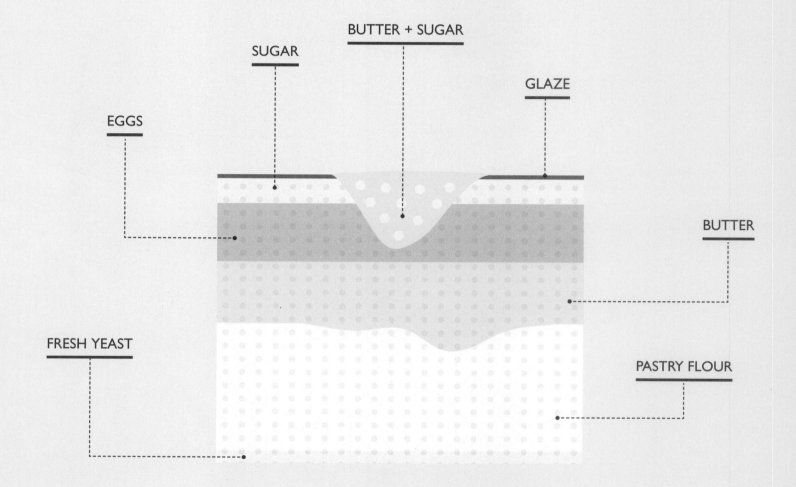

EGGS

SUGAR

BUTTER + SUGAR

GLAZE

BUTTER

FRESH YEAST

PASTRY FLOUR

WHAT IT IS

A brioche dough with dimples filled with butter and sugar after being flattened into a round.

CHARACTERISTICS

–Weight: 1¾ ounces (50 g)
–Size: 6 inches (15 cm) in diameter
–Crumb: tight, soft

COMPLETION TIME

–Preparation time: 50 minutes
–Fermentation time: 16 hours (30 minutes rising, 1 night rising, 30 minutes resting, 2½ hours proofing)
–Baking time: 5 to 7 minutes

EQUIPMENT

–Stand mixer fitted with the dough hook (optional)
–Bench scraper
–Rolling pin
–Sieve
–Pastry brush

CHALLENGE

Rolling the dough.

SKILLS TO MASTER

–Kneading (pages 30 and 32)
–Turning (page 37)
–Preshaping a Round (page 38)
–Glazing (page 48)

USEFUL TIP

Turn the dough slightly and frequently when rolling it out to help maintain the circular shape.

IT'S READY

When the tart is lightly browned.

SHELF LIFE

One or two days, at room temperature.

MAKES 8 LOAVES

BRIOCHE DOUGH

2 cups (245 g) pastry flour (or use T45 flour)
3 large (150 g) eggs
1 packed teaspoon (8 g) fresh yeast
3 tablespoons plus ½ teaspoon (40 g) sugar
¾ teaspoon (5 g) salt
8½ tablespoons (120 g) unsalted
    butter, cut into cubes

GLAZE

1 large (50 g) egg
½ teaspoon (3 g) whole milk
Pinch of salt

TOPPING

5½ tablespoons (80 g) unsalted butter
¼ cup plus 1 tablespoon (65 g)
    granulated or brown sugar

1 Using the technique on page 37, make the brioche dough. Divide the dough into eight pieces using the bench scraper. Preshape each piece into a round (see page 38).

2 Cover the rounds in plastic wrap and let rest in the refrigerator for at least 30 minutes.

3 Roll out (see page 283) each round into a fairly thin round (about ¼ inch/5 mm) using a rolling pin, flouring the work surface and the tops of the rounds.

4 Place the rounds on a baking sheet lined with parchment paper, cover them with a towel, and let rise for 2½ hours in a warm place, 77 to 82°F (25 to 28°C), for the proofing.

5 Preheat the oven to 350°F (180°C). Make the glaze (see page 49) and glaze the rounds using the pastry brush.

6 Using the tips of your index and middle fingers, make 5 indentions in the top of each disk. Place a small (about ½-teaspoon/2 g) piece of butter in each indention and sprinkle the sugar on top (about 2 teaspoons/8 g per brioche).

7 Bake for 5 to 7 minutes.

BRIOCHE BORDELAISE
GARNISHED WITH CANDIED CITRUS

Understanding

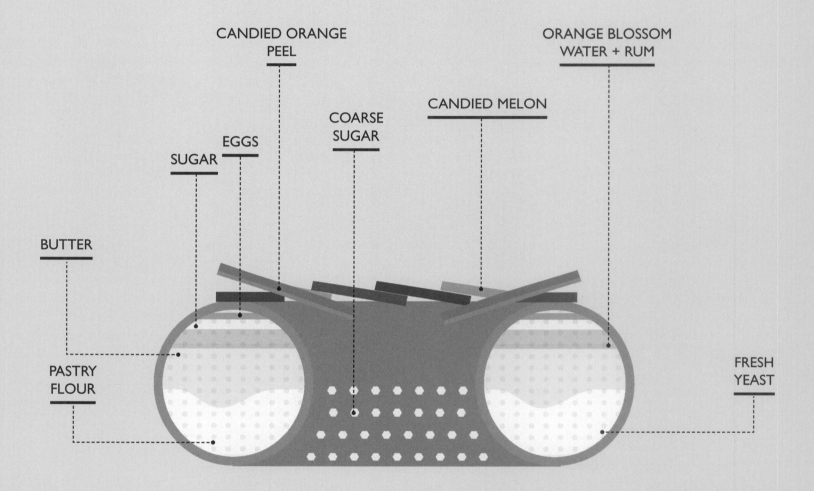

CANDIED ORANGE PEEL

ORANGE BLOSSOM WATER + RUM

CANDIED MELON

COARSE SUGAR

EGGS

SUGAR

BUTTER

PASTRY FLOUR

FRESH YEAST

WHAT IT IS

A brioche dough flavored with orange blossom water and filled with candied fruit, shaped into a ring, and covered with coarse sugar and candied fruit garnishes.

CHARACTERISTICS

−Weight: 1⅛ pounds (500 g)
−Size: 9¾ inches (25 cm) outside diameter
−Crumb: tight, soft

COMPLETION TIME

−Preparation time: 10 minutes
−Fermentation time: 10½ hours
  (30 minutes rising, 1 night refrigerated,
  30 minutes resting, 1½ hours proofing)
−Baking time: 30 minutes

EQUIPMENT

−Stand mixer fitted with the dough hook
−Sieve
−Pastry brush

CHALLENGE

Incorporating the butter into the dough without melting the butter.

SKILLS TO MASTER

−Kneading (pages 30 and 32)
−Turning (page 37)
−Preshaping a Round (page 38)
−Shaping a Couronne (page 46)
−Glazing (page 48)

IT'S READY

When the brioche is golden, and decorated.

SHELF LIFE

Two days, at room temperature.

MAKES 1 BRIOCHE RING

1 tablespoon plus 1 teaspoon (20 g)
    orange blossom water
2 teaspoons (10 g) rum
1⅔ cups (200 g) pastry flour (or use T45 flour)
2 large (100 g) eggs
⅔ teaspoon (4 g) salt
¾ packed teaspoon (6 g) fresh yeast
1 tablespoon plus ½ teaspoon (15 g) sugar
8½ tablespoons (120 g) unsalted
    butter, cut into cubes
½ cup (45 g) roughly chopped orange peel
2½ teaspoons (5 g) grated lemon zest

GLAZE

1 large (50 g) egg

½ teaspoon (3 g) whole milk
Pinch of salt

FINISHING

¼ cup (50 g) coarse sugar
2 tablespoons (20 g) candied orange peel
2 tablespoons (20 g) candied melon peel

1   Refrigerate the ingredients 2 days before making
the brioche. Before making the dough, bring the cubes
of butter to cool room temperature (see page 66). Using
the technique on page 67, make the brioche dough,
combining the orange blossom water and the rum with
the flour. At the end of the kneading time, add the
orange peel and lemon zest and knead briefly to fully
incorporate. Let rise for 30 minutes, then turn the
dough (see page 37). Cover the dough with plastic wrap
and refrigerate it overnight.

2   Preshape the dough into a round (see page 38)
and refrigerate it for 30 minutes to rest. Dip your
index finger into flour and pierce the center of
the dough by pressing your finger all the way
through it until you touch the work surface.

3   Shape the dough into a couronne (see page 46) to
obtain an inside diameter of about 3 inches (8 cm).

4   Place the ring on parchment paper. Make the
glaze (see page 49) and glaze the brioche using the
pastry brush. Let stand for 1½ hours in a warm
place, 77 to 82°F (25 to 28°C), for the proofing.

5   Glaze the ring again. Sprinkle the top edge with
the coarse sugar and place the candied fruits on top.
Preheat the oven to 500°F (260°C) with a baking sheet
placed in the oven. Slide the ring onto the hot baking
sheet with the parchment paper. Bake for 30 minutes.

CREAM-FILLED
BRIOCHE CAKE
(TARTE TROPÉZIENNE)

Understanding

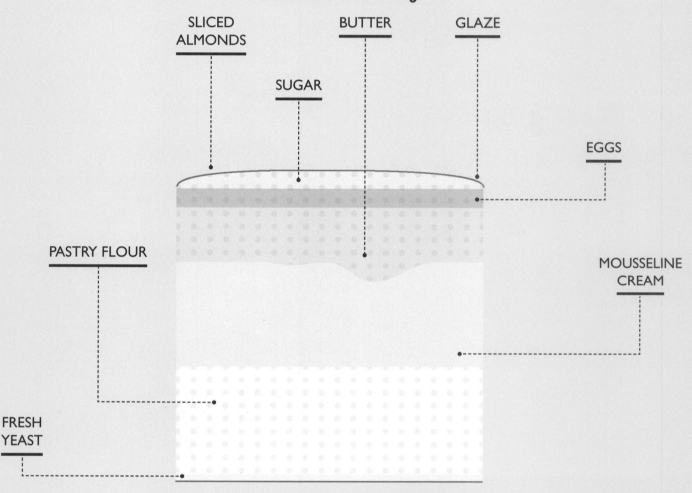

SLICED ALMONDS

BUTTER

GLAZE

SUGAR

EGGS

PASTRY FLOUR

MOUSSELINE CREAM

FRESH YEAST

WHAT IT IS

A brioche filled with a mousseline cream, flavored with orange blossom water and vanilla, and covered with sliced almonds.

CHARACTERISTICS

–Weight: 1¾ pounds (800 g)
–Size: 9½ inches (24 cm) in diameter
–Crumb: tight, soft

COMPLETION TIME

–Preparation time: 25 minutes
–Fermentation time: 14 hours (30 minutes rising, 1 night rising, 1½ hours proofing)
–Baking time: 35 minutes

EQUIPMENT

–Stand mixer fitted with the dough hook (optional)
–Rolling pin
–Pastry ring 9½ inches (24 cm) in diameter
–Pastry brush
–Icing spatula

SKILLS TO MASTER

–Kneading (pages 30 and 32)
–Turning (page 37)
–Shaping a Boule (page 42)
–Glazing (page 48)
–Whisking until Lightened (page 284)

IT'S READY

When the brioche has a golden brown color and when the mousseline cream is creamy and very well lightened.

SHELF LIFE

Two to three days, chilled.

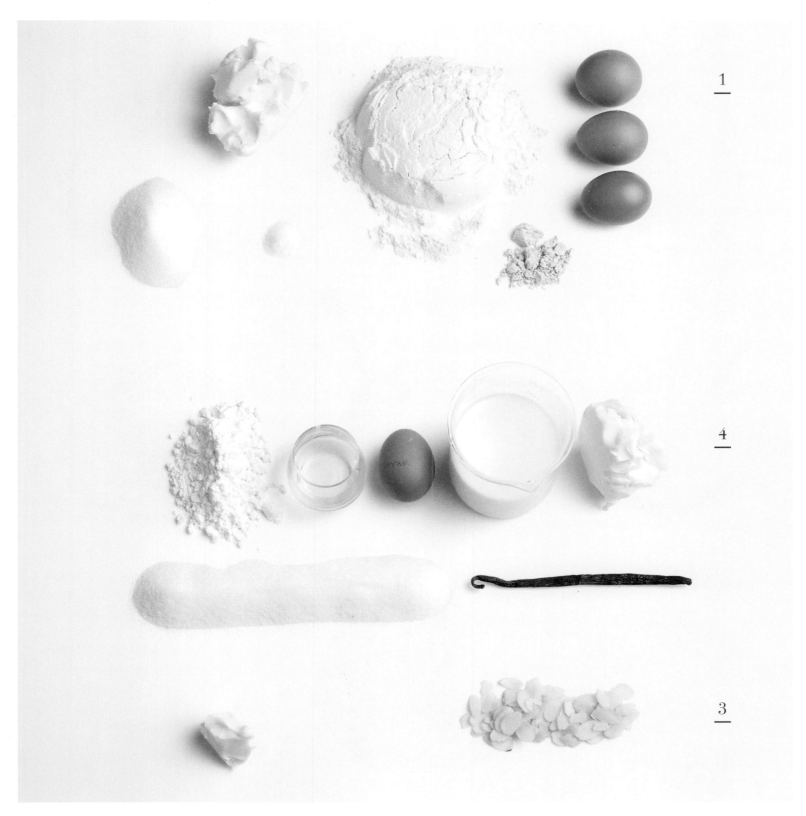

SERVES 8

1 BRIOCHE DOUGH

1¾ cups plus 1 tablespoon (220 g)
    pastry flour (or use T45 flour)
3 large (150 g) eggs
⅞ packed teaspoon (7 g) fresh yeast
2 tablespoons plus 2½ teaspoons (35 g) sugar
⅔ teaspoon (4 g) salt
7 tablespoons plus 4 teaspoons (120 g)
    Beurre en Pommade (page 284)

2 GLAZE

1 large (50 g) egg
½ teaspoon (3 g) whole milk
Pinch of salt

3 TOPPING

1 tablespoon (10 g) sliced almonds

4 MOUSSELINE CREAM

1 large (50 g) egg
¼ cup plus 2 tablespoons (80 g) sugar
¼ cup (25 g) cornstarch
2 teaspoons (10 g) orange blossom water
1 cup plus 2 teaspoons (250 g) whole milk
½ vanilla bean
9 tablespoons (125 g) unsalted butter

1 Using the technique on page 67, make the brioche dough, reserving 2 teaspoons (10 g) beurre en pommade for the molds. The next day, shape the dough into a boule (see page 42). Roll it out to the diameter of the pastry ring while maintaining a round shape. Using a pastry brush, grease the mold with the remaining 2 teaspoons (10 g) beurre en pommade. Place the dough in the pastry ring on a baking sheet lined with parchment paper.

2 Make the glaze (see page 49) and glaze the dough using the pastry brush. Let rest for 1½ hours in a warm place, 77 to 82°F (25 to 28°C), for the proofing.

3 Preheat the oven to 325°F (160°C). Glaze the dough again, then sprinkle it with the sliced almonds. Bake for 35 minutes. Let cool.

4 Make the mousseline cream: In a bowl, combine the egg, sugar, cornstarch, and orange blossom water.

5 In a saucepan, bring the milk to a boil over low heat with the vanilla bean that has been split lengthwise in half and its seeds scraped into the cream. Whisk the mixture into the mixing bowl, then pour the entire mixture back into the saucepan. Heat for 2 minutes while whisking continuously (the cream thickens very quickly), then remove the pan from the heat.

6 Add half the butter to the hot mixture and whisk to combine.

7 Transfer the cream to another bowl then press plastic wrap onto its surface (see page 285) to prevent a skin from forming. Let cool to room temperature.

8 Add the remaining butter to the cream, then beat the cream in the bowl of a stand mixer fitted with the paddle until the cream is lightened in color (see page 284).

9 Cut the brioche horizontally in half and spread the cream over the bottom portion using an icing spatula. Replace the top.

KUGELHOPF

Understanding

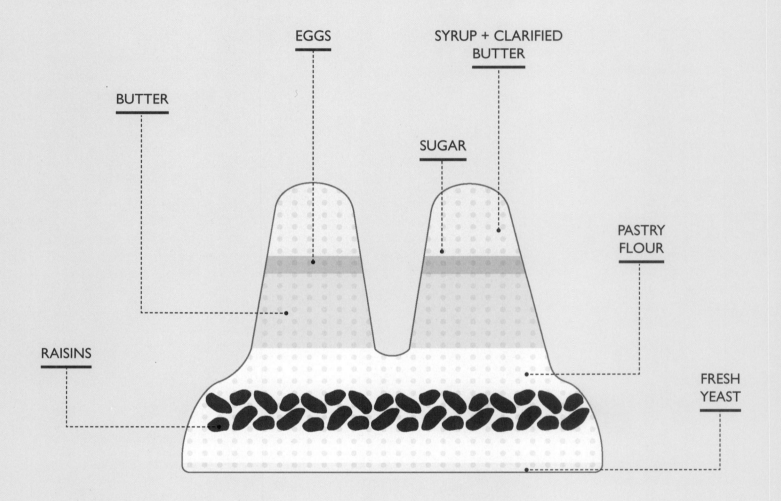

BUTTER

EGGS

SYRUP + CLARIFIED BUTTER

SUGAR

PASTRY FLOUR

RAISINS

FRESH YEAST

WHAT IT IS
A brioche-style cake studded with raisins, baked in a kugelhopf mold, soaked in syrup and clarified butter, then dusted with confectioners' sugar.

CHARACTERISTICS
–Weight: 10½ ounces (300 g)
–Size: 6 inches (15 cm) in diameter
–Crumb: tight

EQUIPMENT
–Stand mixer fitted with the dough hook
–Pastry brush
–Kugelhopf mold 6 inches (15 cm) in diameter

COMPLETION TIME
–Preparation time: 1 hour
–Fermentation time: 1 night + 3½ hours
  (30 minutes rising, 30 minutes of refrigeration, 2½ hours proofing)
–Baking time: 30 minutes

SKILLS TO MASTER
–Kneading (page 32)
–Turning (page 37)
–Shaping a Boule (page 42)

IT'S READY
As soon as the kugelhopf is lightly browned.

SHELF LIFE
Two to three days, wrapped in plastic wrap.

WHY IS THE KUGELHOPF FIRST DUNKED IN THE SYRUP THEN IN THE CLARIFIED BUTTER?

Soaking contributes flavor and moistness. The soaking occurs in two steps because sugar does not dissolve in fat. If you combine the butter and sugar to make a single soaking solution, the sugar will not absorb well into the loaf and could therefore leave an unpleasant graininess on the surface.

1

2

3

MAKES 1 (10½ OUNCE/300 G) KUGELHOPF, OR 2 MINI KUGELHOPF

1 DOUGH

¼ cup (30 g) raisins
1 cup plus 2 tablespoons (140 g) pastry
    flour (or use T45 flour)
2 large (100 g) eggs
½ packed teaspoon (4 g) fresh yeast
1½ tablespoons (20 g) sugar
½ teaspoon (3 g) salt
5 tablespoons (70 g) unsalted
    butter, cut into cubes
2 teaspoons (10 g) Beurre en Pommade
    (page 284), for greasing the mold

2 SYRUP

3½ tablespoons (50 g) water
¼ cup (50 g) sugar

3 FINISHING

1 tablespoon plus 1 teaspoon
    (20 g) unsalted butter
1½ tablespoons (10 g) confectioners' sugar

Making the kugelhopf

<u>2</u>

<u>4</u>

<u>5</u>

<u>6</u>

<u>9</u>

<u>10</u>

THE DAY BEFORE

1   Soak the raisins in warm water. Place the rest of the ingredients in the refrigerator.

2   Using the technique on page 67, make the brioche dough. At the end of the kneading time, add the drained raisins. Let rest for 30 minutes on a floured work surface, covered with a towel.

3   Turn the dough (see page 37). Place the dough in a mixing bowl, press plastic wrap onto its surface (see page 285) and let rest in the refrigerator overnight.

THE SAME DAY

4   Roll the dough over onto itself and shape it into a boule (see page 42). Refrigerate for 30 minutes in the mixing bowl, with plastic wrap pressed onto its surface.

5   Grease the kugelhopf mold with the beurre en pommade using the pastry brush. Form a hole in the center of the dough ball by pressing through the center with both thumbs. Invert the dough and place it in the bottom of the kugelhopf mold, pressing firmly with your fingers so that it fits snugly into the fluted sections of the mold.

6   Cover the mold with a towel and let rest for 2 to 2½ hours in a warm place, 77 to 82°F (25 to 28°C), for the proofing.

7   Preheat the oven to 350°F (180°C) and bake for 30 minutes. Unmold, and let cool on a rack.

8   Clarify the butter (see page 284).

9   Make the syrup: bring the water and sugar to a boil in a saucepan and remove it from the heat. Dip the kugelhopf into the syrup for 5 to 10 seconds, rotating it to evenly absorb the syrup.

10   Drain the kugelhopf for 30 seconds, then dip it into the clarified butter for 5 to 10 seconds.

11   Drain the kugelhopf for 30 seconds, let stand for 5 to 10 minutes for the butter to solidify, then dust the top with confectioners' sugar.

PANETTONE

Understanding

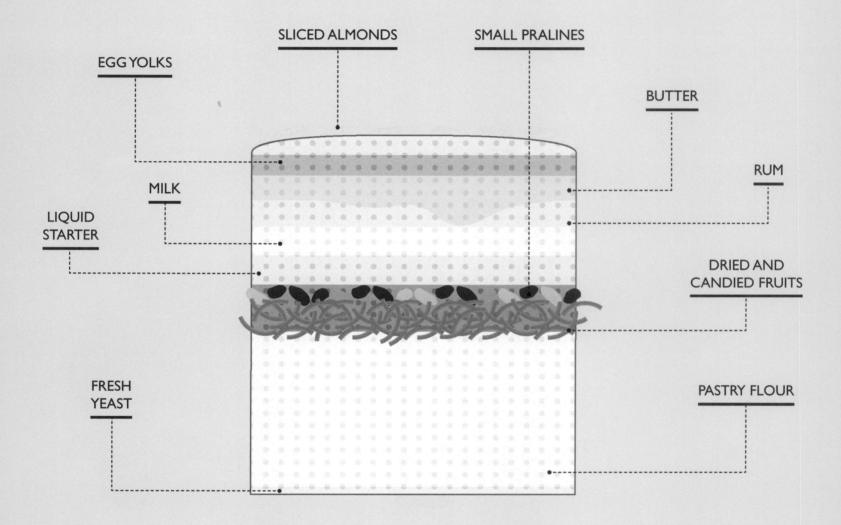

EGG YOLKS

SLICED ALMONDS

SMALL PRALINES

BUTTER

MILK

RUM

LIQUID STARTER

DRIED AND CANDIED FRUITS

FRESH YEAST

PASTRY FLOUR

WHAT IT IS

An Italian brioche-style cake, filled with candied fruits and raisins, and flavored with rum.

CHARACTERISTICS

–Weight: 1⅛ pounds (500 g)
–Size: 8 × 9¾ inches (20 × 25 cm)
–Crumb: tight, moist

EQUIPMENT

–Stand mixer fitted with the dough hook (optional)
–Large panettone mold (1⅓-pound/600 g capacity)
–Pastry bag

COMPLETION TIME

–Preparation time: 45 minutes
–Fermentation time: 4 hours (1 hour rising, 3 hours proofing)
–Resting time: 2 nights
–Baking time: 45 minutes

SKILLS TO MASTER

–Kneading (pages 30 and 32)
–Turning (page 37)
–Shaping a Boule (page 42)

VARIATION

Small panettones. Shape the dough into boules about 3 ounces (80 g) each and bake for 25 minutes.

OPTION WITHOUT A STARTER

For a dough that does not use a liquid starter add an additional ⅝ packed teaspoon (5 g) of fresh yeast and 1 tablespoon plus 1 teaspoon (20 g) of water.

USEFUL TIP

If the fruits have not absorbed all of the rum, drain the excess rum before adding them to the dough.

IT'S READY

When the panettone is well browned.

SHELF LIFE

One week, wrapped well in plastic wrap.

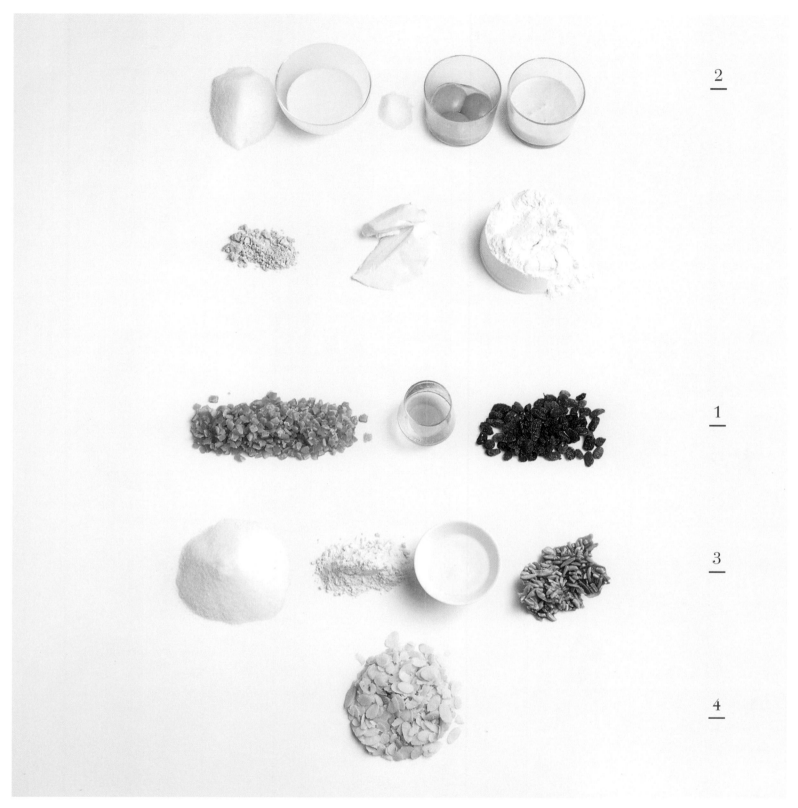

MAKES 1 PANETTONE

1 FRUITS

¼ cup (35 g) raisins
⅓ cup (70 g) candied orange peel
1 tablespoon (15 g) rum

2 DOUGH

1½ cups (180 g) pastry flour (or use T45 flour)
3 tablespoons plus 1 teaspoon (50 g) whole milk
3 tablespoons plus ½ teaspoon (40 g) sugar
3⅛ packed teaspoons (25 g) fresh yeast
1¾ ounces (50 g) Liquid Starter (page 20)
3 large (54 g) egg yolks
½ teaspoon (3 g) salt
4 tablespoons plus 1 teaspoon (60 g)
    unsalted butter, cut into cubes

3 PANETTONE TOPPING

¼ cup plus 3 tablespoons (90 g) sugar
¼ cup (25 g) small pralines
2 tablespoons (15 g) pastry flour (or use T45 flour)
1 large (32 g) egg white

4 FINISHING

⅓ cup (30 g) sliced almonds

Making the panettone

TWO DAYS BEFORE

1 Place the raisins, candied orange peel, and rum in a container and let macerate overnight.

THE DAY BEFORE

2 Knead (see page 32) together the flour, milk, sugar, crumbled yeast, starter, egg yolks, and salt in the bowl of a stand mixer fitted with the dough hook for 6 minutes on medium speed. Knead in the butter at the same speed until the dough detaches from the sides of the bowl. (For kneading by hand, see page 30.)

3 Add the drained macerated fruit and knead on speed 1 until fully incorporated.

4 Transfer the dough to a mixing bowl, cover the bowl with plastic wrap, and let rise for 1 hour in a warm place, 77 to 82°F (25 to 28°C).

5 Turn the dough (see page 37). Place the dough back in the mixing bowl, press plastic wrap onto its surface (see page 285), and let rest in the refrigerator overnight.

THE SAME DAY

6 Shape the dough into a boule (see page 42) and place it in the panettone mold.

7 Let rest for 3 hours, covered with a towel, in a warm place, 77 to 82°F (25 to 28°C), for the proofing.

8 Preheat the oven to 350°F (180°C). Make the panettone topping: Combine the sugar, small pralines, and flour in a bowl. Add the egg white and stir until the mixture is smooth.

9 Spoon the panettone topping onto the top of the dough. Sprinkle with the sliced almonds and bake for 45 minutes.

PISTACHIO-APRICOT
TART

Understanding

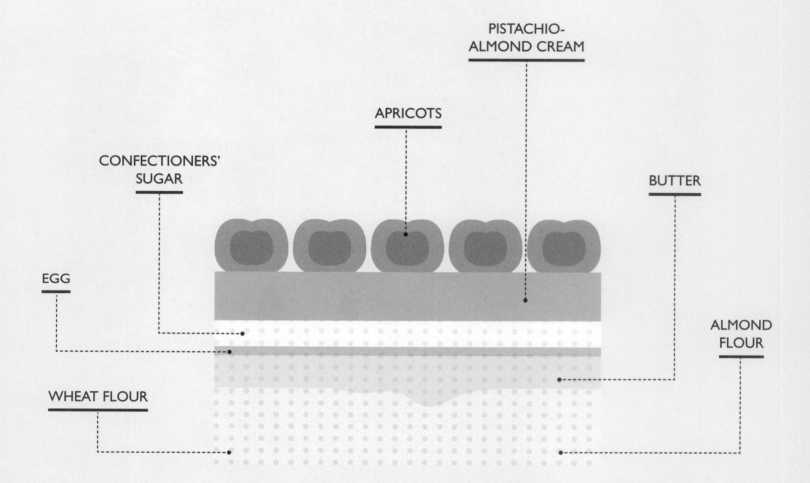

PISTACHIO-
ALMOND CREAM

APRICOTS

CONFECTIONERS'
SUGAR

BUTTER

EGG

ALMOND
FLOUR

WHEAT FLOUR

WHAT IT IS
A sweet pastry crust (*pâte sucrée*) filled with a pistachio-almond cream and topped with wedges of apricot.

COMPLETION TIME
– Preparation time: 1 hour
– Refrigeration time: 4 hours
– Baking time: 35 to 40 minutes

EQUIPMENT
– Stand mixer fitted with the paddle and dough hook
– Whisk
– Rolling pin
– Pastry ring 8 inches (20 cm) in diameter
– Pastry bag

CHALLENGES
– Shaping.
– Baking.

SKILLS TO MASTER
– Kneading (pages 30 and 32)
– Whisking until Lightened (page 284)
– Lining a Pan or Pastry Ring (page 283)

USEFUL TIP
If using drained apricot halves in syrup, drain them well before using.

IT'S READY
When the ends of the apricots begin to brown and the crust is golden.

SHELF LIFE
Two to three days, in the refrigerator.

WHAT HAPPENS WHEN
ALMOND CREAM IS BAKED?
Egg proteins coagulate and the starch in the flour thickens. The cream swells and becomes creamier.

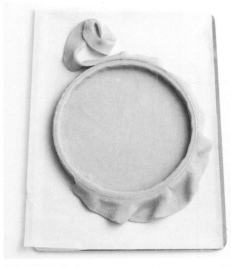

SERVES 6

SWEET PASTRY DOUGH (PÂTE SUCRÉE)

11 tablespoons (155 g) unsalted butter
1 cup (100 g) confectioners' sugar
¼ cup (30 g) almond flour
2 cups minus 1 tablespoon (260 g) high-protein all-purpose flour (or use bread flour or T65 flour)
⅛ teaspoon (1 g) salt
1 large (50 g) egg

PISTACHIO-ALMOND CREAM

3½ tablespoons (50 g) unsalted butter
¼ cup (50 g) sugar
½ cup minus 1 tablespoon (50 g) almond flour
½ teaspoon (5 g) cornstarch
1 large (50 g) egg
1 tablespoon (20 g) pistachio paste

TOPPING

10 fresh apricots or 20 apricot halves in syrup

1 Using the technique on page 75, make the sweet pastry dough and refrigerate it for 2 hours.

2 Using the technique on page 79, make the almond cream. Whisk in the pistachio paste and refrigerate it for 2 hours.

3 Cut the apricots into quarters.

4 Roll out (see page 283) the dough to ⅛ inch (3 mm) thick, line the pastry ring (see page 283) with the dough and place it on a baking sheet lined with parchment paper.

5 Pipe the pistachio-almond cream over the bottom of the tart to a depth of ⅓ inch (1 cm) using the pastry bag.

6 Arrange the apricots on top of the cream in concentric circles.

7 Preheat the oven to 375°F (190°C) and bake for 35 to 40 minutes.

FLAN TART
(FLAN PÂTISSIER)

Understanding

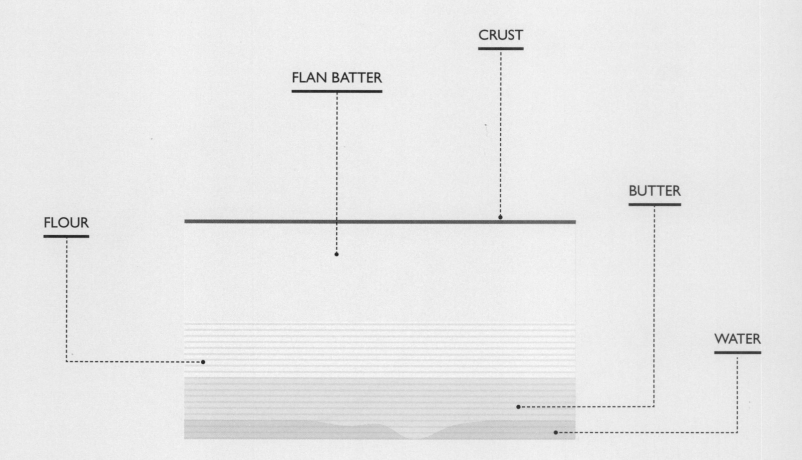

CRUST

FLAN BATTER

BUTTER

FLOUR

WATER

WHAT IT IS

An inverse puff pastry crust filled with a cooked cream made from eggs, milk, sugar, and cornstarch.

COMPLETION TIME

– Preparation time: 1 hour
– Refrigeration time: 12 hours
– Baking time: 35 to 40 minutes

EQUIPMENT

– Stand mixer fitted with the paddle and dough hook

– Pastry ring 10¼ inches (26 cm) in diameter and 1 inch (3 cm) in height
– Pastry brush
– Rolling pin

VARIATIONS

– Coconut flan tart: add 2 cups (200 g) grated coconut.
– Apricot flan tart: place canned syrup-packed apricot halves in the bottom of the pan, then pour the cream over the top.

CHALLENGE

Making the cream.

SKILLS TO MASTER

– Kneading (pages 30 and 32)
– Lining a Pan or Pastry Ring (page 283)
– Whisking until Lightened (page 284)

USEFUL TIP

Let the cooked cream cool completely before baking in order to obtain a nice crust over the top that doesn't crack.

IT'S READY

When the flan is very golden brown, with some dark spots on top of the cream.

SHELF LIFE

Two days, in the refrigerator.

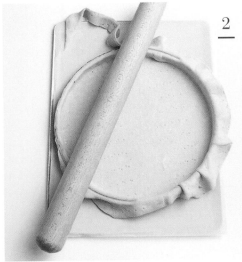

SERVES 10

INVERSE PUFF PASTRY

BEURRE MANIÉ

7 tablespoons (100 g) unsalted butter, cut into cubes, softened
¼ cup plus 1 tablespoon (40 g) high-protein all-purpose flour (or use bread flour or T65 flour)

DOUGH LAYER (DÉTREMPE)

⅔ cup (90 g) high-protein all-purpose flour (or use bread flour or T65 flour)
¾ teaspoon (5 g) salt
2½ tablespoons (40 g) cold water
2 tablespoons (30 g) Beurre en Pommade (page 284)

¼ teaspoon (1 g) white vinegar

RING MOLD

2 tablespoons (10 g) Beurre en Pommade (page 284)

FLAN BATTER

3 large (150 g) eggs
1 cup (200 g) sugar
⅔ cup plus 2 tablespoons (80 g) cornstarch
4 cups (1 liter) whole milk

1   Using the technique on page 69, make the inverse puff pastry. Roll out the dough to ¹⁄₁₀ inch (2 mm) thick.

2   Preheat the oven to 350°F (180°C). Grease the ring mold with the beurre en pommade using the pastry brush. Line the ring (see page 283) with the puff pastry and place it on a baking sheet lined with parchment paper. Place the crust in the refrigerator.

3   Make the flan batter: whisk together the eggs and sugar until lightened. Add the cornstarch and whisk to combine.

4   Bring the milk to a boil. Whisk one-third of the hot milk into the egg-sugar mixture, then pour the mixture back into the saucepan.

5   Whisk continuously for 1 minute over the heat.

6   Pour the batter into the lined ring. Let cool to room temperature, then bake for 35 to 40 minutes. Let cool for 1½ hours.

SPICED LOAF CAKE
(PAIN D'ÉPICE)

Understanding

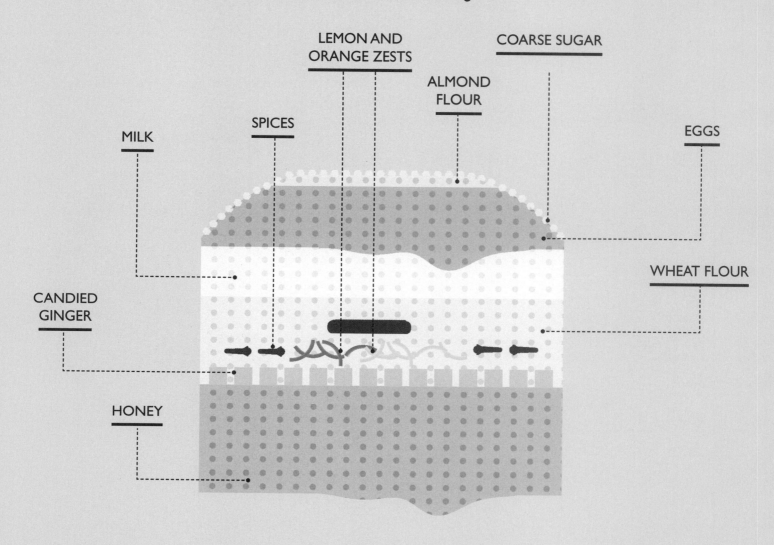

MILK

SPICES

LEMON AND
ORANGE ZESTS

ALMOND
FLOUR

COARSE SUGAR

EGGS

CANDIED
GINGER

WHEAT FLOUR

HONEY

WHAT IT IS

A loaf cake very rich in honey, embellished with spices and citrus zest.

COMPLETION TIME

– Preparation time: 30 minutes
– Baking time: 45 minutes

EQUIPMENT

– One 8-inch (20 cm) loaf pan
– Wooden spoon
– Strainer
– Pastry brush

CHALLENGE

Do not boil the milk-honey mixture. As soon as small bubbles appear, immediately remove the pan from the heat.

USEFUL TIPS

– After unmolding, wrap the loaf in plastic wrap to keep it moist.
– If, at the time of adding the honey-milk mixture to the batter, the temperature of the mixture is lower than 140°F (60°C), rewarm it over low heat.

IT'S READY

When the tip of a knife inserted into the center comes out clean.

SHELF LIFE

One week, wrapped in plastic wrap.

WHY MUST THE MILK NOT BE BOILED?

To avoid burning the spices when they are infused, which can cause them to release unpleasant flavors.

MAKES 1 LOAF

½ cup (170 g) honey
⅓ cup (80 g) whole milk
½ teaspoon (1 g) ground ginger
½ teaspoon (1 g) ground cinnamon
½ teaspoon (1 g) cloves
1 cup (140 g) high-protein all-purpose flour
  (or use bread flour or T65 flour)
2 tablespoons (15 g) almond flour
1¼ teaspoons (5 g) baking soda
⅛ teaspoon (1 g) salt
2 large (100 g) eggs
1½ tablespoons (3 g) orange zest
1½ tablespoons (3 g) lemon zest
2½ tablespoons (28 g) diced candied ginger

FINISHING

½ cup (100 g) coarse sugar

1 Heat the honey and milk in a saucepan over low heat; remove the mixture from the heat before it begins to boil. Add the ginger, cinnamon, and cloves and let steep for 15 minutes.

2 Strain through a sieve (see page 285) and discard the cloves. Let cool.

3 Preheat the oven to 300°F (150°C). Sift together the wheat flour, almond flour, and baking soda into a mixing bowl. Add the salt, eggs, and orange and lemon zests and stir to combine using the wooden spoon.

4 Carefully pour in the infused milk mixture while stirring to obtain a smooth mixture. Add the candied ginger and stir with the wooden spoon.

5 Line the loaf pan with parchment paper and sprinkle half the coarse sugar on top.

6 Scrape the batter into the mold, sprinkle the top with the remaining sugar, and bake for 45 minutes. Let cool, then unmold.

FRUIT CAKE

Understanding

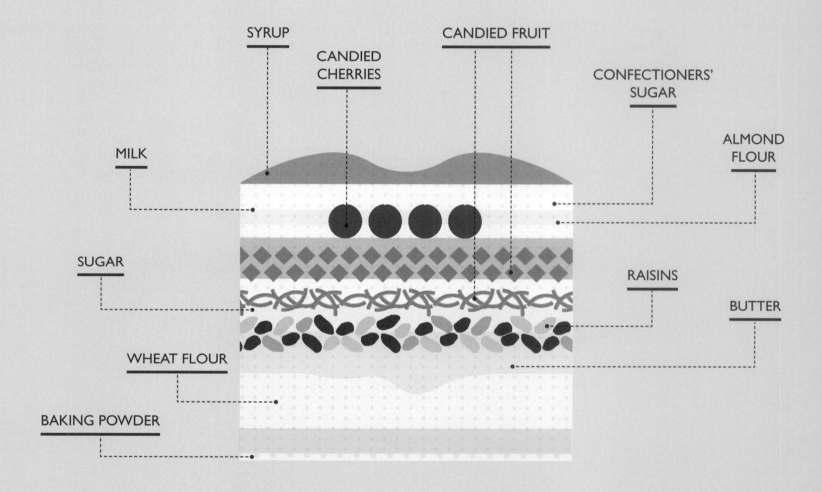

SYRUP

CANDIED
CHERRIES

CANDIED FRUIT

CONFECTIONERS'
SUGAR

MILK

ALMOND
FLOUR

SUGAR

RAISINS

BUTTER

WHEAT FLOUR

BAKING POWDER

WHAT IT IS
A loaf cake filled with candied fruits and soaked with syrup after baking.

COMPLETION TIME
–Preparation time: 30 minutes
–Baking time: 45 minutes

EQUIPMENT
–One 8-inch (20 cm) loaf pan
–Wooden spoon
–Sifter
–Pastry brush

CHALLENGE
Preventing the candied fruits from falling to the bottom of the batter during baking.

SKILLS TO MASTER
Creaming (page 284)

USEFUL TIP
After unmolding, wrap the cake in plastic wrap to keep it moist.

IT'S READY
When the tip of a knife inserted into the center comes out clean.

SHELF LIFE
One week, wrapped in plastic wrap.

WHY SHOULD YOU REHYDRATE THE RAISINS BEFORE BAKING?
To prevent them from absorbing all the water from the batter, which is necessary for the starch it contains to cook.

1

2

4

MAKES I LOAF

1 BATTER

¼ cup (50 g) granulated sugar
½ cup (50 g) confectioners' sugar
5½ tablespoons (80 g) Beurre en
    Pommade (page 284)
2 large (100 g) eggs
1 tablespoon (15 g) whole milk
⅔ cup (90 g) high-protein all-purpose flour
    (or use bread flour or T65 flour)
3 tablespoons (20 g) almond flour
1¼ teaspoons (5 g) baking powder

2 FRUIT

¼ cup plus 3 tablespoons (65 g) raisins
⅓ cup (50 g) diced candied fruits
1 tablespoon (10 g) candied cherries
1½ tablespoons (15 g) candied orange peel

3 PAN

2 teaspoons (10 g) Beurre en
    Pommade (page 284)

4 SYRUP

2½ tablespoons (40 g) water
¼ cup (50 g) sugar
3 tablespoons (40 g) dark rum

Making the fruit cake

1   Place the raisins in a saucepan, cover them with water, and bring to a boil. Remove the pan from the heat and let soak several minutes in the water until the raisins have absorbed a great deal of liquid and are swollen. Drain on paper towels and let cool.

2   Cream together the granulated and confectioners' sugars and beurre en pommade using the large spatula or in a stand mixer fitted with the paddle.

3   Add the eggs and beat until the mixture is smooth. Add the milk and beat to combine.

4   Sift together the wheat and almond flours with the baking powder. Incorporate two-thirds of this mixture into the previous mixture.

5   Place the candied fruits and the cooled drained raisins together in a separate mixing bowl. Add the remaining one-third of the flour mixture and combine well so that all the fruits are generously coated.

6   Scrape the fruit-flour mixture into the batter and stir gently to combine.

7   Grease the loaf pan with the beurre en pommade using the pastry brush. Scrape the batter into the pan. Bake for 45 minutes. Unmold and let cool completely.

8   Make the syrup: bring the water and sugar to a boil in a saucepan and remove it from the heat. Add the rum, stir to combine, and let cool. Soak the cake with the warm syrup.

GENOA CAKE
(PAIN DE GÊNES)

Understanding

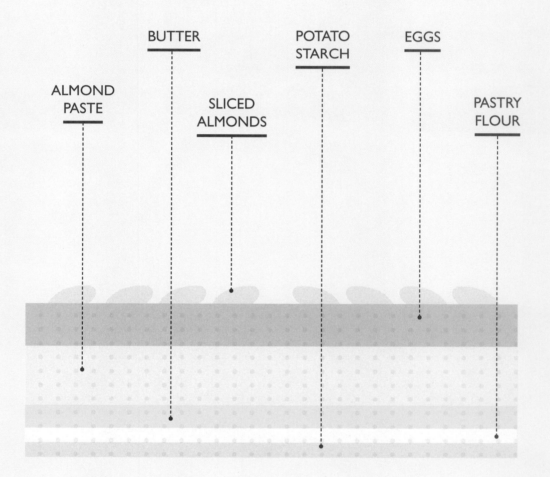

ALMOND
PASTE

BUTTER

SLICED
ALMONDS

POTATO
STARCH

EGGS

PASTRY
FLOUR

WHAT IT IS
A very moist cake made with almond paste.

COMPLETION TIME
–Preparation time: 25 minutes
–Baking time: 25 minutes

EQUIPMENT
–Cake pan measuring 5½ inches (14 cm)
  in diameter and 2 inches (5 cm) deep
–Stand mixer fitted with the
  paddle and whisk
–Sifter
–Wooden spoon
–Pastry brush

TRADITIONAL USE
As a sponge base for a dessert

CHALLENGE
Baking. If it is overbaked, it loses moistness.

USEFUL TIP
Use Beurre en Pommade (page 284) so
that the sliced almonds stick to the pan.

IT'S READY
When the cake is pale golden.

SHELF LIFE
Two to three days.

CAN YOU REPLACE THE
ALMOND PASTE WITH
ALMOND FLOUR?
*With almond flour, the cake will be less
sweet (because almond paste contains
a great deal of sugar). Also, the gluten
network will form more easily, giving this
cake a more open crumb and making
it drier than a typical cake layer.*

MAKES I CAKE

1 GENOA CAKE BATTER

4 tablespoons plus 1 teaspoon
(60 g) unsalted butter
7 ounces (200 g) almond paste
(50 percent almonds)
3 large (150 g) eggs
2½ tablespoons (20 g) pastry
flour (or use T45 flour)
2 tablespoons (20 g) potato starch

2 PAN

2 teaspoons (10 g) Beurre en
Pommade (page 284)
1 tablespoon (10 g) sliced almonds

Making the Genoa cake

3A

3B

4

5

6

7

1 Melt the butter in a saucepan over low heat; let cool.

2 Place the almond paste in the bowl of a stand mixer fitted with the paddle. Add 2 eggs, one at a time, and beat on medium speed after each addition; the dough should be soft and smooth.

3 Add the remaining egg, attach the whisk to the mixer, then beat for about 5 minutes until a smooth batter falls like a ribbon from the whisk when the whisk is raised.

4 Sift the flour then potato starch into the batter; gently combine using the wooden spoon.

5 Add the cooled melted butter and gently combine using the wooden spoon.

6 Preheat the oven to 300°F (150°C). Grease the pan with the beurre en pommade using the pastry brush. Sprinkle the sliced almonds into the pan to coat the bottom and sides; they should stick to the pan in the butter. Invert the pan and lightly tap it to release any excess almond pieces.

7 Scrape the batter into the pan and bake for 25 minutes. Let cool for 10 minutes, then unmold.

SABLÉS

Understanding

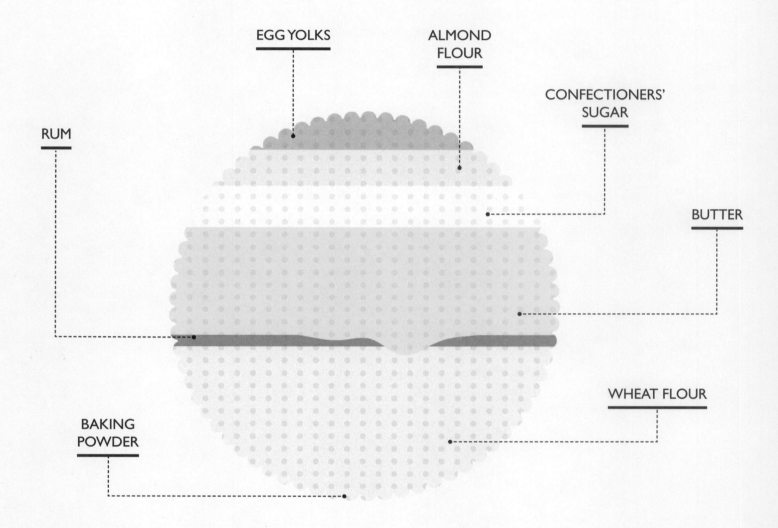

EGG YOLKS

ALMOND FLOUR

CONFECTIONERS' SUGAR

RUM

BUTTER

WHEAT FLOUR

BAKING POWDER

WHAT IT IS
Tender and crumbly cookies rich in butter.

COMPLETION TIME
–Preparation time: 20 minutes
–Refrigeration time: 1 hour
–Baking time: 20 minutes

EQUIPMENT
–Stand mixer fitted with the paddle
–Rolling pin
–Fluted cookie cutter 5 inches
  (13 cm) in diameter
–Sieve
–Pastry brush

VARIATIONS
Chocolate chips, sliced almonds

CHALLENGE
Not overcooking the egg yolk.

SKILL TO MASTER
Glazing (page 48)

USEFUL TIP
When removing the sablés from
the oven they should still be soft,
but will firm up once cooled.

IT'S READY
When the cookies are golden brown.

SHELF LIFE
Two to three days, in an airtight container.

WHY MUST YOU COOK THE EGG YOLKS FIRST?

To get the desired sandy texture. When the yolks are cooked, certain egg proteins coagulate. Once incorporated into the dough, they limit the formation of the gluten network. In other words, the less tight the gluten strands in the dough, the more sandy and crumbly the texture of the sablés will be after baking. Conversely, the tighter the gluten strands, the more compact the texture of the sablés will be.

MAKES 4 SABLÉS

2 large (36 g) egg yolks
1⅔ cups (225 g) high-protein all-purpose flour (or use bread flour or T65 flour)
14 tablespoons plus 2½ teaspoons (210 g) unsalted butter
¾ cup (75 g) confectioners' sugar
⅓ cup (40 g) almond flour
2½ teaspoons (11 g) rum
¼ teaspoon (1 g) fleur de sel sea salt
¼ teaspoon (1 g) baking powder

1 Cook the egg yolks in the microwave for 1 minute, then press them through a strainer with the back of a spoon or spatula.

2 Combine all the ingredients in the bowl of a stand mixer fitted with the paddle for 5 minutes on low speed (speed 1; or combine them together in a mixing bowl using a wooden spoon).

3 Form the dough into a ball then flatten it into a disk. Wrap it in plastic wrap and place it in the refrigerator for 1 hour.

4 Preheat the oven to 350°F (180°C). Roll out (see page 283) the dough to ⅛ inch (4 mm) thick. Cut out 4 rounds using the cookie cutter.

5 Place the sablés on a baking sheet lined with parchment paper. Make the glaze (see page 49) and glaze the sablés using the pastry brush. Score the sablés in a crisscross using the tines of a fork.

6 Bake for 20 minutes.

PALMIERS
(PALM LEAVES)

Understanding

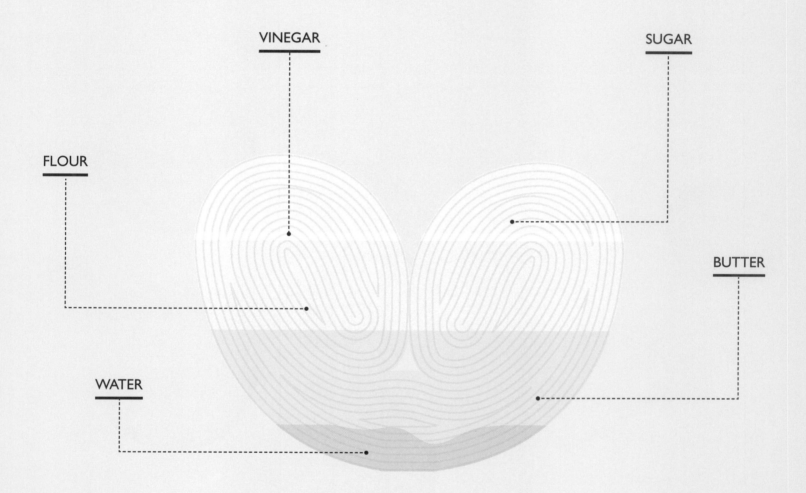

VINEGAR

SUGAR

FLOUR

BUTTER

WATER

WHAT IT IS
A puff pastry sprinkled with sugar, rolled from both ends into the shape of a palm leaf, then cut into slices and baked.

COMPLETION TIME
−Preparation time: 45 minutes
−Refrigeration time: 12 hours and 15 minutes
−Baking time: 15 to 20 minutes

EQUIPMENT
−Stand mixer fitted with the paddle and the dough hook
−Rolling pin

CHALLENGES
−Do not roll out the dough too firmly to prevent the layers of butter and dough from combining.
−Ensure the folds are tight so that there is no air between the different layers of dough.

SKILLS TO MASTER
−Kneading (pages 30 and 32)
−Rolling Out (page 283)

USEFUL TIP
Dust the work surface with confectioners' sugar rather than flour; the sugar will caramelize during baking.

IT'S READY
When they are deep golden and caramelized.

SHELF LIFE
A few days, in an airtight container.

WHY SPRINKLE WITH SUGAR
AFTER EVERY TURN?
When baked, the sugar melts and caramelizes. It acts as a glue between the layers, allowing the pastry to hold its shape better.

MAKES 15 PALMIERS

INVERSE PUFF PASTRY

BEURRE MANIÉ
14 tablespoons (200 g) unsalted butter,
  cut into cubes, softened
½ cup plus 2 tablespoons (80 g) high-protein all-
  purpose flour (or use bread flour or T65 flour)

DOUGH LAYER (DÉTREMPE)
1⅓ cups (180 g) high-protein all-purpose
  flour (or use bread flour or T65 flour)
1⅔ teaspoons (10 g) salt
⅓ cup plus ¾ teaspoon (80 g) cold water
4 tablespoons (60 g) Beurre en
  Pommade (page 284)
½ teaspoon (2 g) white vinegar

FINISHING

1 cup (200 g) sugar

1 Using the technique on page 69, make the inverse puff pastry, following Steps 1 through 3.

2 Make a single turn: Roll out the dough to 24 × 8 inches (60 × 20 cm) using the rolling pin. Fold the dough in thirds onto itself (like a wallet) to form a rectangle. Wrap it in plastic wrap and refrigerate it for 2 hours to rest.

3 Make a double turn: Roll out the dough to 24 × 8 inches (60 × 20 cm) and fold one-fourth of the dough from each end in toward the center. Fold the dough in half from the center (like a book). Wrap it in plastic wrap and refrigerate it for 2 hours to rest.

4 Make another double turn, sprinkling ½ cup (100 g) of the sugar over the dough before folding it. Wrap it in plastic wrap and refrigerate it for 2 hours.

5 Make another single turn, sprinkling ¼ cup (50 g) of the sugar over the dough before folding it. Wrap it in plastic wrap, and refrigerate it for 2 hours.

6 Roll out the dough to 30 inches (96 cm) long and 6 inches (15 cm) wide. Fold over a 6-inch (16 cm) portion of the dough from each short end. Fold over both ends again, then fold in half to finish.

7 Roll the dough in the remaining sugar to coat all sides. Wrap in plastic wrap. Freeze for about 15 minutes.

8 Preheat the oven to 325°F (160°C). Cut the dough into ⅓-inch (1 cm) slices. Place the slices flat on a baking sheet without parchment paper. Bake for 15 to 20 minutes.

RASPBERRY STRIPS

Understanding

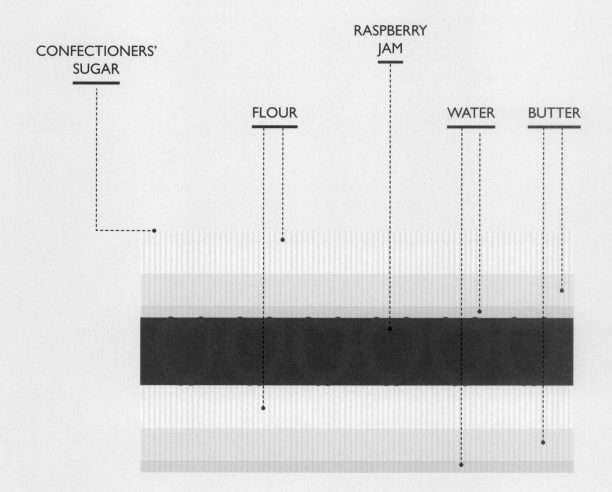

CONFECTIONERS' SUGAR

RASPBERRY JAM

FLOUR

WATER   BUTTER

WHAT IT IS

Squares of puff pastry baked then topped with raspberry jam.

COMPLETION TIME

– Preparation time: 25 minutes
– Refrigeration time: 12 hours
– Baking time: 20 minutes

EQUIPMENT

– Stand mixer fitted with the dough hook and the paddle
– Rolling pin

CHALLENGE

Obtaining a uniform caramelization.

SKILLS TO MASTER

– Kneading (pages 30 and 32)
– Rolling Out (page 283)

IT'S READY

When the pastry is pale golden.

SHELF LIFE

Two to three days, in an airtight container.

MAKES 5 PIECES

1   INVERSE PUFF PASTRY DOUGH

BEURRE MANIÉ

7 tablespoons (100 g) unsalted butter,
    cut into cubes, softened
¼ cup plus 1 tablespoon (40 g) high-
    protein all-purpose flour (or use
    bread flour or T65 flour)

DOUGH LAYER (DÉTREMPE)

⅔ cup (90 g) high-protein all-purpose flour
    (or use bread flour or T65 flour)
2 tablespoons (30 g) Beurre en
    Pommade (page 284)
¾ teaspoon (5 g) salt
2½ tablespoons (40 g) cold water
¼ teaspoon (1 g) white vinegar

2   RASPBERRY JAM

¼ cup plus 2½ teaspoons (60 g) sugar
1⅔ teaspoons (15 g) pectin
1 cup (125 g) raspberries

3   FINISHING

Confectioners' sugar

1 Using the technique on page 69, make the inverse puff pastry.

2 Make the raspberry jam: Stir together 2½ teaspoons (10 g) of the sugar and all of the pectin. Place the raspberries and the remaining sugar in a saucepan over low heat and cook until reduced to a liquid.

3 Add the sugar-pectin mixture to the pan. Whisk to combine, then simmer for several minutes, whisking frequently. Transfer the mixture to a separate container and let cool.

4 Preheat the oven to 350°F (180°C). Roll out (see page 283) the dough into a rectangle measuring 8 × 19½ inches (20 × 50 cm). Cut out ten 4-inch (10 cm) squares.

5 Brush the squares with water using the pastry brush. Stack five squares on top of each other, to form two stacks.

6 Cut slices ¾ inch (2 cm) wide.

7 Place the slices layered side (cut side) up on a baking sheet lined with parchment paper. Bake for about 20 minutes, until golden and flaky. Let cool.

8 Spread raspberry jam over the top of one of the strips, then top it with a second strip. Repeat with the remaining strips and jam. Dust with confectioners' sugar.

FINANCIERS

Understanding

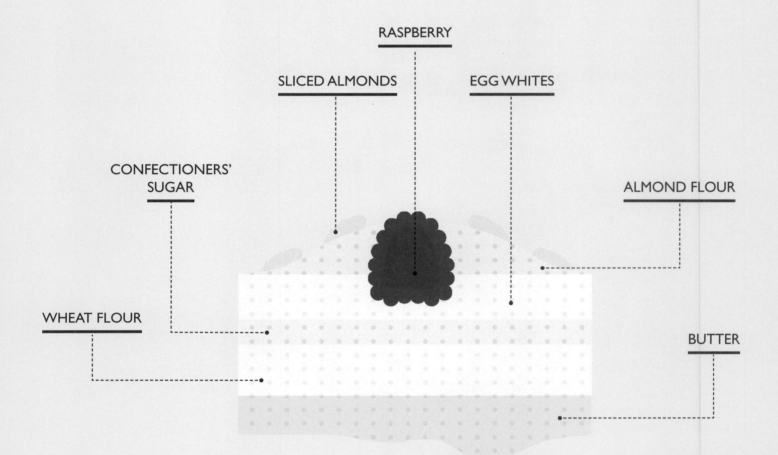

RASPBERRY

SLICED ALMONDS

EGG WHITES

CONFECTIONERS' SUGAR

ALMOND FLOUR

WHEAT FLOUR

BUTTER

WHAT IT IS

A small soft sponge cake made from almond flour and egg whites.

COMPLETION TIME

– Preparation time: 15 minutes
– Fermentation time: minimum
  2 hours, refrigerated
– Baking time: 20 to 25 minutes

EQUIPMENT

– Financier mold with eight cavities
– Sieve
– Piping bag (optional)

CHALLENGE

Making the Brown Butter (*beurre noisette*; page 284).

SKILL TO MASTER

Piping (page 285)

IT'S READY

When the financiers are pale golden.

SHELF LIFE

Two to three days, wrapped in plastic wrap.

WHY LET THE BATTER REST IN THE REFRIGERATOR?

Through whisking, air is incorporated into the batter and becomes trapped in the batter thanks to the eggs (they contain proteins that hold air). The addition of the melted butter coats this structure. When chilling, the butter will harden and evenly set the aerated batter. After baking, the financiers will be more uniform in shape.

MAKES 8 FINANCIERS

FINANCIER BATTER

3½ tablespoons (30 g) high-protein all-purpose
    flour (or use bread flour or T65 flour)
¼ cup (25 g) almond flour
½ cup plus 2 tablespoons (65 g)
    confectioners' sugar
2 large (64 g) egg whites, at room temperature
3 tablespoons plus ½ teaspoon
    (45 g) unsalted butter

DECOR

8 raspberries
1 tablespoon (10 g) sliced almonds

PAN

1 teaspoon (5 g) Beurre en Pommade (page 284)

1   Sift (see page 285) together the wheat and
almond flours and confectioners' sugar. Add
the egg whites and whisk to combine.

2   Make the brown butter: Melt the butter in
a saucepan over medium heat until it becomes a
golden color. When the butter is no longer "spitting"
and stops foaming, strain it through a sieve.

3   Add the hot brown butter to the previous
mixture and continue whisking until the mixture
is well blended.

4   Press plastic wrap onto the surface of the
batter (see page 285) and refrigerate it for
at least 2 hours and up to overnight.

5   Preheat the oven to 325°F (165°C). Grease the
financier molds with the beurre en pommade using
the pastry brush. Fill the pans or cavities using a spoon
or a piping bag.

6   Place 1 raspberry in the center of each
financier then sprinkle them with sliced
almonds. Bake for 20 to 25 minutes.

MADELEINES

Understanding

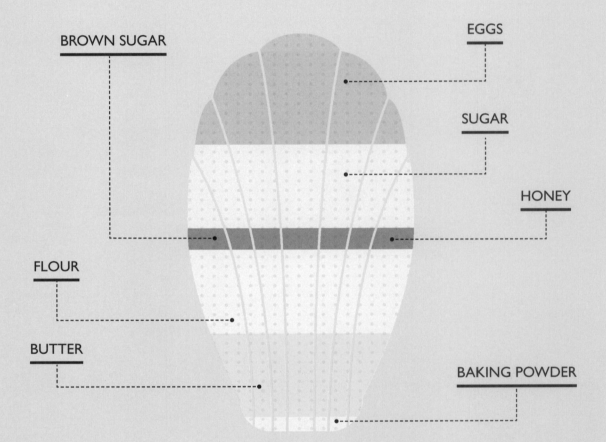

BROWN SUGAR

EGGS

SUGAR

HONEY

FLOUR

BUTTER

BAKING POWDER

WHAT IT IS

Small moist sponge cakes in the shape of a scallop shell

COMPLETION TIME

−Preparation time: 20 minutes
−Refrigeration time: 24 hours
−Baking time: 8 to 10 minutes

EQUIPMENT

−One madeleine mold with twenty cavities
−Sifter
−Pastry bag
−Pastry brush

CHALLENGE

Allowing the batter to rest sufficiently.

SKILL TO MASTER

Piping (page 285)

IT'S READY

When the cakes are golden and the characteristic bump has formed in the centers.

SHELF LIFE

Several days, in an airtight container.

WHAT CAUSES THE BUMP TO FORM IN THE CENTER?

Using a cold batter (directly from the refrigerator) and placing the cakes immediately in a hot oven will give the bump a better chance of developing because:
−the cold increases the thickness of the dough, which will tend to spread less in the mold and therefore rise more, and
−the high temperature of the oven causes the rapid formation of steam and therefore the rising of the batter.

Learning

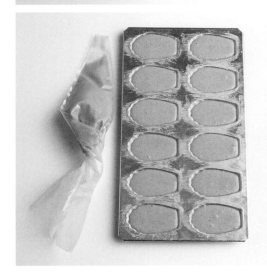

MAKES 20 MADELEINES

BATTER

13 tablespoons plus 1 teaspoon (190 g)
    Beurre en Pommade (page 284)
¾ cup (150 g) granulated sugar
1½ tablespoons (20 g) brown sugar
⅔ teaspoon (4 g) salt
1 tablespoon plus 1 teaspoon (30 g) honey
4 large (200 g) eggs, lightly beaten
1½ cups minus 1½ tablespoons (190 g)
    high-protein all-purpose flour (or
    use bread flour or T65 flour)
1¾ teaspoons (7 g) baking powder

FLAVORING

1 vanilla bean

MOLD

1 teaspoon (5 g) Beurre en Pommade (page 284)

THE DAY BEFORE

1   Combine the beurre en pommade,
granulated and brown sugars, and salt in a bowl
using a wooden spoon. Add the honey and
eggs, then stir to obtain a smooth dough.

2   Flatten the vanilla bean with the back of the
paring knife. Split it lengthwise in half and scrape
out the seeds with the tip of the knife. Add the seeds
to the mixing bowl but do not add the empty pod.

3   Sift the flour and baking powder into
the mixing bowl and stir to combine.

4   When the mixture is smooth, press plastic
wrap onto its surface (see page 285), and let
rest for at least 24 hours in the refrigerator.

THE SAME DAY

5   Preheat the oven to 400°F (210°C). Grease
the cavities of the madeleine mold with the
beurre en pommade using the pastry brush.
Fill the cavities three-fourths full with the
batter using the piping bag or a large spoon.

6   Bake for 8 to 10 minutes, until the cakes are
golden and a bump has formed in their centers.

273

ALMOND TUILE

Understanding

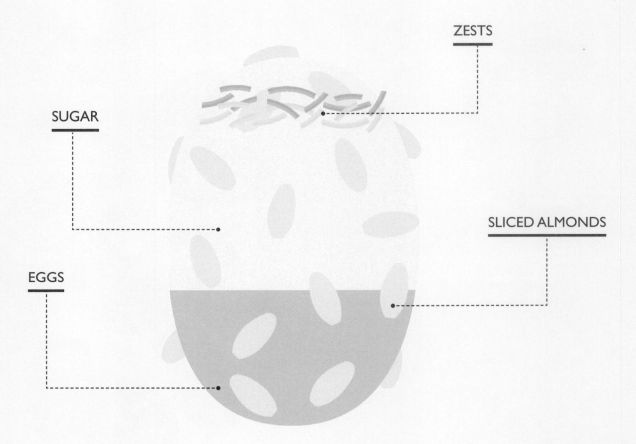

ZESTS

SUGAR

SLICED ALMONDS

EGGS

WHAT IT IS
A very thin and crisp cookie
laced with sliced almonds.

COMPLETION TIME
– Preparation time: 20 minutes
– Refrigeration time: 2 hours minimum
– Baking time: 8 minutes

EQUIPMENT
– A semisphere-shaped mold, such as
  a rolling pin (or a baguette pan)
– A large offset spatula
– Paring knife

VARIATION
Tuiles with chopped hazelnut pieces

CHALLENGE
Shaping the tuiles.

USEFUL TIP
Bake the tuiles in batches; they
need to be shaped quickly while
warm to prevent breaking.

IT'S READY
When the edges of the tuiles are pale golden.

SHELF LIFE
A few days, in an airtight container.

WHY SHOULD YOU LEAVE
THE DOUGH TO RISE FOR
TWO HOURS?
When resting, the sugar is dissolved in the
water contained in the egg whites. This
will limit the crystallization during baking
and therefore create a less grainy texture.

MAKES 25 TUILES

1 vanilla bean
2¼ cups (250 g) sugar
4 large (200 g) eggs
1½ teaspoons (2 g) lemon zest
1½ teaspoons (2 g) orange zest
5 cups (250 g) sliced almonds

1 Flatten the vanilla bean with the back of the paring knife. Split the bean lengthwise in half and scrape out the seeds with the tip of the knife. Place the vanilla bean seeds in a mixing bowl. Add the sugar, eggs, and zests, and whisk to combine into a smooth mixture.

2 Carefully incorporate the sliced almonds into the batter. Press plastic wrap onto the surface of the batter (see page 285) and refrigerate for at least 2 hours to overnight.

3 Preheat the oven to 325°F (170°C). Using a teaspoon, make eight small mounds of tuile batter on a baking sheet lined with parchment paper or on a silicone baking mat, spacing them far apart, as the batter will spread.

4 Dip the back of a fork into water and press the small mounds into rounds, making circular movements from the center to the outside of the tuile.

5 Bake for about 8 minutes.

6 Quickly remove the tuiles from the baking sheet using an offset spatula and drape them over a semisphere-shaped mold such as a rolling pin. Gently form the tuiles over the rolling pin, using your hands; they should cool and dry in a curved shape. Repeat with the remaining tuile batter.

SUGAR PUFFS
(CHOUQUETTES)

Understanding

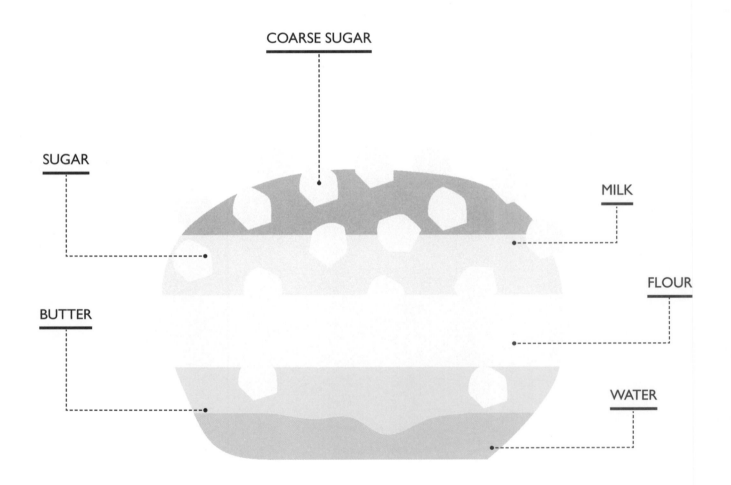

COARSE SUGAR

SUGAR

MILK

FLOUR

BUTTER

WATER

WHAT IT IS

Small cream puffs with no filling, sprinkled with coarse sugar.

COMPLETION TIME

– Preparation time: 15 minutes
– Baking time: 20 minutes

EQUIPMENT

– Stand mixer fitted with the paddle
– Wooden spoon
– Plastic dough scraper
– Pastry bag
– Number 10 plain pastry tip

CHALLENGES

– Thoroughly drying the choux dough without burning it.
– Baking the puffs.

USEFUL TIP

To prevent the puffs from collapsing, do not open the oven door while they still appear moist.

IT'S READY

When the puffs are well inflated, golden, and the grains of sugar have slightly caramelized.

SHELF LIFE

Consume immediately.

WHY DOES THE COARSE SUGAR NOT MELT WHEN BAKING?

The sugar is sucrose (table sugar), which melts above 320°F (160°C). The puffs bake at a lower temperature of 300°F (150°C). As a result, the coarse sugar maintains its shape and does not melt.

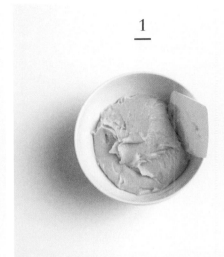

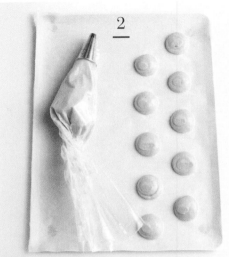

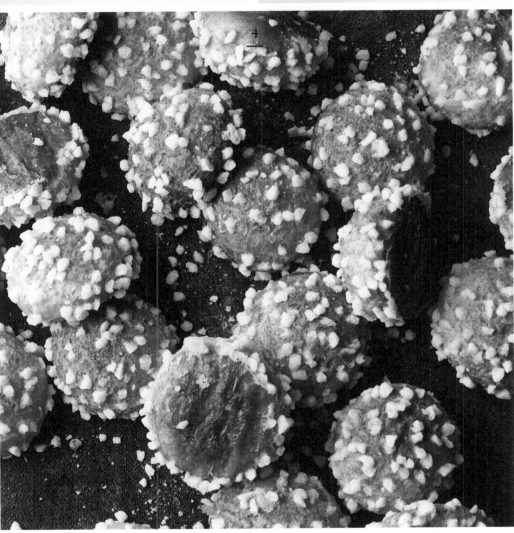

MAKES 50 SUGAR PUFFS (CHOUQUETTES)

CHOUX DOUGH (PÂTE À CHOUX)

⅔ cup (165 g) whole milk
⅓ cup plus 2½ teaspoons (90 g) water
8 tablespoons minus ¾ teaspoon (110 g) unsalted butter
½ teaspoon (2 g) sugar
⅓ teaspoon (2 g) salt
1 cup plus 2 tablespoons (150 g) high-protein all-purpose flour (or use bread flour or T65 flour)
4 large (200 g) eggs

FINISHING

1 cup (200 g) coarse sugar

1 Using the technique on page 73, make the choux dough.

2 Preheat the oven to 325°F (165°C). Scrape the dough into a pastry bag fitted with a plain pastry tip. Pipe twenty-five rounds between ¾ to 1 inch (2 to 3 cm) in diameter on a baking sheet lined with parchment paper, placing the tip of the pastry tip close to the baking sheet and holding it perpendicular to it.

3 Generously sprinkle each puff with coarse sugar.

4 Bake for 20 minutes. Pipe twenty-five more rounds with the remaining dough, sprinkle with the coarse sugar, and bake for 20 minutes.

CHAPTER 3
ILLUSTRATED GLOSSARY

EQUIPMENT

BENCH SCRAPER 280
PLASTIC DOUGH SCRAPER 280
LAME...280
SCISSORS 280
SERRATED KNIFE 280
INSTANT-READ THERMOMETER 280
DIGITAL KITCHEN SCALE........................280
MIXING BOWL, TOWEL..........................280
STAND MIXER
    (PADDLE AND DOUGH HOOK)..............280
PULLMAN LOAF PAN..............................281
PARISIAN BRIOCHE MOLD 281
KUGELHOPF MOLD 281
PANETTONE MOLD 281
MADELEINE PAN 281
FINANCIER PANS 281
BAKING SHEET.......................................281
PASTRY BAG + TIPS 281
ROLLING PIN 281
PASTRY BRUSH......................................281

DOUGH SKILLS DEFINED

SPRITZING 282
STRETCHING 282
PUNCHING DOWN 282
FORMING A CRUST (OR SKIN) 282
SCRAPING 282
SEAMING 282
SHAPING A BOULE (BALL) 282
"FRASAGE" (KNEADING/SMEARING) 282
EXTENSIBLE DOUGH 283
ELASTIC DOUGH 283
ROLLING OUT..283
LINING A PAN OR PASTRY RING 283
NOTCHING A BORDER 283
MAKING A SINGLE TURN 283
MAKING A DOUBLE TURN 283

BUTTER AND EGG TECHNIQUES

GREASING A MOLD 284
BEURRE EN POMMADE
    (BEATEN BUTTER) 284
CREAMING 284
BROWN BUTTER (BEURRE NOISETTE)... 284
CLARIFIED BUTTER.................................284
SEPARATING AN EGG 284
BEATING TO RIBBON STAGE....................284
WHISKING UNTIL LIGHTENED 284

BASIC SKILLS

SIFTING..285
STRAINING...285
TOASTING FRUITS/SEEDS 285
PIPING...285
PRESSING PLASTIC WRAP ONTO
    A SURFACE 285
CONVENTIONAL OVEN HEAT....................285
CONVECTION OVEN HEAT........................285
STEAMING 285
MAILLARD REACTION..............................285

EQUIPMENT

1 BENCH SCRAPER

A tool (plastic or metal) used to divide or cut dough cleanly.

2 PLASTIC DOUGH SCRAPER

A plastic tool for scraping a batter from a bowl into a container.

3 LAME

A sharp blade used to score (slash) bread dough.

4 SCISSORS

A tool used for making notches in bread dough, such as an épi.

5 SERRATED KNIFE

A wide-toothed knife used to cut bread after it is baked.

6 INSTANT-READ THERMOMETER

A thermometer used to check the temperature of the dough at the end of the kneading time. The temperature should be between 72° and 75°F (22° and 24°C) for optimal fermentation.

7 DIGITAL KITCHEN SCALE

A scale used to weigh ingredients precisely. You will need a scale with metric weights or one that allows you to switch between metric and imperial measurements.

8 MIXING BOWL, TOWEL

A stainless-steel container used for mixing batters and doughs or for raising bread dough. During rising, the bowl is covered with a towel to prevent a crust from developing on the surface of the dough.

9 STAND MIXER (PADDLE AND DOUGH HOOK)

A machine that makes it possible to knead bread dough, and to perform many other tasks that can be long and tiring when performed by hand. It permits the development of a stronger dough because the kneading is more intense. Kneading is performed with the dough hook. The paddle is used to beat soft or semiliquid doughs or creams. The whisk beater is used to increase the volume of creams or egg whites.

EQUIPMENT

1

4

7

2

5

8

3

6

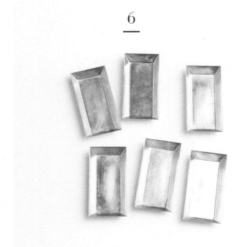

9, 10

1 PULLMAN LOAF PAN

A loaf pan with a lid. It can be purchased in specialty baking shops.

2 PARISIAN BRIOCHE MOLD

A metal rounded and fluted mold used to bake the bottom of Parisian brioches. It can be purchased in specialty baking shops.

3 KUGELHOPF MOLD

A traditional clay mold used to bake the kugelhopf. Metal pans are also available.

4 PANETTONE MOLD

A baking-paper mold. Metal hinged molds are also available.

5 MADELEINE PAN

A pan with multiple scallop-shaped cavities. Metal pans ensure better baking than silicone pans.

6 FINANCIER PANS

Available in pans with multiple cavities or as individual pans. Metal pans ensure better baking than silicone pans.

7 BAKING SHEET

A flat metal pan used for baking breads. They should be lined with parchment paper if the coating is not nonstick.

8 PASTRY BAG + TIPS

These are used for piping batters in a decorative way (such as for cream fillings on cakes) or for filling baked goods (filled doughnuts, almond croissants, etc.), filling uniformly (such as in a king cake), neatly decorating small cakes (financiers, madeleines, etc.), or for piping choux doughs, such as for sugar puffs (chouquettes). Typically when filling a pastry, plain pastry tips of a medium diameter (about ⅓ inch/ 8 to 10 mm) are used. Choose disposable bags, which are more practical and hygienic.

9 ROLLING PIN

A thick wooden dowel used to evenly roll out dough. Turn the dough a quarter of a turn between each pass to ensure even thickness.

10 PASTRY BRUSH

A food-grade brush used to glaze pastries and breads for browning.

DOUGH SKILLS DEFINED

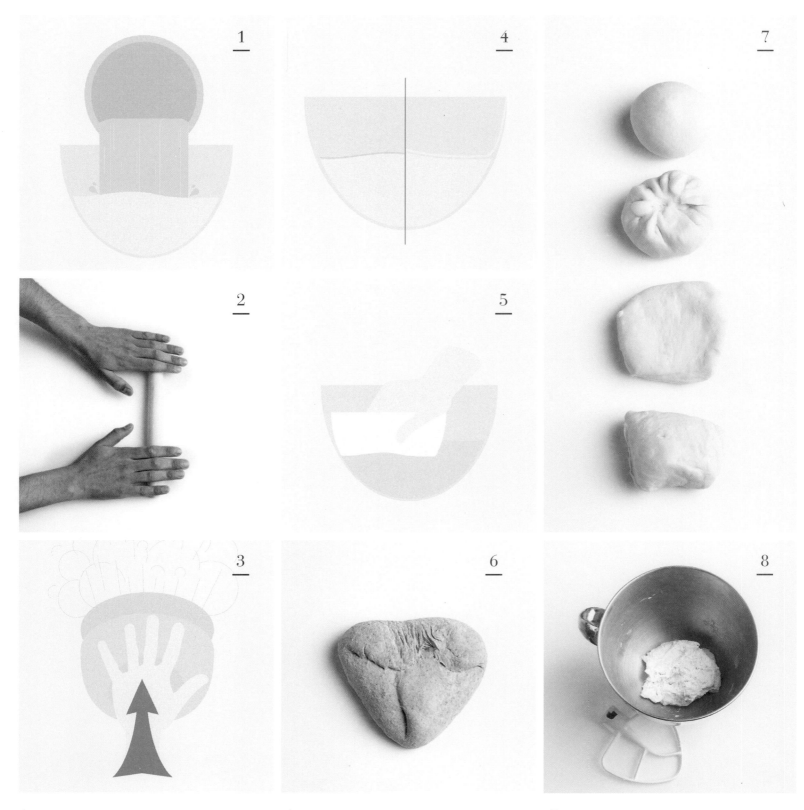

1 SPRITZING

Adding water to a dough at the end of the kneading time in order to increase its hydration if the dough is too dense.

2 STRETCHING

Preshaping an oblong dough. Place the palms of your hands at each end of the dough and roll gently, pressing until you reach the desired length.

3 PUNCHING DOWN

Flattening the dough with your hands to expel gases. This action helps to better distribute air bubbles created during the rise. As a result, the baked good will have a more open crumb.

4 FORMING A CRUST (OR SKIN)

A dough (or cream) develops a crust (or skin) on the surface if exposed to air; it oxidizes.

5 SCRAPING

Extracting a dough or batter from a container using a plastic tool called a "dough scraper."

6 SEAMING

Joining two parts of the same piece of dough. For breads, the seam is usually placed underneath during baking. In some cases, the bread is baked with the seam on top. If this is the case, this action replaces the need to score the bread.

7 SHAPING A BOULE (BALL)

To shape a boule: flatten the dough slightly. Fold the edges in toward the center as you go. Pinch the folded edges to join them, then turn the boule over seam side down onto a floured work surface. Smooth the dough by passing the palms of your hands several times over the entire surface.

8 "FRASAGE" (KNEADING/SMEARING)

In bread baking, this refers to mixing the ingredients of a dough before kneading them. In pastry, this refers to smearing the dough (shortbreads, pie doughs, tart doughs) with the palm of the hand on the work surface to finish incorporating the ingredients without overworking the dough.

DOUGH SKILLS DEFINED

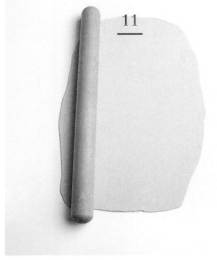

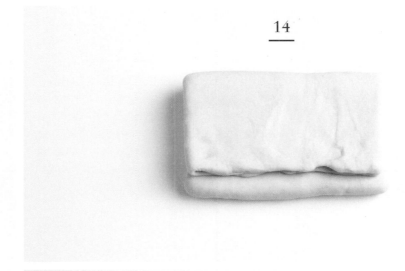

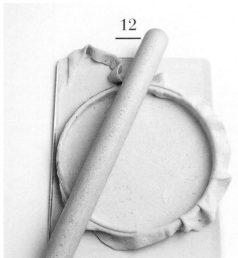

9 EXTENSIBLE DOUGH

Dough that can be easily rolled out.

10 ELASTIC DOUGH

Dough that is difficult to roll out; when rolled out, it retracts automatically.

11 ROLLING OUT

Flattening the dough (puff pastry, shortbread, pie dough, pizza dough, etc.) using a rolling pin. Place the dough onto a lightly floured work surface. Using a lightly floured rolling pin, apply a steady pressure on the dough as you roll it out into a circle, rectangle, or other desired shape, lightly flouring the dough if needed to prevent it from sticking.

12 LINING A PAN OR PASTRY RING

Lining a pan or a pastry ring with a round of dough. After rolling out the dough, roll it up around a floured rolling pin. Place the rolling pin on the edge of the pan and unroll the dough over it. Carefully and gently tuck the dough down into the pan along the bottom and against the sides. Trim off any excess dough above the rim.

13 NOTCHING A BORDER

Making small, uniform notches all around the edge of a dough using a small knife. This allows the dough to rise more quickly during baking and to have a more attractive appearance. Make notches about ¼ inch (5 mm) long starting from the outside edge and moving in toward the center of the dough.

14 MAKING A SINGLE TURN

A type of folding of puff pastry into three thicknesses while turning it. Roll out the dough with the folded edge on the left to a rectangle three times longer than it is wide. Fold one-third of the dough in toward the middle and then another one-third over the top (like a wallet). Wrap the dough in plastic wrap and let rest in the refrigerator.

15 MAKING A DOUBLE TURN

A type of folding of puff pastry into four thicknesses while turning it. Roll out the dough with the folded edge on the left to a rectangle three times longer than it is wide. Fold one-fourth of the dough from each end in toward the center. Fold it in half in the middle (like a book). Wrap the dough in plastic wrap and let rest in the refrigerator.

BUTTER AND EGG TECHNIQUES

1 GREASING A MOLD

Using a pastry brush, coat the whole surface of the mold with beurre en pommade (see below). Greasing the mold facilitates unmolding after baking.

2 BEURRE EN POMMADE (BEATEN BUTTER)

Butter that is very soft (but still cool) and has been worked until creamy. To make beurre en pommade, cut the butter into pieces, place them in a bowl, and let sit at cool room temperature for 1 to 2 hours before working them in a stand mixer fitted with the paddle until creamy but still cool.

3 CREAMING

Beating a beurre en pommade (see above) with sugar to obtain a creamy mixture.

4 BROWN BUTTER (BEURRE NOISETTE)

Butter cooked until the solids have browned.

5 CLARIFIED BUTTER

Butter cooked until only the fat remains and from which all the solids and impurities have been removed. To clarify butter, melt the butter over very low heat. Once fully melted, skim off the impurities from the surface using a spoon. Pour the butter (the yellow portion) into a bowl, being careful to leave the whey (the white particles) in the bottom of the pan.

6 SEPARATING AN EGG

Separating the egg yolk from the egg white. Start by cracking the eggshell in half. Working over a small bowl, use your thumbs to gently pry the halves apart. Let the yolk settle in the lower half of the eggshell while the egg whites run off the sides of the egg and into the bowl. Taking care not to break the egg yolk, gently transfer the yolk back and forth between the eggshell halves, letting the remainder of the egg whites drip into the bowl below. Place the egg yolk in a separate bowl.

7 BEATING TO A RIBBON STAGE

Whisking eggs and sugar together until smooth and homogeneous. The mixture falls from the whisk without separating, like a ribbon falling onto itself.

8 WHISKING UNTIL LIGHTENED

Vigorously whisking together egg yolks or butter with sugar until the mixture "lightens" in color, becoming a pale yellow.

BASIC SKILLS

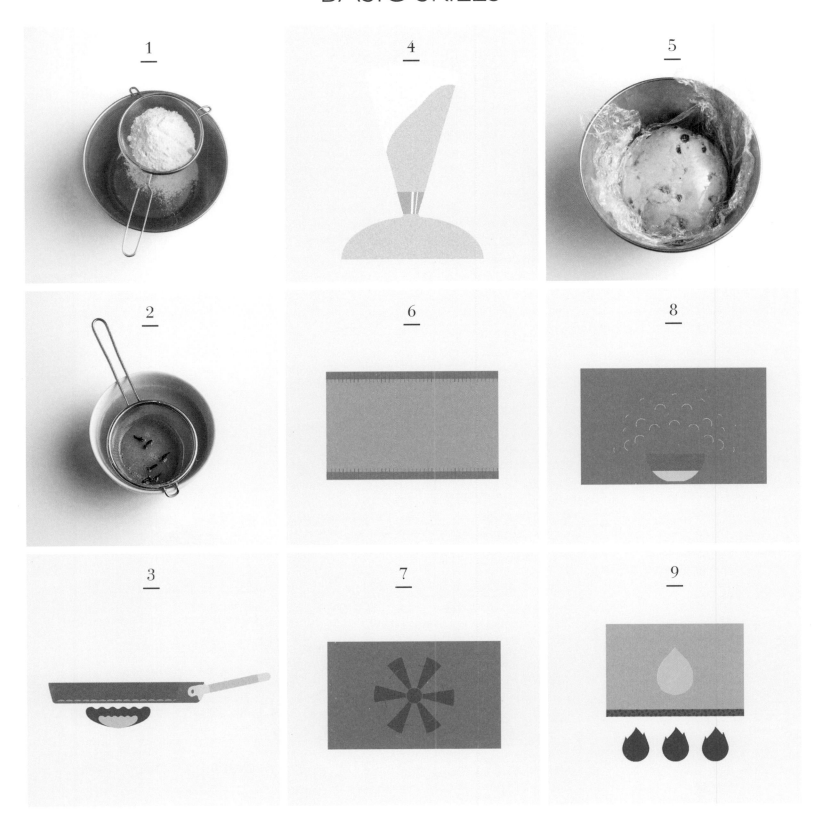

1 SIFTING

Passing a powdered substance (such as flour) through a sieve (or sifter) to remove foreign particles or lumps.

2 STRAINING

Straining a liquid through a sieve or "chinois" to remove any residue or solid pieces.

3 TOASTING FRUITS/SEEDS

Browning dried fruits and seeds to bring out their aromas. Bake for about 10 minutes at 350°F (180°C) or dry-sauté in a pan, shaking the pan regularly. Be careful of burning.

4 PIPING

Using a pastry bag with or without a pastry tip to create shapes (disks, domes, fingers, puffs).

5 PRESSING PLASTIC WRAP ONTO A SURFACE

Gently applying plastic wrap against the surface of a mixture to make direct contact with it so that the mixture does not come into contact with the ambient air. This prevents the mixture from forming a skin or from drying out.

6 CONVENTIONAL OVEN HEAT

Heat released by an oven equipped with two heating elements, which are found in the top and bottom of the oven. (Note that an older oven may have just one heating element.) The heat increases slowly. It is not recommended to bake with several pans in the oven at the same time.

7 CONVECTION OVEN HEAT

Heat released by an oven equipped with two heating elements and a fan. The heat is evenly distributed in the oven, so you will need to set the temperature about 25°F (10°C) higher than for a conventional oven.

8 STEAMING

Water introduced into the oven as steam to maintain a humid environment. This creates shine and a beautiful crust, helps the formation of the slashes, and limits evaporation so the bread has a longer shelf life.

9 MAILLARD REACTION

Chemical reactions between the proteins and the sugars that occur as soon as there are more molecules of water on the surface (at the end of baking of bread). They create a brown color and caramelized aromatic notes.

INDEX TO RECIPES AND BREAD-BAKING BASICS

BAGUETTES

Baguette 84
"French tradition" baguette...........................88
"French tradition" baguette with
  mixed seeds 92

BREADS MADE WITH OIL
(FLAT BREADS)

Ciabatta..158
Crunchy breadsticks (grissini) 168
Focaccia...160
Fougasse 164

BRIOCHES

Braided brioche (challah)...........................224
Flaky brioche 228
Parisian brioche 216
Pink praline brioche..................................220

BRIOCHE-STYLE CAKES

Brioche bordelaise garnished with
  candied citrus 234
Cream-filled brioche cake
  (tarte Tropézienne) 236
Kugelhopf...240
Panettone 244
Sugar tart (tarte au sucre) 232

ESSENTIAL INGREDIENTS

Alternative flours.......................................14
Fats, milk 28
Fresh yeast...18
Gluten-free flours......................................16
Liquid starter 20
Poolish 24
Salt 27
Sourdough starter (levain) 19
Stiff starter 22
Sugar, eggs 29
Water 26
Wheat flour 12

FERMENTATION STAGES

Baking..52
Fermentation 34
Final shaping 40
Glazing...48
Kneading by hand......................................30
Kneading mechanically...............................32
Scoring...50

FILLED BREADS

Cheese bread 146
Cheese ficelles with seeds 150
Chocolate loaf..138
Mixed seeds ring.......................................132
Small hazelnut-fig loaves 142
Small Italian loaves....................................148
Small muesli loaves 144
"Surprise" loaf 154
Walnut loaf...136

FUNDAMENTAL CUSTARDS
AND CREAMS

Almond cream (crème d'amandes) 78
Apple compote filling 80
Pastry cream (crème pâtissière) 76

FUNDAMENTAL DOUGHS

Brioche dough 66
Choux dough (pâte à choux)........................72
"French tradition" straight dough.................56
Inverse puff pastry......................................68
Leavened puff pastry...................................62
Pizza dough...58
Straight dough 54
Sweet pastry dough
  (pâte sucrée/pâte sablée) 74
Vienna dough 60

ILLUSTRATED GLOSSARY

Basic skills 285
Butter and egg techniques..........................284
Dough skills defined 282
Equipment 280

LEAVENED PUFF PASTRIES

Almond croissant 192
Chocolate-filled croissant rolls
  (pain au chocolat)...................................184
Croissant 180
Pain Suisse 190
Raisin and cream croissant spirals
  (pain aux raisins) 186

LOAF AND SINGLE-LAYER CAKES
(GÂTEAUX DE VOYAGE)

Fruit cake 254
Genoa cake (pain de Gênes).........................258
Spiced loaf cake (pain d'épice) 252

PUFF PASTRY–BASED CAKES
AND TARTS

Flaky apple tart...202
King cake (galette des rois).........................204

SMALL BITES: SPONGE CAKES,
PUFFS, AND CRISP COOKIES

Almond tuile 274
Financiers 270
Madeleines 272
Palmiers (palm leaves)...............................264
Raspberry strips..266
Sablés 262
Sugar puffs (chouquettes) 276

SOFT BREADS AND BUNS

Bagel...172
Pullman loaf sandwich bread
  (pain de mie) 170
Sesame seed bun 176

SPECIALTY BREADS

Beer bread 128
Chestnut sourdough...................................122
Cornmeal loaf 124
Gluten-free loaf 126
Lemon sourdough rye................................118
Multigrain brown loaf (pain noir) 120
Sourdough rye...114

TARTS

Flan tart (flan pâtissier).............................250
Pistachio-apricot tart.................................248

TRADITIONAL PUFF PASTRIES

Apple tart with lattice 198
Apple turnover (chausson aux pommes).......194

YEAST-RAISED BREADS

Basic poolish loaf (pain maison)....................96
Multigrain loaf..108
Old-world loaf (pain d'antan) 104
Rustic loaf with rye (pain de campagne) 100
Stone-ground wheat loaf 106
Whole wheat sourdough 112

YEAST-RAISED SWEET BREADS
AND DOUGHNUTS

Filled doughnuts.......................................212
Sweet loaves 208
Vienna baguette..210

INGREDIENT INDEX

ALMONDS

Almond croissant 192
Almond tuile 274
Cream-filled brioche cake
   (tarte Tropézienne) 236
Financiers 270
Fruit cake 254
Genoa cake (pain de Gênes) 258
King cake (galette des rois) 204
Panettone 244
Pistachio-apricot tart 248
Sablés 262

APPLE

Apple tart with lattice 198
Apple turnover (chausson aux pommes) 194
Flaky apple tart 202

APRICOT

Pistachio-apricot tart 248

BEER

Beer bread 128

BUCKWHEAT FLOUR

Gluten-free loaf 126

CANDIED FRUIT

Brioche bordelaise garnished with
   candied citrus 234
Fruit cake 254
Panettone 244

CANDIED GINGER

Spiced loaf cake (pain d'épice) 252

CHEESE

Cheese bread 146
Cheese ficelles with seeds 150
"Surprise" loaf 154

CHESTNUT FLOUR/CHESTNUTS

Chestnut sourdough......................................122

CHOCOLATE

Chocolate-filled croissant rolls
   (pain au chocolat)....................................184
Chocolate loaf...138
Pain Suisse..190
Vienna baguette.. 210

COCOA POWDER

Chocolate loaf...138

CORNMEAL

Cornmeal loaf 124

DARK RYE FLOUR (OR T170)

Beer bread...128
Cheese bread 146
Lemon sourdough rye 118
Multigrain brown loaf (pain noir) 120
Multigrain loaf 108
Rustic loaf with rye (pain de campagne) 100

Sourdough rye.. 114
"Surprise" loaf 154

DRIED FRUIT

Small hazelnut-fig loaves 142
Walnut loaf..136

FIG

Small hazelnut-fig loaves 142

HONEY

Chestnut sourdough......................................122
Madeleines 272
Spiced loaf cake (pain d'épice) 252

LEMON

Lemon sourdough rye 118

LIQUID STARTER

Chocolate loaf...138
Ciabatta...158
"French tradition" baguette with
   mixed seeds 92
"French tradition" baguette..........................88
Panettone 244
Pullman loaf sandwich bread
   (pain de mie) 170
Walnut loaf..136
Whole wheat sourdough 112

MOLASSES

Multigrain brown loaf (pain noir) 120

MUESLI

Small muesli loaves.......................................144

OLIVE

Fougasse 164
Small Italian loaves....................................... 148

OLIVE OIL

Focaccia... 160
Fougasse 164

ORANGE BLOSSOM WATER

Braided brioche (challah)..............................224
Brioche bordelaise garnished with
   candied citrus... 234
Cream-filled brioche cake
   (tarte Tropézienne) 236

PINK PRALINES

Pink praline brioche......................................220

RAISINS

Fruit cake 254
Kugelhopf 240
Panettone 244
Raisin and cream croissant spirals
   (pain aux raisins) 186

RASPBERRY

Filled doughnuts 212
Financiers 270
Raspberry strips 266

RICE FLOUR

Gluten-free loaf 126

RUM

Braided brioche (challah)..............................224
Brioche bordelaise garnished with
   candied citrus 234
Fruit cake 254
Panettone 244
Sablés 262

PASTRY FLOUR (OR T45)

Bagel..172
Brioche bordelaise garnished with
   candied citrus 234
Chocolate-filled croissant rolls
   (pain au chocolat)....................................184
Cream-filled brioche cake
   (tarte Tropézienne) 236
Croissant... 180
Filled doughnuts 212
Flaky brioche 228
Kugelhopf 240
Pain Suisse..190
Panettone 244
Parisian brioche 216
Pink praline brioche......................................220
Raisin and cream croissant spirals
   (pain aux raisins) 186
Sugar tart (tarte au sucre) 232
Sweet loaves 208

SEEDS

Bagel..172
Cheese ficelles with seeds 150
"French tradition" baguette with
   mixed seeds 92
Mixed seeds ring..132
Multigrain brown loaf (pain noir) 120
Multigrain loaf 108
Sesame seed bun 176
Small hazelnut-fig loaves 142

STIFF STARTER

Beer bread...128
Chestnut sourdough......................................122
Lemon sourdough rye 118
Old-world loaf (pain d'antan) 104
Rustic loaf with rye (pain de campagne) 100
Small hazelnut-fig loaves 142
Sourdough rye..114
Stone-ground wheat loaf..............................106

WHOLE WHEAT FLOUR
(OR "INTEGRAL" T150 FLOUR)

Beer Bread...128
Multigrain loaf 108
Whole wheat sourdough 112

WHOLE WHEAT FLOUR
(OR STONE-GROUND T110)

Multigrain brown loaf (pain noir) 120
Old-world loaf (pain d'antan) 104

WHOLE WHEAT PASTRY FLOUR
(OR STONE-GROUND T80)

Old-world loaf (pain d'antan) 104
Stone-ground wheat loaf...............................106

ACKNOWLEDGMENTS FROM RODOLPHE

Thank you to the teams of Maison Landemaine, who work hard every day.

ACKNOWLEDGMENTS FROM ANNE

Thank you to everyone on the team who participated in the creation of this book.

ACKNOWLEDGMENTS FROM YANNIS

Thanks to Flours T65 and T175, with whom I spent a delicious weekend. To you also, gluten-free bread, who allowed me to discover something new and trendy. And finally, a big thank-you to my favorite *chouquette*, who fills me with joy with every bite!

First published in France by Hachette Livre (Marabout) in 2016.
Copyright © 2016 by Hachette Livre (Marabout).

HarperCollins books may be purchased for educational, business, or sales promotional use. For information please email the Special Markets Department at SPsales@harpercollins.com.

First published in 2020 by
Harper Design
An Imprint of HarperCollins*Publishers*
195 Broadway
New York, NY 10007
Tel: (212) 207-7000
Fax: (855) 746-6023
harperdesign@harpercollins.com
www.hc.com

Distributed throughout North America by
HarperCollins*Publishers*
195 Broadway
New York, NY 10007

ISBN: 978-0-06-288713-9
Library of Congress Control Number: 2019026139

Printed in China

First Printing, 2020

Graphic Design: Yannis Varoutsikos
Styling: Orathay Souksisavanh
Translation: Zachary R. Townsend, Townsend Language Services, Inc.